# A
# BETTER
# PILL

# A BETTER PILL

## FIRST STEPS TO A CONSCIOUS, NONLOCAL HEALTHCARE PARADIGM

EVELYN M. BRODIE

ILLUSTRATIONS BY GEORGE CHRISTIE

The Book Guild Ltd

First published in Great Britain in 2018 by
The Book Guild Ltd
9 Priory Business Park
Wistow Road, Kibworth
Leicestershire, LE8 0RX
Freephone: 0800 999 2982
www.bookguild.co.uk
Email: info@bookguild.co.uk
Twitter: @bookguild



Typeset in Aldine401 BT

Printed and bound in Great Britain by CPI Group (UK) Ltd, Croydon, CR0 4YY

ISBN 978 1912362 080

British Library Cataloguing in Publication Data.
A catalogue record for this book is available from the British Library.

*This book is dedicated to George, Alastair, Katrina and all the pioneers of nonlocality who have paved the way towards the new paradigm, often in the face of ridicule and censorship.*

# CONTENTS

# ACKNOWLEDGEMENTS

I give deep and heartfelt thanks to all those who took the time and trouble to read and re-read the various drafts of this book as it progressed and developed. In particular my husband George Christie, who made version after version of the many illustrations that bring the words to life and my daughter Katrina Ferron who spent hours asking searching questions that forced me to clarify my thinking and my writing.

I am also deeply indebted to Dr Govin Murugachandran and Dr Marianna Santos who read the medical chapters from a place of much deeper practical knowledge and experience than my own and corrected any anatomical and physiological errors I had made. Any remaining errors of course are down to me.

Others that gave me invaluable comments and perceptive questions as I developed my thinking include Dr Harry Bush, Andrew Klein, Anna Miller, Cathy Warren, Lindsay Williams and Maya. And Jasmin Naim once more did an incredibly detailed and thorough proof-reading of the manuscript for which I am very grateful.

I also acknowledge the following authors and publishers for giving me permission to reprint quotations from their publications.

Al-Khalili, Jim and McFadden, Johnjoe. 2014. *Life on the Edge: The Coming of Age of Quantum Biology* London, UK: Bantam Press, Reproduced by Permission of The Random House Group Ltd.

Aurobindo, Sri. 2001. *A Greater Psychology* Pondicherry, India: Sri Aurobindo Ashram Publications Trust

Botkin, Allan L. PsyD and Hogan, R. Craig, PhD. 2005, 2014. *Induced After-Death Communication: A New Therapy for Healing Grief and Trauma* Charlottesville, VA, USA: Hampton Roads Publishing c/o Red Wheel/Weiser, LLC Newburyport, MA, www.redwheelweiser.com

Brown, David Jay. 2013. *The New Science of Psychedelics: At the Nexus of Culture, Consciousness and Spirituality* Rochester, Vermont, USA: Inner Traditions International and Bear & Company, http://www.Innertraditions.com

Halifax, Joan, PhD. 1991. *Shamanic Voices: A survey of visionary narratives* New York, NY, USA: Viking Penguin. Reproduced by permission of Brockman, Inc.

Hancock, Graham. 2005. *Supernatural: Meetings with the Ancient Teachers of Mankind* London, UK: Century. Reproduced by permission of The Random House Group Ltd.

Hancock, Graham. 2015. *The Divine Spark: Psychedelics Consciousness and the Birth of Civilization* London, UK: Hay House, Inc.

Laszlo, Ervin. 2007. *Science and the Akashic Field: An Integral Theory of Everything (Second Edition)* Rochester, Vermont, USA: Inner Traditions International and Bear & Company, http://www.Innertraditions.com

Laszlo, Ervin. 2009. *The Akashic Experience: Science and the Cosmic Memory Field* Rochester, Vermont, USA: Inner Traditions International and Bear & Company, http://www.Innertraditions.com

Levine, Peter A. PhD. 2010. *In An Unspoken Voice: How the Body Releases Trauma and Restores Goodness* Berkeley, California, USA: North Atlantic Books

Lewis, Thomas, M.D., Amini, Fari M.D., Lannon, Richard, M.D. 2000. *A General Theory of Love* New York, USA: Vintage Books, Random House

Lipton, Bruce H. PhD. 2005. *The Biology of Belief* Carlsbad, CA, USA: Hay House Inc.

Mason Boring, Francesca. 2012. *Connecting to Our Ancestral Past: Healing through Family Constellations, Ceremony, and Ritual* Berkeley, California, USA: North Atlantic Books

McGilchrist, Iain. 2009. *The Master and his Emissary: The Divided Brain and the Making of the Western World* New Haven and London: Yale University Press

Myss, Caroline. 1997. *Anatomy of the Spirit* London, UK: Bantam, Random House Group Ltd.

Narby, Jeremy. 1999. *The Cosmic Serpent, DNA and the Origins of Knowledge* New York, NY, USA: Jeremy P. Tarcher/Putnam

Pribram, Karl H. M.D. 2013. *The Form Within: My Point of View* Westport, CT, USA: Prospecta Press

Rankin, Lissa, Dr. 2013. *Mind over medicine: Scientific Proof That You Can Heal Yourself* Carlsbad, CA, USA: Hay House Inc.

Romijn, Herms. 2002. Journal of Consciousness Studies, Volume 9, Number 1, 1 January 2002, Imprint Academic

Ruppert, Franz. 2012. *Symbiosis and Autonomy, Symbiotic Trauma and Love Beyond Entanglements* Steyning, UK: Green Balloon Publishing

Schneider, Jakob Robert. 2007. *Family Constellations: Basic Principles and Procedures* Heidelberg, Germany: Carl-Auer-Systeme

Schore, Allan N. 2012. *The Science of the Art of Psychotherapy* New York, USA: W.W. Norton & Company

Strassman, Rick, M.D. 2000. *DMT: The Spirit Molecule* Rochester, Vermont, USA: Inner Traditions International and Bear & Company, http://www.Innertraditions.com

Strassman, Rick, M.D., Wojtowicz, Slawek M.D., Luna, Luis Eduardo, PhD, and Frecska, Ede, M.D.. 2007. *Inner*

*Paths to Outer Space* Rochester, Vermont, USA: Inner Traditions International and Bear & Company, http://www.Innertraditions.com

Van Der Kolk, Bessel. 2014. *The Body Keeps the Score: Mind, Brain and Body in the Transformation of Trauma* USA: Viking Penguin

Van Lommel, Pim, M.D. 2010. *Consciousness Beyond Life: The Science of the Near-Death Experience* New York, NY, USA: Harper Collins Publishers

# ABOUT THE AUTHOR

*What happens when I have got rid of everyone else's voices telling me, or even forcing me to do something I don't want to; when I see the world with my own eyes and know my own truth?*[1]

(Franz Ruppert)

I work as a shamanic practitioner and integrated healer. In the 1970s I gained degrees in economics from Glasgow University in Scotland and Stanford University in California. For thirty years I enjoyed a lucrative career as an economist, financial journalist and communications executive, including ten years, five days a week, as a live financial-TV correspondent. I did not have any religious or spiritual beliefs and the result of my societal conditioning was to work and play hard, achieve excellent academic credentials and have a varied, interesting and successful (but highly conventional) career and family life.

Despite the outward success, while working in the corporate environment and being driven by financial measures of achievement, I also felt very judged. I was obsessed by

---

1 Ruppert, Franz. 2012. *Symbiosis and Autonomy, Symbiotic Trauma and Love Beyond Entanglements* p.269 Steyning, UK: Green Balloon Publishing

what people thought about me. I appeared confident and controlling, but that was my mask. In fact I had very little self-esteem and depended on the approval of others, particularly men, both in my personal life and the workplace.

Then in 2004 I had an experience that forced me to change my belief system. I was exposed to an altered state of consciousness for the first time when I attended a remote viewing seminar. That experience of sitting in a room in the UK while being able to experience and describe events at a different place and time, forced me to change my way of living, but if you had told me back then what I would be doing today I would have said you were in need of therapy!

The experience was so vivid and undeniable that to try and understand it, I felt compelled to embark on a dual track quest for knowledge. In the early days when I first started connecting with elements outside the physical body, my rational left-brain was overwhelmed and fought desperately to understand what was happening to me. Since then I have been on an intense double track of investigation which you could say was to meet the needs of both the right- and the left-hand sides of the brain. The right-brain track was to experience a variety of altered states of consciousness and find out how best to use the information available in these states. This has included work with Alberto Villoldo's Light Body School,[2] as well as many trips to Peru to work directly with the Q'ero shamans in the Andes and the Shipibo shamans (and their plant medicine) in the Amazon. The left-brain track was to try to find and understand the science of where the information comes from when we are in an altered state of consciousness and how it reaches us: the physics and biology of an expanded consciousness including quantum physics, psychoneuroimmunology, neurobiology and epigenetics.

---

2 http://thefourwinds.com

Over the past decade my investigative travels have taken me to North, Central and South America, India, and Southeast Asia and in 2013 I published a book describing my ten-year journey, *Corporate Bitch to Shaman: A journey uncovering the links between 21st century science, consciousness and the ancient healing practices.*[3]

The outcome of my work so far is that I feel my personal calling is to be a bridge between the worlds of psychosomatic and nonlocal healing (principally but not entirely based on shamanic techniques) and the scientific, medical world. To present the knowledge I had available at that time, in 2015 I published a second book, *Temenos Touch: The Art and Science of Integrated Medicine and Non-local Healing.*[4]

I now live in London, England and run a successful private healing practice and integrated healing training courses. Over the past decade, working with people has taught me that the key underlying source of most people's unhappiness stems from a lack of love, including self-love and even from the feeling that they are unlovable. Within the family this belief can stem from a huge array of systemic sources and entanglements, including the inadequacies of our parents and the wounds we carry on behalf of our genealogical lineage. In the wider societal picture the unhappiness is representative of our Western world alienation from any form of true internal spiritual connection, or any form of connection and symbiosis with this beautiful planet that is our home.

Along with the lack of love people also frequently have a sense of powerlessness, a dissociation from their own bodies and from any form of community as well as a feeling of being

---

3 Brodie, Evelyn M. 2013. *Corporate Bitch to Shaman: A journey uncovering the links between 21st century science, consciousness and the ancient healing practices* Beauchamp, Leicestershire: Matador

4 Brodie, Evelyn M. 2015. *Temenos Touch: The Art and Science of Integrated Medicine and Non-local Healing* California, USA: Waterside Press

a victim to external forces. Governments, the media and the medical profession can often exacerbate this with their incessant portrayals of the world as a dangerous place, where at any minute we may face annihilation from terrorist bombs, floods and earthquakes resulting from climate change, or the fear created by diagnoses of diseases from cancer to dementia.

During my journey of intellectual investigation and experiential exploration I have built an increasingly large toolbox of techniques for my work. People come to me seeking help with a wide range of problems, including physical ailments, stress and anxiety, emotional loss and a sense of existential crisis – of losing the way, or suffering the debilitating effects of trauma on their sense of self-worth.

My toolbox has gradually extended out from fairly mainstream bodymind treatments like craniosacral therapy and psychotherapy to increasingly energetic treatments including shamanic practices such as soul retrieval, cleansing the energy field and working with the ancestors. This has followed the gradual growth in my academic understanding of the intricate connections between first the brain and the body and secondly between the physical brain and the nonlocal mind or what might be called a wider field of consciousness, which has many names according to your metaphysical and philosophical standpoint as I will discuss in much greater depth in subsequent chapters.

This journey of enquiry has shown me a wide array of solutions, ways to break out of our stories, conditioning and alienation. Many of these techniques were used by our ancestors and have survived and continue to be used by indigenous people today, those still in touch with the lands that they live on and the communities that they live in. But for the past few centuries these ways were dismissed by mainstream scientists as irrational and delusional. Rupert Sheldrake challenges this in *The Science Delusion* when he asks:

*Should science be a fundamentalist belief-system? Or should it be based on open-minded enquiry into the unknown?*[5] He lists ten unspoken beliefs and assumptions that science is often unquestioningly based upon and demonstrates that these have now been proven false by modern science, and yet they remain the underlying paradigm. When they are finally overthrown, the nature of the scientific questions that we ask will change and the paradigm will shift.

One of my teachers Alberto Villoldo notes the negative impact that the old paradigm has helped to create: *The story of victimhood has become ubiquitous, creating a culture of powerlessness that expresses itself in many ways... The self-help movement is rife with people who spend all their energy exploring themselves and their 'issues', honing their stories again and again rather than breaking out of them.*[6]

This book is my attempt to help people break out of the stories of victimhood. It presents what is known within academia, but is still struggling to make its way into public awareness. I hope it will be of use to all those who are willing to make an open-minded enquiry into the unknown, seeking greater awareness and being prepared to step into greater responsibility.

I particularly hope it will attract interest from those who can spread this knowledge more widely and start to make the changes that our health service and planet so desperately need: journalists, health professionals, policy makers, legislators and those responsible for research and health budgets.

5 Sheldrake, Rupert. 2013. *The Science Delusion* p.257 London, UK: Coronet, Hodder & Stoughton Ltd.

6 Villoldo, Alberto, PhD. 2009. *Courageous Dreaming: How the Shamans Dream the World into Being* p.47 London, UK: Hay House Inc.

# INTRODUCTION

Many leading doctors and psychologists now recognise that stress, unresolved trauma and alienation from any sense of community are responsible for many of the chronic diseases of Western populations. The body and brain learn and then default to a maladaptive reaction to stress and life events, thus becoming unable to maintain normal healthy behaviour and immune function. The psyche splits into a traumatised self and a survivor self. We dissociate internally from the traumatised self and our bodies to avoid feeling their pain. We dissociate externally from our communities and our planet to avoid feeling their suffering. We suffer from a lack of sense of purpose or meaning in life. We feel lost and turn to food, alcohol, sex, pornography, drugs, shopping, work and unhealthy dependent relationships to try to find meaning and happiness.

In this book I want to investigate what I believe is a widespread delusion of victimhood and the tools that are now available to help us to step out of this delusion into a place of autonomy and consciousness. These tools include things that in the past have been variously described as woo-woo, new age, alternative and counter-cultural. They include physical bodymind work, energy healing, meditation, dance, chanting, work with the ancestors, work with the land and for some people possibly even the exploration of a greater, nonlocal consciousness through the ceremonial use of psychedelic compounds. I do emphasise here the conscious, ceremonial use of these compounds, or else their use as part of a clinical trial, and not mindless recreational use of these compounds. I write much more about this in Chapter 6.

My objective is to explain in modern medical and scientific terms why these tools are necessary to an integrated healthcare system for the 21st century, that recognises it is no longer enough to treat symptoms pharmacologically, but seeks root causes of disease and disconnection.

I don't want to adopt an 'us and them' attitude to the medical establishment, but I do want to validate the need for the integration into public health services of a range of holistic services beyond those that are usually available within the NHS and equivalent bodies in other countries, yet which are being proven to be useful by a growing number of peer-reviewed scientific trials.

If you want to continue reading, are you prepared to step outside the box of your 'knowns', the hidden conditioning imposed predominantly by your cultural upbringing and schooling? Maybe you have already achieved this and are just interested in the scientific validation of what you intuitively feel and believe. Maybe the answer is not clear as yet, because of course it can be comfortable to be a victim. If we are victims then the state we find ourselves in is not our fault!

As many pioneering individuals have done before, are you prepared to step into a world of uncertainty, with many dimensions and a consciousness that exists outside your physical body? Are you prepared to step into the 21st century science of neuroplasticity and connection with a nonlocal energy greater than our own, which if we use the realisations of quantum physics, allows us to consciously become an active participant of the world we live in, with autonomy, power, influence, choice – but also responsibility?

I am going to be discussing some challenging concepts. For some people they may appear to be difficult partly because they are underpinned by some seriously complicated mathematics, but don't worry, there are no equations in this book. For others they may be difficult because they may challenge your view of reality and what we are capable of. I will try to lead you through the concepts one step at a time and, in an attempt to be clear, I will define some of the key words I am going to use within each chapter. There is great confusion about language and words like energy, spirit, consciousness, mind, placebo, can mean many different things to different people and so clarity in this area is essential to eliminate misunderstanding as much as possible.

Research into psychedelic compounds and particularly the remarkable properties of the tryptamines in dealing with a wide range of psychological problems is finally being permitted again after an 18-year ban in the Western world. This ban, under which the endogenously produced di-methyl-tryptamine (DMT) was categorised as a Class A drug, was passed by the United States Congress in 1970, over the objections of nearly every scientist in the field at the time[7]. Perhaps fortunately they did not put serotonin and melatonin into the same Class A category, or there would be no understanding of how these mood molecules (which both chemically and physiologically are very close to the tryptamines) work in our brains.

Why did this happen despite the extremely positive results

---

7 Including for instance the co-founder of Alcoholics Anonymous, Bill Wilson and Dr Albert Kurland, one of the world's leading experts on LSD who continued to study the benefits of the drug until his death in 2008, at which time he was writing a book titled *LSD: An Investigational Odyssey*.

of the clinical trials in the 1960s which pointed to the potential of these drugs to improve the lives of millions of people? Arguably because the increasing use of psychedelics in the 1960s was also highly associated with a rapidly escalating counter-culture that questioned the establishment and its values.

And yes, this book will also question the conditioning and values of the old establishment rooted in materialism and wielding a fundamental disregard for this planet that is our home. Stepping into the world of a nonlocal consciousness outside our physical bodies gives us much greater control over our own health and well-being than we are taught is possible, but it also gives us a much greater sense of our impact throughout space and time, hence the extent of our power (which can be used wisely or otherwise) and responsibility to ourselves and others, including the environment that we live in.

The reason we can now start to validate the use of an array of healing tools which have always been used by 'the primitive peoples' comes as a result of the emerging implications of quantum physics and 21st century neurological answers to the questions that I pose below, which are 180 degrees from the answers which the Newtonian scientific and medical paradigms have provided. The latter are the answers which have led us increasingly to social isolation and dependence on pharmaceutically manufactured medication, stripping away our personal power and autonomy.

I emphasise that the questions are not new – they are the existential questions that philosophers and mystics have pondered since modern man emerged. Some of the answers are not new either, they are the answers that those self-same philosophers and mystics often arrived at over the aeons, but which have been dismissed during the reign of scientific materialism.

What I am attempting to present here is the modern medical and scientific rationale for some 'irrational' viewpoints that have been decried and denigrated by our scientific communities for around four hundred years, but which at an intuitive, emotional level have always had such appeal to humanity.

So the questions I will discuss in the following chapters are:

1. Do you think that we believe what we see, or see what we believe? In other words do you see things as they are, or does your conditioning determine what you perceive is around you, governing how you behave and what you think it is possible to achieve in your life?
2. Do you believe you are a victim or a co-creator of your world? Can you influence what happens and accept autonomy, or are you the product of what others tell you about yourself, limited by what they believe you should do and say? Are you stuck in a trauma of the past, neurologically programmed to react unconsciously to conditioning, or are you able to learn new ways of being that free you to step into your power and potential?
3. Do you believe that placebos and alternative medicine therapies have a real impact on the physical and mental health of a patient? This can be taken to refer first to the impact of placebo substances on the patient, and secondly to the impact of placebo services given to the patient.
4. Which do you think is more important in perception – the functionality of the right-hemisphere of the brain, or that of the left-hemisphere? Alternatively phrased, are emotions, intuition and creativity more or less important than language, logic and compartmentalisation?
5. Do you believe anything travels faster than the speed of light and how do you think microscopic quantum effects impact our macroscopic everyday reality? The answer to this will impact your belief in quantum biology and the interaction between brain, mind and consciousness.

6. Do you think consciousness is held within the physical brain or in some sort of field outside the brain? In other words are you a materialist or a dualist? If the latter do you believe in the emerging field theories of consciousness?
7. Do you think psychedelic compounds are helpful or dangerous and if so in what circumstances? Do you support further research into these chemicals that interact with neurotransmitters to assist people suffering from disorders such as post-traumatic stress disorder (PTSD), addiction, cluster headaches and depression, as well as those facing death as a result of a terminal illness?
8. What do you think shamanic healing involves and is it genuinely effective? And do you believe that the shamans have had access for centuries to information which more advanced civilisations are only now re-discovering?
9. What do you think happens at death? When your physical body dies do you believe that 'you' become extinct, do you reincarnate in a different form, does your individual consciousness continue in some other dimension, or does your individual consciousness in some way re-join a collective consciousness in a different dimension or within an omniscient and omnipresent field of energy?
10. Do you think it is possible to carry emotional or physical pain on behalf of another member of the family system that you are in whether they are dead or alive? In other words are we energetically entangled with our ancestors?

Before proceeding, I invite you to ponder each of these questions for a few minutes and acknowledge your current belief system and response to each.

In order to provide answers to these questions, I am attempting to put the research of hundreds of doctors and scientists, covering thousands of pages of journals across the globe, into language that everybody can understand. This will undoubtedly lead to some lack of depth as far as academic experts are concerned, but I want journalists, politicians, teachers and people working throughout the medical professions, as well as everyone else trying to live their lives on this planet, to be able to access these emerging concepts which are so crucial for our individual and collective health.

Ervin Laszlo has been professor of philosophy, systems theory and future studies in the USA, Europe and the Far East. He is founder and president of the international think-tank, the Club of Budapest and the General Evolution Research Group. He has spent more than forty years searching for an *Integral Theory of Everything*, searching for meaning through science, writing 75 books which have been translated into 20 languages.

He calls the journey into a nonlocal consciousness the Akashic experience, in honour of the Indian concept of the Akasha as the source of everything. He writes: *The Akashic experience testifies that we are subtly yet effectively linked with each other, with nature, and with the cosmos. It inspires solidarity, love, empathy, and a sense of responsibility for each other and the environment. These are ineluctable elements of the mind-set we need to pull out of the global crisis that threatens our world and to create peace and sustainability on this perilously ravaged planet.*[8]

So if you want to become more conscious, more aware of the healthcare paradigm shift our global society is moving towards, more aware of your potential and hence more responsible, read on. If you would prefer to stay as a victim of the old paradigm, you will probably choose to close the book right now, but I would ask at the very least that you don't denigrate from prejudice theories and modalities that you have

---

8 Laszlo, Ervin. 2009. *The Akashic Experience: Science and the Cosmic Memory Field* pp7–8 Rochester, Vermont, USA: Inner Traditions International and Bear & Company, www.Innertraditions.com

chosen not to investigate objectively. Remember the perennial wisdom, we don't know what we don't know! Or as stated by British theologist William Paley: *There is a principle which is a bar against all information, which is proof against all argument, and which cannot fail to keep a man in everlasting ignorance. This principle is, contempt prior to examination.*[9]

## GLOSSARY FOR THE INTRODUCTION

**Autonomy**: the right or condition of self-government, independence, freedom.

**Consciousness**: self-awareness. Being able to observe and influence your actions.

**Dissociation**: a profound detachment when people watch events as if they were out of their own body, like an independent witness. The person is unable to feel their body or their emotions.

**Nonlocality**: action at a distance. Distant particles can have simultaneous effects on other particles in the system, which involves information being transmitted faster than the speed of light.

**Nonlocal consciousness**: consciousness located outside a particular time or place. Complete and endless consciousness existing in a dimension that is not tied to time or place.

**Psychedelic**: hallucinogenic substances.

**Shaman**: someone who can journey into nonlocal consciousness at will and gain information that will benefit their community.

---

9 Paley, William. 1794. *A View of the Evidences of Christianity*

# CHAPTER 1: SEEING IS BELIEVING?

**Do you think that we believe what we see, or see what we believe? In other words do you see things as they are, or does your conditioning determine what you perceive is around you, governing how you behave and what you think it is possible to achieve in your life?**

> *The model we choose to use to understand something determines what we find.*[10]
>
> (Iain McGilchrist)

## Introduction

In this chapter I present some basic anatomy of the brain, the endocrine system and the nervous system, which is necessary if we are to be aware of what is happening inside our bodies and hence how we can potentially change those reactions.

In the old paradigm seeing is believing. The body and the

10 McGilchrist, Iain. 2009. The Master and his Emissary: The Divided Brain and the Making of the Western World p.97 New Haven and London: Yale University Press

brain are considered to be mechanisms that function according to deterministic systems. Emotions are independent from our physical bodies and our health, and our minds have no control over our health or our subjective experiences. Everything is objective and systemically determined.

Modern biology and neuroscience have moved towards understanding that there is much greater symbiosis between the body and the brain and the way in which our subjective experiences in the past determine the neural pathways by which we perceive things in the present. There is a deepening knowledge of the extent to which emotional stress and trauma has a lasting physiological impact on the brain, the physical body and our health.

## The impact of observation on outcome

Historically the scientific answer to the question 'Do we believe what we see, or see what we believe?' would have been the former. The conventional view is that evidence, in terms of what is observed in an experiment, is what turns a hypothesis into a proven fact. But, just as it has been shown in physics that the position, expectations and attitude of the observer can have a huge impact on the outcome of any scientific experiment,[11] so too our current beliefs, expectations and previous life experiences can create a large auto-feedback on our perception of what we observe and experience, whether they be physical objects or events in the world around us, or even what's happening inside us.

Events that we perceive and react to can be stressful and even

11 This phenomenon is known as the Copenhagen interpretation of quantum physics and derives from the work of Niels Bohr, Werner Heisenberg and Max Born.

traumatic incidents, such as redundancy, criticism, accidents, medical diagnoses and the death or departure of a loved one. These events can also be less personal and more societal, such as immigration, global warming, whether a particular political candidate is honest or evil or even how we react to different people walking down the street – whether they are black or white, wearing a hoodie, a mini-skirt, a turban or a burka. Other events include positive happenings such as compliments, praise, getting a promotion or a new job, moving to a new home, meeting a loved one or having a baby. On a wider level they can include winning a war, a new piece of legislation or a particular person being elected to a position of authority and power.

To understand how our expectations and beliefs have such a significant impact on our perception of objects and events, it's necessary to have at least a basic understanding of the anatomy and physiology of the brain and the interaction of the brain and the body through the endocrine system and the nervous system. This is the modern medicine of the bodymind and how what happens in the mind controls what happens in the body, including how we perceive and then react to events. There is also a biofeedback mechanism between body and the mind, so the flow of causality is two-way. In this chapter I will talk about the intricate links between what happens in the physical brain and the body, while in later chapters I talk about the links between a wider non-physical mind or consciousness, via the brain to the body and back again.

The knowledge that I present here is based on huge volumes of medical and scientific research. Some of the main sources I have used are the biological, neurological and psychological compilations put together over many years by the recognised experts in their various fields, including Drs Peter Levine,[12] Bruce

12 Levine, Peter A. PhD. 2010. *In An Unspoken Voice: How the Body Releases Trauma and Restores Goodness* Berkeley, California, USA: North Atlantic Books

Lipton,[13] Iain McGilchrist,[14] Karl Pribram,[15] Allan Schore[16] and Bessel Van Der Kolk.[17] I quote from and reference all of them at length and I am grateful to them and their publishers for the permissions granted to use their material. For readers wanting the original research papers and sources for the conclusions that these authors present, I refer you to the extensive references provided in their published works as cited.

As background information on these important medical figures spanning a wide range of disciplines, Dr Peter Levine received his PhD in medical biophysics from the University of California, Berkeley and also holds a doctorate in psychology from the International University. He has worked in the field of stress and trauma for over 40 years. His contribution to the field of body psychotherapy was honoured in 2010 when he received the Lifetime Achievement award from the United States Association for Body Psychotherapy.

Dr Bruce Lipton began his scientific career as a cell biologist and received his PhD from the University of Virginia at Charlottesville. In 1982 he began examining the principles of quantum physics and how they might be integrated into understanding the cell's information processing systems. He produced breakthrough studies on the cell membrane and his research at Stanford University's School of Medicine, between 1987 and 1992, revealed that the environment,

---

13 Lipton, Bruce H. PhD. 2005. *The Biology of Belief* Carlsbad, CA, USA: Hay House Inc.

14 McGilchrist, Iain. 2009. *The Master and his Emissary: The Divided Brain and the Making of the Western World* New Haven and London: Yale University Press

15 Pribram, Karl H. M.D. 2013. *The Form Within: My Point of View* Westport, CT, USA: Prospecta Press

16 Schore, Allan N. 2012. *The Science of the Art of Psychotherapy* New York, USA: W.W. Norton & Company

17 Van Der Kolk, Bessel. 2014. *The Body keeps the Score: Mind, Brain and Body in the Transformation of Trauma* USA: Viking Penguin

operating through the membrane, controlled the behaviour and physiology of the cell, turning genes on and off. His discoveries presaged today's science of epigenetics.

Dr Iain McGilchrist is a psychiatrist, doctor, writer and literary scholar. He was Clinical Director of the Acute Mental Health Services at the then Bethlem Royal and Maudsley NHS Trust in London, and is a Fellow of the Royal College of Psychiatrists.

Dr Karl Pribram's distinguished career, spanning six decades, was devoted to brain/behaviour research. He taught neurophysiology and physiological psychology at Yale University and for 30 years was at Stanford University where he received a lifetime career award from the National Institutes of Health as Professor of Neuroscience in the Departments of Psychology and Psychiatry. His most recent award was presented by the Society of Experimental Psychologists for his seminal role in the cognitive revolution and for his pioneering contributions to the computational, theoretical and physiological foundations of brain function and behaviour.

Dr Allan Schore is on the clinical faculty of the Department of Psychiatry and Biobehavioral Sciences, UCLA David Geffen School of Medicine, and at the UCLA Center for Culture, Brain, and Development. The American Psychoanalytic Association has described Dr Schore as: *a monumental figure in psychoanalytic and neuropsychoanalytic studies.*[18]

Bessel Van Der Kolk M.D. has been active as a clinician, researcher and teacher in the area of post-traumatic stress and related phenomena since the 1970s. He was co-principal investigator of the DSM IV Field Trials for Post-Traumatic Stress Disorder (PTSD) and his current research is on how trauma affects memory processes and brain-imaging studies of PTSD. He is past President of the International Society for

18 www.allanschore.com

Traumatic Stress Studies, Professor of Psychiatry at Boston University Medical School, and Medical Director of the Trauma Center at JRI in Brookline, Massachusetts.

These are some of the authorities on whom I base my work and to whom I am indebted for blazing the trail, often being initially subjected to ridicule and ostracised by their peers before being recognised as ahead of their time.

## Simple anatomy and physiology of the brain

Figure 1 shows some of the major areas of the brain which are key to understanding the bodymind, the way the cells throughout the entire body are influenced from the brain and our thoughts and emotions. The brain stem is situated just above the foramen magnum, where the spinal cord enters our skull. Above the brain stem is the limbic brain (see figure 2 for a description of what is included within the limbic brain) and around it are the basal ganglia, then the cingulate gyrus, then

Figure 1: key areas for the bodymind

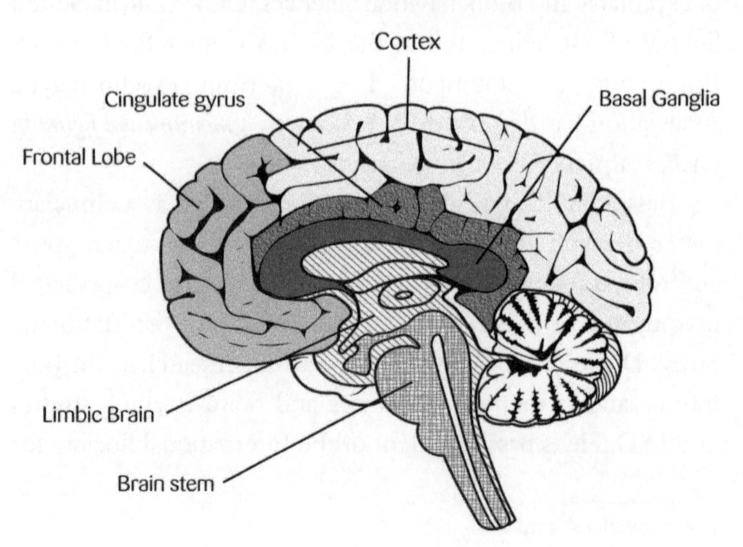

the cerebral cortex including the frontal lobe, containing the two separate hemispheres (left and right) of the cortex.

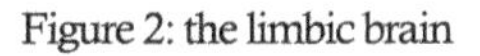
Figure 2: the limbic brain

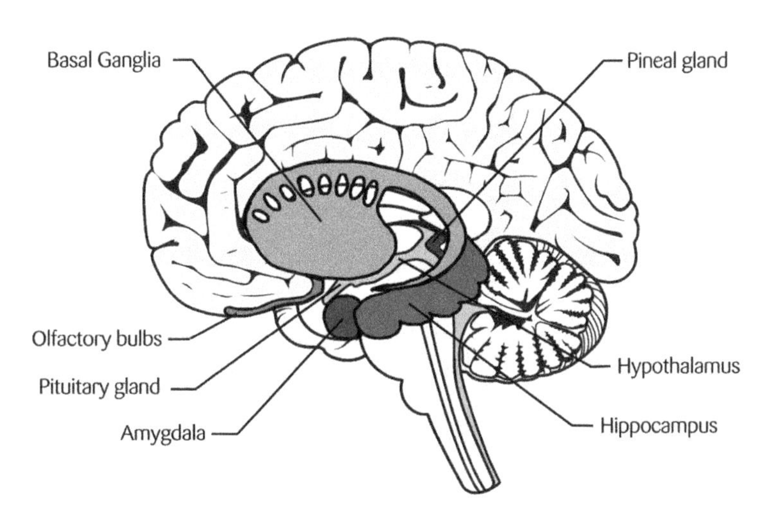


Figure 2 delves into the enormously important limbic section of the brain in more detail. As shown it is comprised of the physical cells which seem to be the source of our emotions and internal awareness of our bodily states. Among other things it includes the hypothalamus, the hippocampus, the limbic basal ganglia, the amygdala, the pituitary gland, the pineal gland and the olfactory bulbs, all of which are deeply connected with our emotions and our brain-body connections.

Emotional feelings are generated when our bodies experience pain or pleasure and it is the amygdala, deep in the limbic brain, which is responsible for intense survival emotions. This emotional centre has direct and extremely fast connections with the cerebral cortex, the sensory organs, the visceral organs (the hollow organs, such as the gut, heart and lungs) and the endocrine system, as I will discuss in greater detail. It is particularly closely connected to the right-hemisphere of the orbitofrontal cortex.[19]

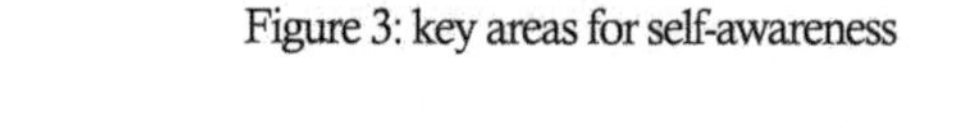
Figure 3: key areas for self-awareness

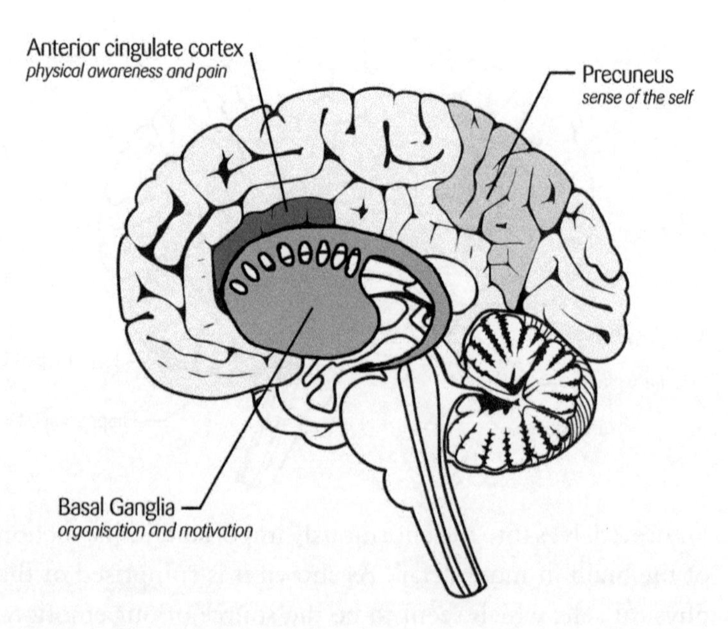


Figure 3 moves to the parts of the brain that make us aware of our physical state, action and our sense of self. The right anterior cingulate cortex (located within the cingulate gyrus, directly under the pre-frontal cortex) is the part of the brain that allows us to be aware of our physical state. It is associated with the appreciation of pain, both our own pain, transferred from the physical body via the nervous system, and empathically with the pain of others.

The upper basal ganglia are involved in organising and

19 McGilchrist, Iain. 2009. *The Master and his Emissary: The Divided Brain and the Making of the Western World* p.58 New Haven and London: Yale University Press

maintaining motivational behaviour, the secondary courses of action.

The precuneus lies between the two hemispheres of the brain and is deeply connected with the sense of the self, of who we are. It has a very high metabolic rate even when resting but it goes quiet in altered states of consciousness when the sense of self is switched off, for instance in deep sleep, anaesthesia and vegetative states.

As shown in Figure 4, towards the surface of the skull is the cerebral cortex which is split laterally into two hemispheres, right and left. Towards the front is the forebrain and at the very front we have the thin sliver of brain tissue called the pre-frontal cortex. This is the most recent, the most highly evolved and the most distinctly human of all the regions of the brain. Anatomically it is located between the cortical systems that modulate our motivations and those that modulate our emotions. It is associated with thinking, planning and decision-making.

Figure 4: the cortex

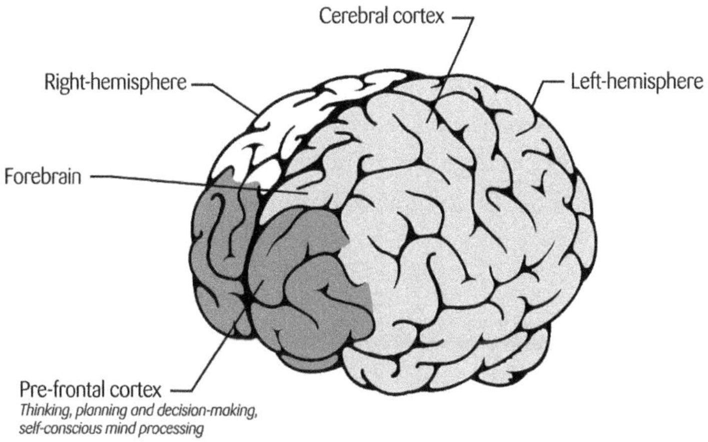

Cerebral cortex
Right-hemisphere
Left-hemisphere
Forebrain
Pre-frontal cortex
*Thinking, planning and decision-making, self-conscious mind processing*

Figure 5: key functional areas

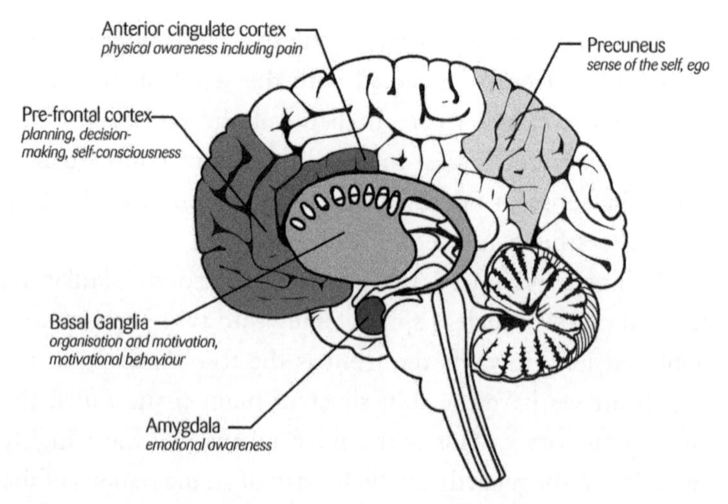


Perhaps most significantly, the pre-frontal cortex is the seat of 'self-conscious' mental processing i.e. it can observe our own behaviours and emotions. Because of its strong connections with the limbic brain (particularly the amygdala) and the endocrine system, it is then able to modify the response of the limbic brain and the endocrine system to external events. In other words it has the capacity to exert control over the other parts of the brain.

Figure 5 summarises what I have described so far about the functions of the various parts of the brain in a very simplified presentation. What is key as I continue is that the pre-frontal cortex has the ability to modify what's happening in all the other parts of the brain. It at least thinks it's the boss!

## Simple anatomy of the nervous system

So how is all this information being communicated around the brain and between the brain and the body? That is the function of the enormously complex nervous system, which is subdivided in different ways as illustrated in Figure 6.

Physically it is split into the central nervous system of the brain and the spinal cord, and the peripheral nervous system, which consists of all the neural tissue outside the central nervous system and which connects the central nervous system to all other parts of the body.

Within the peripheral nervous system there are sensory neurons which bring information from the receptors in tissues and organs into the central nervous system. This information comes from touch, taste, pressure, pain, temperature, smell, vision, hearing and balance. The motor neurons carry commands from the central nervous system to the muscles and glands.

Figure 6: the nervous system

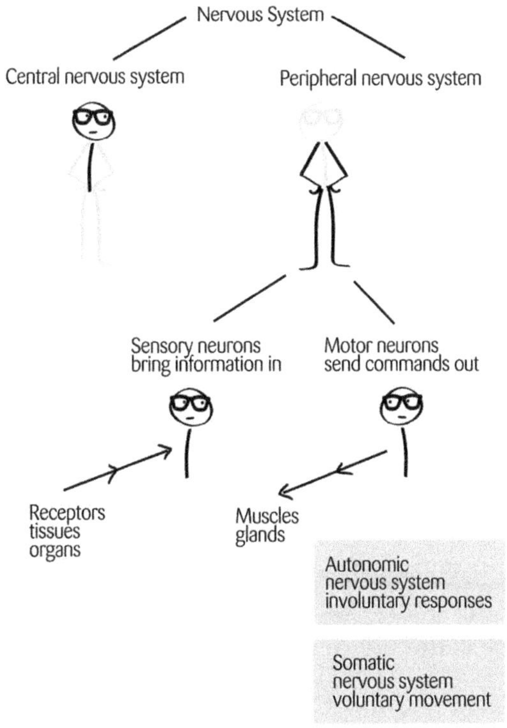

Nervous System

Central nervous system

Peripheral nervous system

Sensory neurons
bring information in

Motor neurons
send commands out

Receptors
tissues
organs

Muscles
glands

Autonomic
nervous system
involuntary responses

Somatic
nervous system
voluntary movement

Then within the motor neurons there is the somatic nervous system, which controls voluntary movements and skeletal muscle contractions and the autonomic nervous system, which in turn controls the involuntary responses of our smooth muscles, cardiac muscle, glands and tissues.

Within the brain, the central nervous system consists of neural tissue, composed of both cell bodies and long connecting axons. Each neuron consists of cytoplasm and a nucleus surrounded by a cell membrane and dendrites. The cell body receives impulses from other cells through the dendrites and transmits electrical impulses away to other cells through the axon. Figure 7 shows a typical neuron.

Figure 7: the structure of a neuron

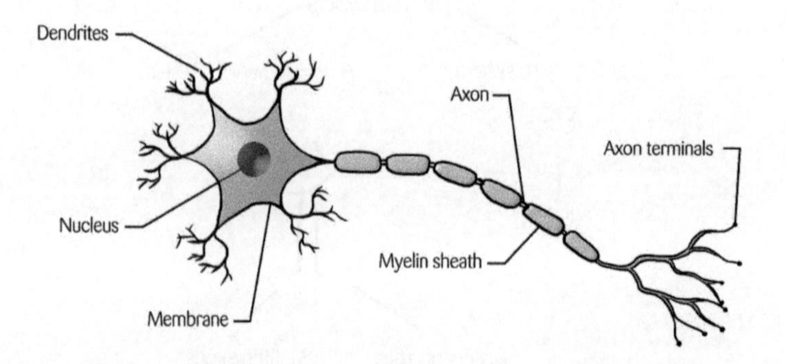


Our nervous system works through a complex network of neuronal pathways each involving a chain of separate neurons through which instructions and information are passed electromagnetically with the help of chemicals called neurotransmitters. These are chemicals synthesised either in the brain itself or in other tissues (particularly the gut) that modify brain function through their effects on nerve cells.[20] The neurotransmitters are released by electrochemical pulses within the neurons. They leave via the axon terminals and are transferred across the gaps between neurons which are known as synapses. They then bind to receptors on the feathery dendrites of adjacent cells. Together these connections in the brain form what is called the synaptodendritic web.[21]

The axons of some neurons are surrounded by a white fatty substance called myelin which greatly speeds up the outgoing transmission of signals between neurons. Areas of the central nervous system that are rich in myelin constitute what is known as the white matter of the brain and are more predominant in the right-hemisphere. These neurons seem capable of a wide-ranging focus. Areas of the central nervous system that largely consist of cell bodies rather than axons do not appear white, and these areas constitute what is known as the grey matter of the brain, which is more predominant in the left-hemisphere which specialises in much more localised attention.

This left-right division of grey and white matter as well as the electromagnetic foundations of our nervous system in communication will be crucial in the later chapters as I move on to the way our brains can connect with the wider field of energy that surrounds us.

From the brain the central nervous system communicates with the rest of the body in a number of ways, in particular through its close interaction with the endocrine system.

---

20 Examples of neurotransmitters are serotonin, melatonin, acetylcholine, dopamine, noradrenaline, gamma amino butyric acid, and glutamate. Note that somewhat confusingly, different cultures use different names for some of these neurotransmitters. Adrenaline is the same as epinephrine and noradrenaline is the same as norepinephrine.

21 For those interested in further details of this process which is highly condensed here, a good source is http://www.human-memory.net/brain_neurons.html

Figure 8: autonomic nervous system

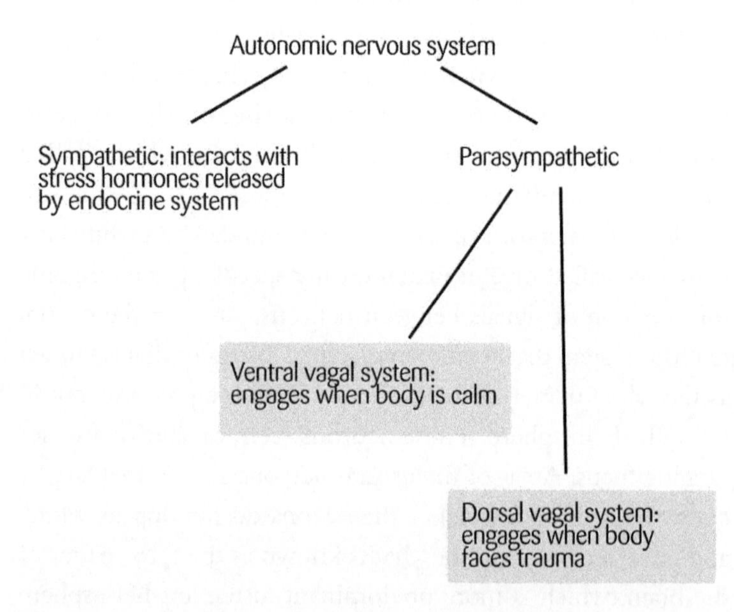


One distinction which is of great relevance to our health or disease is the division of the autonomic nervous system into the sympathetic and the parasympathetic branches as shown in Figure 8. The sympathetic nervous system interacts with the hormones released by the endocrine system when the body is under stress and agitated.

The parasympathetic nervous system further subdivides into two branches. The first branch interacts with the hormones released by the endocrine system when the body is relaxed and calm. It is mediated by the ventral vagal system and regulates cardiac output to foster engagement or disengagement with the social environment. The second branch interacts with the hormones released by the endocrine system when the person moves beyond stress to true trauma and fight or flight have failed. This is mediated via the dorsal motor nucleus of the vagal system which is associated with intense emotional states and acts to shut down metabolic activity during immobilisation, death feigning and hiding behaviour.[22]

## The brain-body connection via the endocrine system in connection with the nervous system

The various parts of the brain talk to the major organs of the body via the nervous system in conjunction with the endocrine system through what is called the hypothalamic-pituitary-adrenal axis, which links the electrical impulses of the brain and the nervous system with the chemical reactions of the body, through the mediation of hormones produced in the endocrine system.

This is getting into the real physiology of how mental and emotional stress impact our health, in particular by shutting down the immune system as we switch to survival mode. As you are reading this, don't worry if you feel this describes how you live your life for a lot of the time – the next chapter goes on to explain how you can change things.

Figures 9 and 10 show the hormones released when we start to perceive danger, fear or anger, and the impact that has on a wide variety of functions via the sympathetic nervous system. Doctors would describe this as an activation of the hypothalamic-pituitary-adrenal axis and the fight-or-flight response.

The hypothalamus (about the size of an almond) is in charge of the stress response located within the limbic brain as shown in Figure 2. It secretes substances known as neuro-hormones that start and stop the secretion of pituitary hormones. At the same time the hippocampus which curves back from the amygdala regulates the pituitary gland's secretion of steroids.

22 Schore, Allan N. 2012. *The Science of the Art of Psychotherapy* p.267 New York, USA: W.W. Norton & Company

To produce the fight-or-flight response, the hypothalamus activates two systems in combination: the sympathetic nervous system and the adrenal-cortical system. The sympathetic nervous system uses nerve pathways to initiate reactions in the body, while the adrenal-cortical system uses the bloodstream.

Figure 9: physical responses to fear or stress stage one

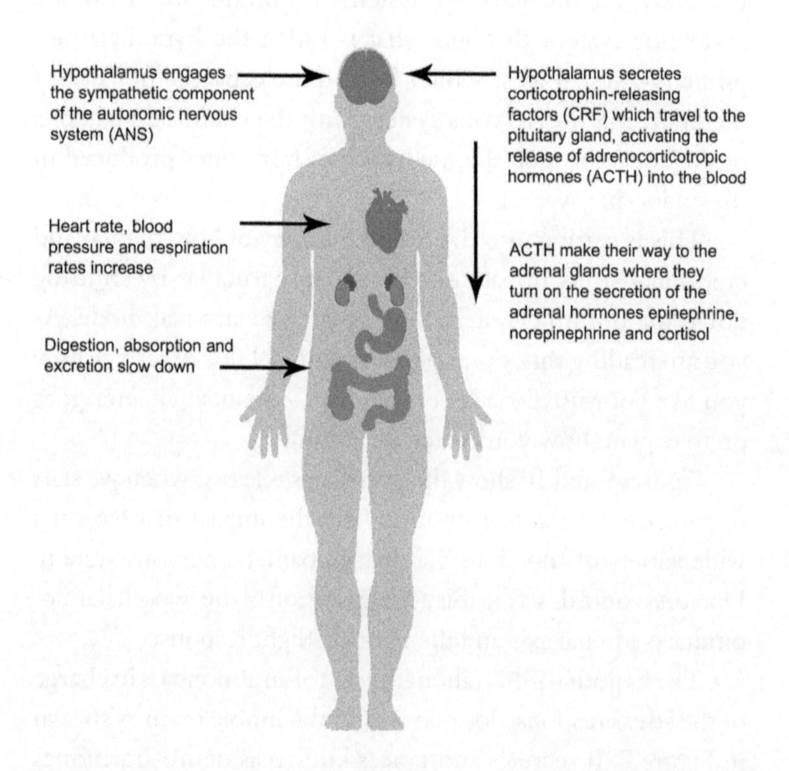


Initially on facing a stressful situation, the hypothalamus releases the main stress hormone, corticotrophin-releasing factor, into the sympathetic component of the autonomic nervous system. Corticotrophin-releasing factor sends several messages to the anterior pituitary gland within the limbic brain:

1. causing it directly to secrete adrenocorticotropic hormone/corticotrophin which in turn stimulates the adrenal cortex to release cortisol;
2. causing it to stimulate the adrenal glands to release corticosteroid, adrenaline and noradrenaline.

These hormones together regulate our metabolism and immune response throughout the body. Via the sympathetic nervous system they have the following impacts:

- the blood vessels travelling to the heart, large muscle groups, lungs and brain dilate;
- the heart and respiratory rates increase and the muscles tense;
- the pupils dilate so that more light can get in;
- glucose is released into the bloodstream giving a boost of energy;
- blood flow to the gastrointestinal tract, hands and feet is constricted:
- the level of acid in the stomach increases and digestive enzymes decrease;
- cortisol suppresses the immune system in order to conserve energy reserves and the reproduction system gets shut off;
- blood flow is redirected to the hindbrain enhancing its life-sustaining reflexes to ensure our short-term survival; and
- the adrenal stress hormones constrict the blood vessels in the forebrain reducing its ability to engage in conscious action, reasoning and logic. There is a diminished ability to think clearly.

The result is that we are in the physical state commonly known as 'fight or flight' and may experience rage or panic.

If the danger then subsides or is resolved by fight or flight, the hypothalamus stops triggering the stress responses and the sympathetic nervous system shuts off again. The ventral vagal branch of the parasympathetic system takes over. Our cortisol and adrenaline levels naturally drop. Our heart rate and breathing decrease, our blood pressure drops and the immune, digestive and reproductive systems switch back on.

Figure 10: physical responses to fear or stress stage two

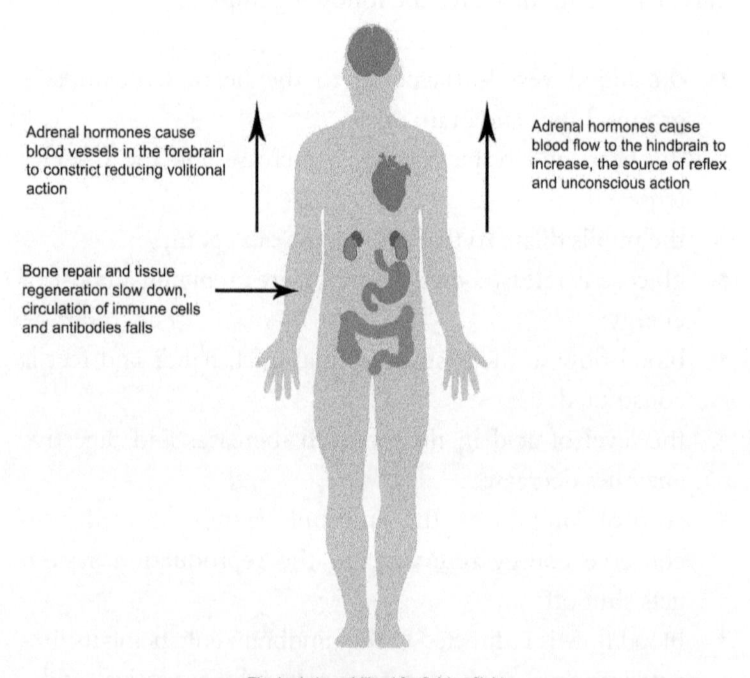


However, if the fear-inducing situation is not resolved but indeed escalates, the next stage is defined as trauma, which arises when the situation is overwhelming and the person feels helpless and hopeless. They fear they will not survive. Fight or flight are impossible, or have failed. At this point as shown in Figure 11, the body switches into the dorsal vagal branch of the parasympathetic system, the state of conservation and withdrawal. The person strives to be 'unseen'. The metabolism shuts down and the heart rate, blood pressure and respiration decrease. The muscles collapse, the person loses all energy to have an impact on their life and enters a state of helplessness. The body freezes and the hypothalamic-pituitary-adrenal axis floods the system with pain-numbing opiates. Medically this is the state known as tonic immobility. It can be seen as an emergency brake.

Figure 11: physical responses to fear or stress stage three

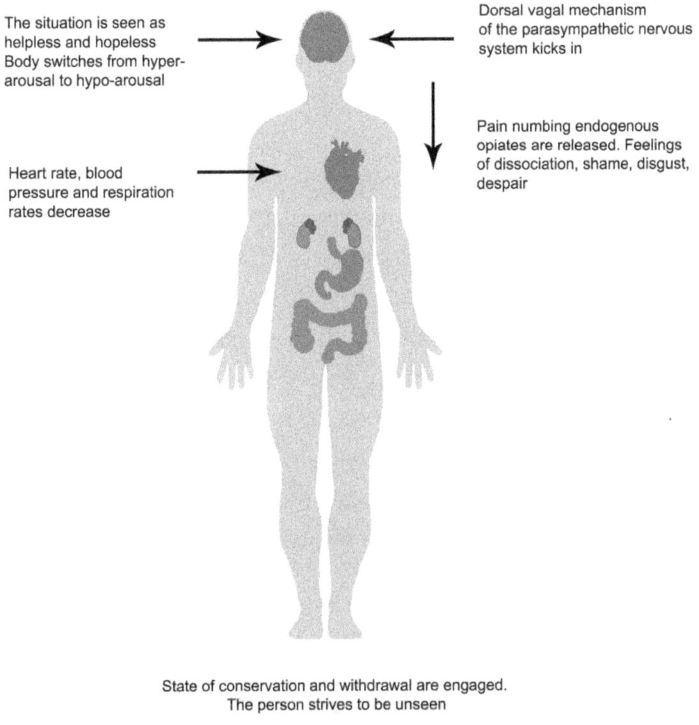

In this hypo-metabolic state the person may feel shame, disgust, hopeless despair and then a profound detachment of dissociation wherein they watch events as if they were out of their own body, like an independent witness. At this stage, the right anterior insula is severely inhibited, such that the person is unable to feel their body or their emotions, a condition known as alexithymia. Dissociatively detached people are remote from their sense of identity and their selves. They don't know who they are. Van Der Kolk reports that: *Almost every brain-imaging study of trauma patients finds abnormal activation of the insula. This part of the brain integrates and interprets the input from the internal organs – including our muscles, joints, and balance (proprioceptive) system – to generate the sense of being embodied... trauma makes people feel like either some body else, or like no body. In order to overcome trauma, you need help to get back in touch with your body, with your Self.*[23]

As trauma specialist Peter Levine describes it: *This collapse, defeat and loss of the will to live are at the very core of deep trauma... Such distancing, called dissociation, helps to make the unbearable bearable.*[24]

Unfortunately many people today are suffering from post-traumatic stress disorder and dissociation from their bodies and their selves. Millions more are suffering from chronically elevated levels of stress and disease, leaving themselves open to infections and viruses as their immune system is operating at a reduced level. As Allan Schore writes: *there is a growing consensus that human disease states fundamentally involve a dysregulation of an organism's psychobiological stress coping systems.*[25]

These reactions in the body resulting from stress in the environment are what the pharmaceutical industry attempts to control with antidepressants.

---

23 Van Der Kolk, Bessel. 2014. *The Body keeps the Score: Mind, Brain and Body in the Transformation of Trauma* p.247 USA: Viking Penguin

24 Levine, Peter A. PhD. 2010. *In An Unspoken Voice: How the Body Releases Trauma and Restores Goodness* pp49–50 Berkeley, California, USA: North Atlantic Books

25 Schore, Allan N. 2012. *The Science of the Art of Psychotherapy* p.224 New York, USA: W.W. Norton & Company

What is known as downer depression is attributed to low levels of the mood molecule serotonin which makes you feel alone, isolated, unloved and unworthy of love. Prescription pharmaceuticals such as Prozac, Zoloft and Paxil raise serotonin levels in the brain in order to improve a person's mood and enhance feelings of well-being.

The stress chemicals dopamine and its derivative noradrenaline increase feelings of alertness, assertiveness, aggression and wakefulness. They heighten energy, speed up thoughts and improve muscle coordination. Levels of dopamine and noradrenaline which are too low can cause depression. Levels which are too high can create anxiety and aggression, at the extreme leading to violent behaviour, schizophrenia, paranoia, and other forms of psychosis. The tricyclic anti-depressants Elavil, Triavil, Amoxapine, Doxepin and Wellbutin are used to alter dopamine and noradrenaline levels.

But all these pharmaceutical compounds are aimed at curing the symptoms of depression or aggression by altering the pharmacology inside our brains, without asking or attempting to deal with why the chemical levels do not naturally return to a state of healthy homeostasis and balance. As Van Der Kolk puts it: *After conducting numerous studies of medications for PTSD, I have come to realize that psychiatric medications have a serious downside, as they may deflect attention from dealing with the underlying issues. The brain-disease model takes control over people's fate out of their own hands and puts doctors and insurance companies in charge of fixing their problems.*[26]

This is at the heart of the division between curing symptoms and healing causes. As Caroline Myss writes: *A 'cure' occurs when one has successfully controlled or abated the physical progression of an illness. Curing a physical illness, however,*

26 Van Der Kolk, Bessel. 2014. *The Body keeps the Score: Mind, Brain and Body in the Transformation of Trauma* pp36–37 USA: Viking Penguin

*does not necessarily mean that the emotional and psychological stresses that were a part of the illness were also alleviated. In this case it is highly possible, and often probable, that an illness will recur.*

*The process of curing is passive; that is the patient is inclined to give his or her authority over to the physician and prescribed treatment instead of actively challenging the illness and reclaiming health. Healing, on the other hand, is an active and internal process that includes investigating one's attitudes, memories, and beliefs with the desire to release all negative patterns that prevent one's full emotional and spiritual recovery.*[27]

So far this explains how things which happen in our lives on any particular stressful or even traumatic occasion impact the brain, the nervous system, the endocrine system and the physical body through highly interconnected pathways. That is the background information we need so that we can understand how what we have experienced in the past impacts our brain's perception of, and body's reaction to, new events. Why we see what we believe rather than believing what we see.

## Brain patterning in response to previous events, known as limbic resonance

In 2000 Thomas Lewis M.D., Richard Lannon, M.D., and Fari Amini, M.D. (at the time clinical professors of psychiatry at the School of Medicine within the University of California, San Francisco) published *A General Theory of Love.*[28] They explain in detail the way that neurons in the cortex learn

27 Myss, Caroline. 1997. *Anatomy of the Spirit* pp47–48 London, UK: Bantam, Reproduced by permission of The Random House Group Ltd

28 Lewis, Thomas, M.D., Amini, Fari, M.D., Lannon, Richard, M.D. 2000. *A General Theory of Love* New York, USA: Vintage Books, Random House

and remember information through the creation of neural networks, which get stronger with use and wither when left unattended. In neurology, the pathways that we use most often are called attractors. In the case of the motor cortex these attractors organise our achievements in the world, our intentions in action. In the case of the limbic cortex, the attractors organise our initial assessment of the relevance of a novel input: what is it?

The problem with attractors is that they lead to the neural network registering new sensory information as if it conformed to past experience. As Lewis, Lannon and Amini put it: *Because human beings remember with neurons, we are disposed to see more of what we have already seen, hear anew what we have heard most often, think just what we have always thought. Our minds are burdened by an informational inertia whose headlong course is not easy to slow. As a life lengthens, momentum gathers.*[29]

Their conclusion is that: *the neural past interferes with the present. Experience methodically rewires the brain, and the nature of what it has seen dictates what it can see.*[30]

After a perception has been formed, the upper basal ganglia then decides what to do. Again we are driven by attractor pathways. So for example if an event has caused stress in the past, we tend to have a stressful reaction to the same event in the present even if the circumstances are very different.

If our attractors are strong enough, then we may even be inclined to manipulate completely novel events to correspond to our old beliefs. So for instance if we have been bitten by a dog in the past, we may see any dog coming towards us as

29 Lewis, Thomas, M.D., Amini, Fari, M.D., Lannon, Richard, M.D. 2000. *A General Theory of Love* p.141 New York, USA: Vintage Books, Random House

30 Lewis, Thomas, M.D., Amini, Fari, M.D., Lannon, Richard, M.D. 2000. *A General Theory of Love* p.135 New York, USA: Vintage Books, Random House

aggressive. If we have been raped by someone we love, we may believe anyone else we love will also rape us. If we have been told in the past that we are stupid or ugly, we may have built up a strong pattern and belief of inadequacy. Hence we may disbelieve anyone who now tells us something different, such as we are smart and beautiful. We hear what we have heard a million times before, even though the information this time is different! We see what we have unconsciously decided we will see, even if that is not really what is there. We react as we have reacted before to a particular stimulus, even when the wider circumstances are different.

The neural network of attractors and what may appear from the outside to be inappropriate reactions to minor stresses or setbacks in life are most pronounced in children who have been systemically abused and adults suffering from PTSD.

Allan N Schore has collated much of the evidence that demonstrates how psychologically stressed children become dissociating adults and this derives from the neural programming in their right-brain that results from repeated trauma. As Schore reports, the work of many including D.F. Watt[31] and D. Kalsched[32] has demonstrated that, as they grow, these children can switch into a dissociated state very quickly, in response to external events that would only cause a minor elevation of the hypothalamic-pituitary-adrenal axis in people whose limbic attractors were less focused on the extreme response of tonic immobility.

31 Watt, D.F. 2003. Psychotherapy in an age of neuroscience: Bridges to affective neuroscience. in J. Corrigall & H. Wilkinson (Eds), 2003. *Revolutionary connections. Psychotherapy and neuroscience.* p.109 London, UK: Karnac Books

32 Kalsched, D. 2005. Hope vs. Hopelessness in the Psychoanalytic Situation and in Dante's Divine Comedy in Lynn Cowan (Ed) 2005 *Barcelona, 2004, Proceedings of the Sixteenth International Congress for Analytical Psychology*, p.174 Einsiedeln, Switzerland: Daimon

Lipton suggests the root cause of ongoing psychobiological stress is even further back than childhood, into the womb during the mother's pregnancy, when the foetus absorbs the hormones that are circulating in the mother's bloodstream. He writes: *Stress hormones prepare the body to engage in a protection response. Once these maternal signals enter the fetal blood stream, they affect the same target tissues and organs in the fetus as they did in the mother... The development of fetal tissue and organs is proportional to both the amount of blood they receive and the function they provide. When passing through the placenta, the hormones of a mother experiencing chronic stress will profoundly alter the distribution of blood flow in her fetus and change the character of her developing child.*[33]

This suggests that the child's physiology is dependent on conditions from conception onwards and this physiology includes the neuronal patterns within the brain and the limbic attractors set in place. This conditioning then leads to a cascading reaction to external events whereby people respond in what appears to others to be an inappropriate way. They see life-threatening trauma when others see a minor threat. They fall into hopeless despair when others see a small setback.

Schore notes that: *Pathological dissociation... is manifest in a maladaptive, highly defensive, rigid, and closed system, one that responds to even low levels of intersubjective stress with parasympathetic dorsal vagal hypoarousal and heart rate deceleration. This fragile unconscious system is susceptible to mind-body metabolic collapse and thereby a loss of energy-dependent synaptic connectivity within the right brain, expressed in a sudden implosion of the implicit self and a rupture of self-continuity. This dis-integration of the right brain and collapse of the implicit self are signalled by the amplification of the parasympathetic*

33 Lipton, Bruce H. PhD. 2005. *The Biology of Belief* pp143–144 Carlsbad, CA, USA: Hay House Inc.

*affects of shame and disgust, and by the cognitions of hopelessness and helplessness.*[34]

This may all sound terribly gloomy, but the third conclusion from recent neuroscience is that we all have the potential for change. We can reprogramme our beliefs and our limbic attractors so that the future may be different from the past and those techniques are the focus of the next chapter.

## Conclusion

The brain works through a combination of electromagnetic and chemical channels. It contains the structures which allow the nervous system to send electrical impulses throughout the body and specifically the endocrine system to release chemicals from different glands. These in turn cause physical reactions in every cell and organ, which send further information back to the brain.

At any time the body may be in a state of fight-or-flight, dominated by the sympathetic nervous system and flooded with stress hormones. It may be in a state of tonic immobility, dominated by the dorsal vagal branch of the parasympathetic system, the state of conservation and withdrawal, flooded with pain-numbing opiates. Or it may be in a state of happy relaxation, under the control of the ventral vagal branch of the parasympathetic system, able to sleep, eat and fight infection.

All parts of the brain develop neural network pathways, which get stronger the more often they are used, becoming attractors, which condition our responses to new events in conformity with learned behaviours from past events.

The limbic brain is deeply connected with our emotions

34 Schore, Allan N. 2012. *The Science of the Art of Psychotherapy* pp83–84 New York, USA: W.W. Norton & Company

and our brain-body connections. The pre-frontal cortex is the seat of the 'self-conscious' mind i.e. it can observe our own behaviours and emotions. These two areas of the brain, limbic and pre-frontal cortex, are very strongly connected and the pre-frontal cortex has the capacity to exert control over the limbic brain.

Whilst we do process things unconsciously in terms of learned behaviour, it is possible to train the pre-frontal cortex to consciously change our perceptions, to believe what we see rather than seeing what we believe, and reacting according to what is truly present now.

## GLOSSARY FOR CHAPTER 1

**Alexithymia**: an inability to feel your body or your emotions.

**Endocrine system**: the collection of glands that produce the hormones that control our metabolism.

**HPA axis**: the hypothalamic-pituitary-adrenal axis which links the electrical impulses of the brain and our nervous system with the chemical reactions of the body, through the mediation of hormones produced in the endocrine system.

**Myelin**: the white fatty substance surrounding the axons of some neurons which greatly speeds up the outgoing transmission of signals between neurons.

**Parasympathetic nervous system**: a part of the autonomic nervous system (traditionally thought to be unconscious) which may be dominated by the dorsal vagal branch, the state of conservation and withdrawal, flooded with pain-numbing opiates, or by the ventral vagal branch, resulting in a state of happy relaxation, able to sleep, eat and fight infection.

**Serotonin**: a neurotransmitter with multiple functions that occurs in the cardiovascular system, the gastrointestinal tract and the nervous system.

**Sympathetic nervous system**: a part of the autonomic nervous system (traditionally thought to be unconscious), which regulates the body's fight-or-flight response.

**Tonic immobility**: the outcome of trauma, at which point the body switches into the dorsal vagal branch of the parasympathetic system, the state of conservation and withdrawal. The person strives to be 'unseen'. The body freezes and the HPA axis floods the system with pain-numbing opiates.

**Trauma**: the person is in a situation which is overwhelming. They feel helpless and hopeless. They fear they will not survive. Fight or flight are impossible, or have failed.

# CHAPTER 2: VICTIM VS AUTONOMOUS CO-CREATOR

**Do you believe you are a victim or a co-creator of your world? Can you influence what happens and accept autonomy, or are you the product of what others tell you about yourself, limited by what they believe you should do and say? Are you stuck in a trauma of the past, neurologically programmed to react unconsciously to conditioning, or are you able to learn new ways of being that free you to step into your power and potential?**

> *Our great challenge is to apply the lessons of neuroplasticity, the flexibility of brain circuits, to rewire the brains and reorganize the minds of people who have been programmed by life itself to experience others as threats and themselves as helpless.*[35]
>
> (Bessel Van Der Kolk)

35 Van Der Kolk, Bessel. 2014. *The Body keeps the Score: Mind, Brain and Body in the Transformation of Trauma* p.167 USA: Viking Penguin

## Introduction

In this chapter I consider some of the growing evidence regarding the extent of our ability to consciously control what were previously believed to be unconscious physical reactions to external events, through neuroplasticity and the mindful engagement of the pre-frontal cortex. This means that the future can be different from the past. We can learn to reprogramme our brains and their neural attractor pathways.

Frequently the quickest and most long-lasting way of doing this is through accessing memories held at a cellular level within the physical body rather than using talking therapies which access the brain (particularly the vocal left-brain), which tends to tell the story over and over. Until the autonomic nervous system's responses to traumatic experiences are accessed in the body, our old patterns remain stuck in the limbic brain, which can only be reprogrammed through physical experience.

## Therapy focused on reprogramming the limbic attractors

Dr Dan Siegel is currently Clinical Professor of psychiatry at the UCLA School of Medicine where he is on the faculty of the Center for Culture, Brain, and Development. He is the founding Co-Director of the Mindful Awareness Research Center and a leader in the field of interpersonal neurobiology. Recent neurobiological research that he has extensively documented demonstrates that, although our neural biology is programmed by our pasts, it is possible for the brain to change structurally and develop new neural connections that might allow us to escape the prison of the old limbic attractor pathways.

Central to this is the concept of neuroplasticity, or the ability of the brain to:

1. stimulate new neurons to grow;
2. create and strengthen synaptic connections; and
3. increase the sheathing along the axonal lengths to enhance the conduction speed of neural electrical impulses (a process known as myelinogenesis).

As described in Chapter 1, myelin is an electrically insulating material that forms around the axons of some neurons in the brain and nerve fibres elsewhere. It increases the speed at which impulses travel from cell to cell within the central nervous system. A new technology called diffusion tensor imaging allows observation of how these myelinated circuits remodel themselves during spatial learning and memory tasks. It has been observed that microstructural changes, that is neuroplasticity, can be seen after as little as two hours of training in a new task.[36]

So how can we encourage positive neuroplasticity in a therapeutic setting?

## Mindwork

Allan Schore's psychotherapeutic model focuses on what he describes as widening the windows of affect tolerance, gradually allowing the client to experience what would previously have been seen as stressful and threatening within a safe space held and mediated by the therapist. This sort of space, what I call a temenos, is one method of allowing a patient to switch from a state of stress, fear and being objectified or even unseen, to a state of relaxation, hope, acknowledgement and acceptance. The patient is encouraged to switch from being controlled

---

36 Siegel, Daniel J. M.D. 2010. *The Mindful Therapist* New York, NY, USA: W.W. Norton & Company, Inc.

by their sympathetic nervous system to being controlled by the ventral vagal branch of the parasympathetic system, which allows the body's own immune system to switch back on to fight infection or disease. At the same time the patient is encouraged to engage in myelination and positive neuroplasticity.

In the Journal of the American Medical Association, psychologist Richard M. Glass reports the studies demonstrating that neuroplasticity does take place in effective psychotherapy. He concludes: *Recent research in brain imaging, molecular biology, and neurogenetics has shown that psychotherapy changes brain function and structure. Such studies have shown that psychotherapy affects regional cerebral blood flow, neurotransmitter metabolism, gene expression, and persistent modifications in synaptic plasticity.*[37]

## Bodywork

Levine's model of working with the bodymind is a second method of inducing neuroplasticity and myelination. Again it is dependent on a therapist holding a safe enough space for the patient to experience frightening physical sensations without shutting down, so that a new neural pathway can be activated. As he describes it: *In order to unravel this tangle of fear and paralysis, we must be able to voluntarily contact and experience those frightening physical sensations; we must be able to confront them long enough for them to shift and change. To resist the immediate defensive ploy of avoidance, the most potent strategy is to move toward the fear, to contact the immobility itself and to consciously explore the various sensations,*

37 Glass, R.M. 2008. Psychodynamic psychotherapy and research evidence. Bambi survives Godzilla? *The Journal of the American Medical Association*, 300, 1587–1589.

*textures, images and thoughts associated with any discomfort that may arise.*[38]

So physiologically, if we can become conscious of tracking our bodily sensations in response to external events via the pre-frontal cortex, we can learn to intentionally modify the emotional responses from the amygdala and decide on a different course of action from the basal ganglia.[39] Siegel's Mindsight process[40] is entirely dependent on the fact that we can sense, shape and modify the flow of energy and information within our own lives and in our interactions with others. This can allow us to face previously avoided emotions knowing that we have the capacity to transform them into tolerated emotions with a different physical response from before.

## Meditation

A third and much more ancient way of inducing neuroplasticity is coming back into vogue with the recent medical understanding of the bodymind connections. This of course is meditation and it can be done without any therapist present, hence is arguably the most self-empowering and autonomous of all.

Dharma Singh Khalsa's book *Meditation as Medicine* is an excellent source of comprehensive information about a variety of different types of meditation to help deal with ailments deriving from a huge range of sources. In it he cites

38 Levine, Peter A. PhD. 2010. *In An Unspoken Voice: How the Body Releases Trauma and Restores Goodness* p.74 Berkeley, California, USA: North Atlantic Books

39 For instance see Cresswell, J.D., Way, B.M., Eisenberger, N.I., and Lieberman, M.D. 2007 Neural correlates of dispositional mindfulness during affect labeling. *Psychosomatic Medicine, 69*, pp560–565

40 http://www.drdansiegel.com/about/mindsight/

the conclusions of studies on meditation by the US Federal Government's Office of Alternative Medicine and Dr Herbert Benson of the Harvard Medical School. Most significantly:

- *Meditation has a profound effect upon three key indicators of ageing: hearing ability, blood pressure, and vision of close objects…*
- *Long-term meditators experience 80% less heart disease and 50% less cancer than non-meditators…*
- *Meditators secrete more of the youth-related hormone DHEA as they age than non-meditators.*[41]

He reports that those who practise transcendental meditation have a lower biological age (measured by physiological determinants rather than chronological age) than those who do not meditate. Those meditating for more than five years were found to be physiologically twelve years younger than non-meditating counterparts.

Again this results from the connections between our thoughts, our emotions and the endocrine system. The conscious act of meditation increases blood flow in the brain and increases activity in the pre-frontal cortex. It shifts the cortex and the amygdala into a relaxed alpha brainwave pattern wherein they send the hypothalamus a message to direct the endocrine system to release the calming hormones melatonin and serotonin, while reducing production of the stress hormone cortisol. The nervous system is dominated by the parasympathetic branch which favours the organs and glands of immunity and you reach the ideal condition for healing.

Singh Khalsa also notes that the ancient Sanskrit mantras often chanted to accompany meditation have the very specific physiological action of vibrating the upper palate of

---

41 Singh Khalsa, Dharma, M.D and Stauth, Cameron. 2001. *Meditation as Medicine* p.8 New York, NY, USA: Fireside

the mouth, which connects upwards to the pituitary gland, thereby altering its secretions into the endocrine system.[42] The vibrations arising from these mantras can also stimulate the hypothalamus and the vagus nerve which travels through the neck and services the heart, lungs, intestinal tract and back muscles.

Siegel has developed a highly effective programme based on the power of the mind to integrate the brain and promote well-being.[43] In his terminology what he defines as the mind has the capacity to change the brain, that is the extended nervous system in this context, because attention on the regulation of the information flows leads to myelinogenesis. As a result, in response to an external event we have: *the power of awareness to focus attention in certain ways to shape the flow of energy and information. As this flow occurs, our mental regulation process drives the firing in the brain by initiating activity in specific patterns of neural connections that can then induce structural changes in the brain's connectivity.*[44]

Siegel has a whole series of exercises that he has developed to enhance awareness, all of which can be conducted on your own, and which are largely based on meditation techniques. This is stepping into true self-responsibility, self-empowerment and choice, knowing we are in the driving seat and that we can change our mental, emotional and physical responses to outside events away from the old patterning of the limbic attractors.

---

42 Singh Khalsa, Dharma M.D. and Stauth, Cameron. 2001. *Meditation as Medicine* p.29 and p.105 New York, NY, USA: Fireside

43 Siegel, Daniel J. M.D. 2010. *Mindsight: The New Science of Personal Transformation* New York, NY, USA: Bantam Books

44 Siegel, Daniel J. M.D. 2010. *The Mindful Therapist* p.218 New York, NY, USA: W.W. Norton & Company, Inc.

## Case studies

I would like to consider how we can work with people effectively when we understand the physical manifestations of stress and trauma and how we can reprogramme our limbic pathways and our reactions to ensure the future is different from the past.

## Case Study Client A

Client A tells me she is suffering from chronic lower back pain and has constant tension in her shoulders. She is having difficulty sleeping at night and feels she has lost her way in the world. I recognise these as some of the classic symptoms of stress.

Initially I ask her to lie on the therapy table and I feel into her lower back with an approach based on craniosacral therapy. The spine starts to relax and the pain in her back starts to ease as the tension in her shoulders starts to lift. I ask her to breathe deeply into the area I am holding, in through the nose and out through the mouth. She starts to cry and says she knows her physical pain comes from her job and her boss at work. When he is away her back pain gets better and when he returns to the office her pain gets worse.

I move up her body to hold the solar plexus, which is the stress centre as it is the site of the adrenal glands. I ask her to try to breathe deeply into the stress and then imagine breathing it out. Let out whatever needs to come. Rage, anger, fear, grief, loss, shame, guilt. I move to her feet and ask her to hold her arms in front of her and shake them as hard as she can. At the same time I shake her legs. Shake it all loose, let it all out. She starts to say how much she hates her boss, he is so unfair and such a bully. She releases the stress and tension physically and verbally.

Then I ask her to bend her knees so her feet are flat on the therapy table and I put two big flat stones under her feet to represent the earth and her connection to it. I ask her to put her own left hand on her heart. Can she really get into her body by feeling her heart beat? That takes some time, but then she starts to feel her pulse, the beating heart. Can she feel the earth under her feet? Yes. I hold her feet and move them slowly as if she is walking on the earth. I ask her to feel into her path from the heart, imagining she is walking a new path, her way forward in life. She recognises that she has to look for a new job, that the current job is making her sick. She also visions that she has to do something that helps people more and is more creative than her current position.

As follow up self-empowering work to take into her everyday life, I suggest that whenever she is feeling stressed she should do kundalini yoga[45] breathing and shaking to release the stress and reset the nervous system from the control of the sympathetic to the vagal parasympathetic. I also suggest that she needs to give her heart a voice as she considers new jobs, not just her head. She recognises that money is not as important to her as health and life satisfaction.

This is an example of identifying problematic aspects of one's environment, and recognising how changing that environment can affect the health and well-being of individual cells and fundamentally improve your life. It demonstrates a longer-term solution to the client's malaise, but also gives her some short-term tools to alleviate her symptoms until the longer-term solution can be implemented.

---

45 Kundalini yoga is called by practitioners 'the yoga of awareness', and it aims to cultivate the creative spiritual potential of a human to uphold values, speak truth, and focus on the compassion and consciousness needed to serve and heal others.

**Case Study Client B**

Client B is quite shy and withdrawn when she comes to see me. She has been suffering from depression but doesn't like taking anti-depressants so wants to see if she can do something else that will allow her to come off the pills. She has heard of the complementary treatment called Reiki (which literally translated means universal life energy) and initially would like to experience a Reiki treatment.

I ask her to lie down on the therapy table and initially I go to her feet and hold them, feeling into her system. I voice to her that we want her body to come back to the perfect template of health and the perfect position, so if it would like to move at any time it is welcome to do so, whether that is tiny millimetres in the spine or the skull (which might be appropriate if she has physical issues such as migraines or back problems) or great big unwindings in the limbs or head or torso (which might be appropriate if she is holding suppressed trauma in the body which needs to be released). I also voice to her that the most important thing is that she must feel safe. In a few minutes I am going to start working on her chakras, the traditional energy centres of Indian and Buddhist philosophy, located at the crown of the head, the forehead, the throat, the heart, the solar plexus, the womb area and the root. I tell her that the only thing she needs to do is tell me if anything doesn't feel good. It is totally OK in this space to say 'no, I don't like that'. She must please tell me if I am coming too close or doing anything she doesn't feel comfortable with.

As I say this she starts to cry and shake. She tells me she was repeatedly abused by her father. No-one has ever told her it is ok to say no. This is an immediate signal to me that I need to be particularly sensitive as I approach her body, and as I continue with the Reiki treatment I check in with her as I work whether it feels safe and comfortable where I am holding her, and at the lower two chakras (the sex organs including the womb) I keep my hands well off her body, just feeling into the energy of the yoni, the yogic name for the collective of the feminine sexual organs. She experiences a safe space without demands and with permission to use her voice.

On the next visit I do some energetic cleansing of the yoni as I guide her to breathe in a particular way, and then I hold into the solar plexus. I ask her to find her voice, to release whatever she wanted to say to her father. I use a rattle and a drum and ask her to make as much noise as she wants, giving the anger to the rattle and the drum. She starts screaming and releasing her anger, venting the voice the child never had. When the anger turns to grief, I bring in a big cushion towards her. If this is something new that approaches her, what can she say? She says 'no – I don't want you near me.' She uses her arms and her legs to fight it off and maintain her space. She has a voice and physical strength to create a boundary. She can even find anger and tell it to go away and leave her alone. She feels powerful and knows that in future she has choice.

To finish the session I ask her to put her own hands on her heart and yoni and feel the energy moving between them. We allow them to connect and talk to each other. As homework I ask her to practise saying no to people, even in very simple situations, and to use a breathing exercise to continue with her heart-yoni connection, linking these two powerful feminine energy centres.

This is an example of how we can retrain our bodies to respond differently and in healthier ways by identifying and then addressing the original trauma in a safe space. It helps to change the neural networks, and offers practical exercises to use every day to reinforce the new limbic attractors and the new way of being in the world.

## Epigenetics

Epigenetics literally means control above genetics and Dr Bruce Lipton and other epigeneticists have developed a different way of taking control of our health. Not neuroplasticity within the brain, but epigenetics, which focuses on altering the behaviour of the nuclei of our cells through changing our environment. This environment includes physical things as diverse as the air we breathe, the water we drink, the food we eat and the toxins we use in our homes. It also includes emotional things such as what sort of family and friends we surround ourselves with, whether we are suffering from stress and trauma or whether we are joyful and relaxed. It also includes our beliefs. In particular, many people live in fear of the genetic codes and sequences carried in the nuclei of their cells. They believe that their health is largely dependent on their genes, which come directly from their parents. They believe they are victims of heredity.

Lipton and his colleagues have discovered that: *DNA blueprints passed down through genes are not set in concrete at birth. Genes are not destiny! Environmental influences, including nutrition, stress, and emotions, can modify those genes without changing their basic blueprint. And those modifications, epigeneticists have discovered, can be passed on to future generations as surely as DNA blueprints are passed on via the double helix.*[46]

How does this work? Surrounding each cell body is the membrane which also turns out to be the cellular 'brain'

46 Lipton, Bruce H. PhD. 2005. *The Biology of Belief* p.37 Carlsbad, CA, USA: Hay House Inc.

because it is the receptor (awareness) and effector (action) proteins embedded in the membrane that interact with what is happening outside the cell to produce the behaviour inside the cell. Scientists are working to classify hundreds of complex information pathways that connect the membrane's reception of environmental signals and the activation of the cell's behaviour-activating proteins.

Hence, while it is true that we inherit specific genes from our parents, and different genes are correlated with our behaviour and characteristics, including health or disease, these genes are not activated until something triggers them. Within each chromosome the gene carrying DNA forms the core, and the cellular membranes with their receptor and effector proteins surround the DNA. When the genes are covered, their information cannot be 'read', but when an environmental signal comes along and causes the proteins to change shape, they may detach from the DNA's double helix, allowing the gene to be read and activated.

As Lipton explains: *Once the DNA is uncovered, the cell makes a copy of the exposed gene. As a result, the activity of the gene is 'controlled' by the presence or absence of the ensleeving proteins, which are in turn controlled by environmental signals.*[47]

He concludes: *the cell's operations are primarily moulded by its interaction with the environment, not by its genetic code... Logically, genes cannot preprogram a cell or organism's life because cell survival depends on the ability to dynamically adjust to an ever-changing environment.*[48]

Taking things a step further, because the pre-frontal cortex is self aware, it can observe any programmed behaviour we are engaged in, including our habitual responses to environmental

47 Lipton, Bruce H. PhD. 2005. *The Biology of Belief* pp38–39 Carlsbad, CA, USA: Hay House Inc.

48 Lipton, Bruce H. PhD. 2005. *The Biology of Belief* p.56 Carlsbad, CA, USA: Hay House Inc.

stimuli, evaluate that behaviour, and consciously decide to change the programme. Therefore as Lipton says: *We can actively choose how to respond to most environmental signals and whether we even want to respond at all. The conscious mind's capacity to override the subconscious mind's preprogrammed behaviours is the foundation of free will.*[49]

We are not stuck with our genes or our self-defeating behaviours. We have choice about how to live, how to react to events and what behaviours to engage in, although frequently this will mean discarding the conditioning of our families, ancestors and societal 'norms'.

**Conclusion**

So far I have explained the brain-body connections we all have, consciously or unconsciously, and how we can help to create our own state of health through engaging in practices and therapies to enhance neuroplasticity, allowing new neural networks to form which help us to escape our previous conditioning and limiting beliefs. At the same time we can mindfully choose to respond to events and observations in a different way from our engrained responses.

But these solutions require us to understand that we have significant control of what is happening in our brains, that we have choice. And if we choose to accept self-responsibility and work to achieve a better life and better health then we can no longer blame others for our misfortunes and unhappiness. If we choose to be victims and tell ourselves that change is impossible, then of course it will be! One of the keys is recognising that we do have this choice. No matter how

49 Lipton, Bruce H. PhD. 2005. *The Biology of Belief* p.104 Carlsbad, CA, USA: Hay House Inc.

depressed we feel, no matter how bad our lives have been until now, things can change. We can react in a different way and set up new neural networks based on a different set of beliefs about ourselves and what we are capable of.

All this is part of the new paradigm that is being pulled together from the growing communication between the previously siloed disciplines of psychology, neurology and immunology.

## GLOSSARY FOR CHAPTER 2

**Chakra**: a Sanskrit term literally translated as wheel or disk, used throughout Indian healing to represent energy centres throughout the body. The chakras are sited at the same places as the main endocrine glands and some of the major nerve plexi of the body.

**Epigenetics**: control above genetics. The way in which genes are turned on and off within the cell as a result of the environment they are operating in, mediated by the cell membrane.

**Mind**: an embodied process that regulates the flow of energy and information.[50]

**Myelinogenesis**: the ability of the brain to increase the sheathing along the axonal lengths to enhance the conduction speed of neural electrical impulses.

**Neural attractors**: the neural pathways that we use most often and with which we tend to assess new events in the light of previous experiences.

**Neuroplasticity**: the ability of the brain to change structurally and develop new neurons, new synaptic connections and new circuits when responding to experience.

---

50 Definition as used by Daniel J. Siegel, M.D.

**Psychoneuroimmunology**: the science which studies the interaction of the brain, psychological processes, the nervous system and the immune system.

**Reiki**: a Japanese term literally translated as universal life energy, it is a healing technique based on activation of the natural healing processes of the patient's body to restore physical and emotional well-being.

**Temenos**: a protected physical and emotional space in which the transforming work of healing takes place through learning and teaching.

# CHAPTER 3: THE POWER OF THE PLACEBO

**Do you believe that placebos and alternative medicine therapies can have a real impact on the physical and mental health of a patient? This can be taken to refer first to the impact of placebo substances on the patient and secondly to the impact of placebo services given to the patient.**

> *The prevailing medical paradigm has no capacity to incorporate the concept that a relationship is a physiologic process, as real and as potent as any pill or surgical procedure.*[51]
>
> (Thomas Lewis, Fari Amini, Richard Lannon)

## Introduction

In Chapters 1 and 2 I presented the modern physiological evidence of the links between our bodies and our mind, our

---

51 Lewis, Thomas, M.D., Amini, Fari, M.D., Lannon, Richard, M.D. 2000. *A General Theory of Love* pp80–81 New York, USA: Vintage Books, Random House

emotional experiences and the resulting health or disease that we experience.

In the Oxford English Dictionary the definition of a placebo is: *a medicine or procedure prescribed for the psychological benefit to the patient rather than for any physiological effect.*[52] In the new paradigm, what are defined as placebos do very frequently lead to a physical improvement in the patient, whether they are administered as substances in drug tests or mentally and emotionally delivered as services by a health care professional that the patient trusts and/or places in a position of authority.

Equally nocebos work – patients that are told they are beyond help will regard themselves as such. The conclusion is that the intention, attention and words of the physician or therapist take on enhanced importance.

## So what exactly is a placebo?

I have wrapped a belief in the impact of placebo drugs and alternative medicine therapies together in the question posed at the top of this chapter. That is because I believe the evidence presented in Chapters 1 and 2 has demonstrated that the body and the brain can no longer be considered to be separate. They are inextricably linked, with our mental and emotional state intricately entangled with our physical health.

When we accept this, then actually the definition of a placebo as *a medicine or procedure prescribed for the psychological benefit to the patient rather than for any physiological effect* becomes a bit of an oxymoron! As soon as there is a psychological benefit there will also be a physiological effect because the impact a medicine or procedure has on our beliefs and our health are inter-connected.

52 https://en.oxforddictionaries.com

The extended definitions of placebo are:

*A substance that has no therapeutic effect*; and *A measure designed merely to humour or placate someone*.

The first of these would by definition rule out a placebo having any real impact on the physical or mental health of a patient so the question posed above becomes completely nonsensical. Placebo is defined as useless. The second is probably closer to the meaning that scientists now think of when they administer placebos in clinical trials.

Therefore for the remainder of the chapter let us take the placebo to mean a medicine or procedure prescribed to humour or placate someone without any direct pharmacological effect. Hence the question that I pose can be taken to first ask about the impact of placebo substances on the patient, while the second part of the question can be taken to ask about the impact of placebo services given to the patient.

## Placebo substances

For many years the gold standard of pharmaceutical trials has been whether a drug performs better in double-blind clinical trials than a placebo. The double-blind condition means that neither those administering the drug nor the patients know who is getting the trial treatment and who is receiving the placebo. It has long been recognised that this is necessary as in earlier trials and experiments, somehow the knowledge of the doctors or nurses about which alternative a patient was receiving, and hence their expectations of the treatment, impacted the outcome.

Irving Kirsch is Associate Director of the Programme in Placebo Studies and Lecturer in medicine at the Harvard Medical School and Beth Israel Deaconess Medical Center. He is also Professor Emeritus of psychology at the University of

Plymouth (UK), and University of Hull (UK), and University of Connecticut (US). He has published 10 books and more than 250 scientific journal articles and book chapters on placebo effects, antidepressant medication, hypnosis and suggestion.

His most famous work is a meta-analysis of the impact of antidepressants relative to placebo and his findings make gloomy reading for the pharmaceutical industry. He concludes: *The serotonin theory is as close as any theory in the history of science to having been proved wrong. Instead of curing depression, popular antidepressants may induce a biological vulnerability making people more likely to become depressed in the future.*[53]

His work on antidepressants and his book, *The Emperor's New Drugs: Exploding the Antidepressant Myth*,[54] has been covered extensively in the international media and has influenced official guidelines for the treatment of depression in the United Kingdom.

He originated the scientific concept of response expectancy in clinical trials, or in other words, what people experience depends on what they expect to experience. Relating this back to Chapter 1, they feel what they believe they will feel rather than believing what they actually feel!

His work also raises serious questions about the way the results of clinical trials are reported and the extent therefore to which they provide accurate information. This is worrying for the patients who believe that strict testing standards ensure the safety and efficacy of the drugs they are provided with by their doctors.

What Kirsch discovered by using the Freedom of Information Act to request trial data from the Food and Drug Administration (FDA) was that a number of clinical trials

---

53 http://www.ncbi.nlm.nih.gov/pmc/articles/PMC4172306/ Antidepressants and the Placebo Effect, 2014 Abstract

54 Kirsch, Irving, PhD. 2009. *The Emperor's New Drugs: Exploding the Antidepressant Myth* UK: Random House

had been completed but were not in the public domain. It turned out that almost half of the antidepressant clinical trials sponsored by the drug companies had not been published and until his work was published their results were known only to the drug companies and the FDA. You may not be surprised to hear that most of the unpublished studies had failed to find a significant benefit of a given drug over placebo.

Also, he uncovered that almost all antidepressant trials include a placebo run-in phase. Before the trial begins, all of the subjects are given a placebo for a week or two. After this run-in period, the subjects are reassessed, and anyone who has improved substantially is excluded from the official trial. These subjects are already much better but have only received the placebo! That leaves subjects who have not benefitted much from the placebo to be tested as to whether they perform better on placebo or on the drug under scrutiny for its effectiveness. Only the results of this second phase are published.

So for example, as shown in Table 1, say there are 100 people entering a trial. In the first placebo run-in phase, 50 of them improve substantially. That leaves 50 people entering the second phase of the trial and 25 get the placebo once again, while 25 get the drug being tested. Say 10 of the placebo group now improve while 15 of the drug group improve.

The results would be reported as being that 40 per cent of subjects improved using the placebo (10 out of 25) and 60 per cent improved using the drug (15 out of 25). This 20 per cent difference would probably be judged to be statistically significant, in other words the drug is 'successful'.

But if the full results were reported they would show that 60 per cent of subjects improved using the placebo (50 from phase 1 plus 10 from phase 2 out of the 100 initial participants) while once again 60 per cent of subjects improved using the drug (15 out of 25 in phase 2 only). An insignificant difference and therefore the drug is unsuccessful.

**Table 1: Different outcomes depending on the presentation of the 100 people entering the trials**

| Run in period, only placebo given | Number responding positively to placebo | Number not responding to placebo |
|---|---|---|
| 100 in total | 50 | 50 – continue to stage 2 |
| Secondary trial | Number responding positively to placebo | Number responding to drug being tested |
| 50 from run in, 25 in each group | 10 | 15 |
| | Percentage responding positively to placebo | Percentage responding positively to drug being tested |
| Figures reported | 10/25=40% | 15/25=60% |
| Full results from both run in period and secondary trial | Percentage responding positively to placebo | Percentage responding positively to drug being tested |
| 100 | (50+10)/100=60% | 15/25=60% |

All sorts of different permutations of these numbers can be conjured, but overall the two conclusions seem to be that:

1. The results of all drug trials should be reported, not just the ones that the pharmaceutical companies deem to be successful.
2. The results for all subjects included throughout the trials should be reported, not just the group that makes it through to the second phase.

For patients, what is important is that they feel better and if the placebo produces an improvement that is just as good from their perspective – possibly even better, as placebos will not produce the pharmaceutical side effects often associated with 'real' drugs. However, there can equally be nocebo side effects if patients believe they are taking something that might have a damaging impact, even if it is non-pharmacologically active. So for instance if people are in drug trials where they know the 'real thing' may have side effects such as hair loss, or weight gain, then they can experience hair loss or weight gain even when they are on the placebo.

Epigeneticist Dr Bruce Lipton whom I introduced in Chapter 2 emphasises that much greater research on the placebo effect would be advantageous, noting that: *If medical researchers could figure out how to leverage the placebo effect, they would hand doctors an efficient, energy-based, side effect-free tool to treat disease.*[55]

This research of course would need to be conducted by altruistic and independent organisations, as it will not be conducted by the pharmaceutical companies who depend on their drugs outperforming placebos.

## Placebo procedures and services

Dr Lissa Rankin attended Duke University, the University of South Florida, and Northwestern University, studying medicine for twelve years before practising as an OB/GYN physician in a conventional medical practice for eight years. Since 2007 she has been working in integrative medicine. Initially she ran her own mind-body medicine practice but

---

55 Lipton, Bruce H. PhD. 2005. *The Biology of Belief* p.108 Carlsbad, CA, USA: Hay House Inc.

these days she is a full-time writer, teacher and speaker. She recently pulled together extensive evidence on the power of the placebo and the nocebo, which she extended beyond pharmacology to psychology.

The results are that for those who have great faith in the wisdom and words of their doctors or other therapists, what they are told by these trusted experts may become a self-fulfilling prediction. As she writes: *When we pronounce upon someone with statistics like 'Nine out of ten people with your condition die in six months' or 'you have a twenty percent chance of five-year survival,' is this far from the voodoo practices of some native cultures? Are we cursing them, triggering fear responses in their mind, and causing their minds to activate stress responses, when the body most needs relaxation responses?*

*When we pronounce our patients 'incurable' or even label them with a 'chronic' disease like multiple sclerosis or Crohn's disease or high blood pressure, and we tell them they will be afflicted their whole lives, are we not, in essence, harming them?*[56]

Dr Bruce Lipton echoes these sentiments writing: *Troublesome nocebo cases suggest that physicians, parents, and teachers can remove hope by programming you to believe you are powerless.*[57]

Part of this programming has been the teaching surrounding the inevitability of suffering from so-called genetic diseases since at least 1987 and the first human genetic map. These beliefs have acted as a huge nocebo on thousands of patients who believe, on the basis of genetic science, that they will suffer from the afflictions of their ancestors as carried in their inherited DNA. But as previously discussed in the section on epigenetics in Chapter 2, Lipton has demonstrated that it is whether a gene is covered or unwrapped that is the

---

56 Rankin, Lissa, Dr. 2013. *Mind over medicine: Scientific Proof That You Can Heal Yourself* p.34 Carlsbad, CA, USA: Hay House Inc.

57 Lipton, Bruce H. PhD. 2005. *The Biology of Belief* p.113 Carlsbad, CA, USA: Hay House Inc.

key to determining whether a genetic illness will develop. Is the inherited gene switched off or on?

This activation can come from environmental toxins, such as chemicals in our food, water, air or homes, or it can come from our social environment, how we are treated by others, or it can come from what we believe and whether we chose a path of self-improvement and healing

In Chapter 1 I discussed how we see what we believe, with our life experiences becoming engrained into neural attractor pathways in the brain which have a tendency to make us behave in the future as we have behaved in the past. Chapter 2 explained how we can take conscious steps to reprogramme the brain and either engage in neuroplasticity or engage in epigenetic control of our gene expression.

The power of the placebo and the nocebo demonstrates that this tendency to be influenced by what we believe to be true does not just derive from our physical and emotional experiences in life, but extends to our health through our attitudes towards, and expectations about, the impact pharmacological drugs will have, and our trust (or distrust) in our healthcare providers.

Rankin hypothesises that at least part of the success reported by patients receiving alternative or complementary therapies derives from the beliefs the patients have about their efficacy (a traditional placebo effect) as well as the dual attitude, attention and intention of the therapist. The practitioner can have a huge positive (or negative) impact on the mental and emotional state of the patient and hence on their physiological state.

Many alternative therapies involve the practitioner truly listening to and seeing a patient, allowing them to express their dark inner fears (the parts that they often don't like to look at, that they are ashamed of or feel guilty about) without judgement, touching them in a non-sexual but caring way, holding them, expressing a belief in the possibility of deep healing, and at their best, creating an empathic space of unconditional love.

One of the difficulties in proving the efficacy of alternative therapies in a way that permits peer-reviewed academic journals to publish the results is that there is no potential for a controlled double-blind placebo trial. Most of these therapies are hands-on, face-to-face and directly connective. Even with something like homeopathy, acupuncture or Reiki, when the patient might not know if the therapist was giving them 'real' treatment, the therapist knows, hence their knowledge could impact the outcome of the trials and as such they are not double blind. When we get to something like Emotional Freedom Technique (EFT), or shamanic practices, both the client and the therapist are fully engaged with what is happening, which is all via real experience, with no possibility that a placebo (that is no treatment) is being given.

Despite this, there are many institutes and journals now collecting trial data for alternative therapies of all descriptions. Among the most comprehensive are the Monroe Institute,[58] the Institute of Noetic Sciences[59] and the Energy Psychology Journal,[60] which together contain a mounting library of scientific, peer-reviewed evidence regarding the efficacy of alternative therapies.

And of course patients are voting with their pocket book, although there are surprisingly few figures available on exactly how much people spend on complementary therapy. In the United States the most recent reliable figures seem to come from a nationwide government survey carried out in 2007, which reported that US adults spent $33.9 billion out-of-pocket

58 https://www.monroeinstitute.org/
59 http://www.noetic.org/
60 http://energypsychologyjournal.org/

on visits to complementary and alternative medicine (CAM) practitioners and on purchases of CAM products, classes, and materials. But these figures are already almost a decade out of date and anecdotal evidence would suggest that the figure has grown enormously during that time. This indicates that, whether the therapies are just psychological placebos or not, the public are convinced that they provide positive results which they are not receiving from their other healthcare providers.

Iain McGilchrist explains another way in which we can rewire our neural programming which can start to explain why self-healing modalities like Reiki, EFT and shamanic journeying are so effective for so many people. This is by actively using our imagination!

Just imagining ourselves doing something (including healing ourselves mentally, physically and emotionally) can rewire our neural programming through what are known as mirror neurons. McGilchrist writes: *Mental representation, in the absence of direct visual or other stimulus – in other words, imagining – brings into play some of the same neurons that are involved in direct perception. It is clear from this that, even when we so much as imagine doing something, never mind actually imitate it, it is, at some level which is far from negligible, as if we are actually doing it ourselves. Imagining something, watching someone else do something, and doing it ourselves share important neural foundations.*

*Imagination, then, is not a neutral projection of images on a screen. We need to be careful of our imagination, since what we imagine is in a sense what we are and who we become.*[61]

With Reiki for instance when working on themselves people already believe they can heal, and they call in the universal energy to allow each and every cell to work in the

---

61 McGilchrist, Iain. 2009. *The Master and his Emissary: The Divided Brain and the Making of the Western World* p.250 New Haven and London: Yale University Press

perfect template of health. There is an optimism, a belief, and an imagining – all powerful placebos at the very least and all working to create optimal conditions for health via the nervous system and the endocrine system. Perhaps there is even more – a genuine downloading from the nonlocal universe of omniscient and omnipresent knowledge and information, but discussion of that as a genuine possibility comes later. For now, even if nothing else, this strong combination of beliefs can lead to a powerful change akin to the placebo effect. In other words the healing works!

**Case Study Client C**

Client C was in her twenties and had previously suffered from a tumour in her spine. That had been surgically removed but she continued to be in chronic pain. Her doctor told her she would just have to take painkillers for the rest of her life as scar tissue resulting from the operation was putting pressure on her nerves and there was nothing else to be done.

We did a series of combined craniosacral and Reiki treatments and in particular visualised Reiki energy wrapping around the scar tissue. We asked it to help the scar tissue to dissolve and be replaced by cells in the optimal template of health. After a few sessions the pain went and the client no longer depended on medication.

Did the treatment 'just' give the client hope instead of despair, switching her nervous system from the sympathetic to the parasympathetic branch and allowing her immune system to function fully once again? Or was there a deeper and harder-to-explain healing going on from an external source? I cannot prove either, but I do know she felt better, and that of course is what is of prime importance.

**Case Study Client D**

Client D comes from a culture where shamanism is prevalent. She has a tumour in her right leg. She feels she has to take care of everyone else in her family, and has put her career on hold to do that. We do some work around roles she takes on including being head of the family, and ways in which she can take care of herself better and not feel so responsible for everyone else to her own detriment.

The next time I see her she has had surgery to remove the tumour, but her leg feels very disconnected from her body and she feels a number of people are trying to harm her with toxic back-stabbing and curses. I do work to cleanse the toxic back-stabbing and at the end give her an exercise to help protect herself energetically.

At our next appointment she feels as if a number of the problems she had been carrying on behalf of the family have been closed but she still feels drained and blocked and her leg is still very troublesome. We do further work cleansing what she has been carrying on behalf of her whole lineage of women, and she gets a real vision of clarity about her path and what she should be doing in her life for herself rather than trying to fulfil the expectations that others have of her. I give her a Reiki visualisation exercise to use on an ongoing basis to help her leg to heal.

After that I don't see her for a while before she returns to see me and proudly shows me the medal she received when she completed a triathlon. She thanks me profusely and tells me she could never have done this without my help with the ancestors.

Again you can debate whether I really removed a curse from the client's energy field, and helped her to return to the lineage what actually belonged to them, but what matters is that she believes I did, which along with our other work gave her the internal resources to trust that she could be well rather than being blighted by ill-wishes from others, and then the strength to follow through with her physical training. This study also illustrates exactly the power that curses can have on any individual.

## Conclusion

I hope Chapters 1 to 3 have provided compelling evidence that we can heavily influence our own reality from our belief systems about what is possible and what is impossible.

We create aspects of our own reality by how we choose to react to any event.

We create aspects of our own reality by choosing what type of medical practitioner to attend and what medications to accept, as well as the attitude with which we then take these medications.

We create our own reality by what we eat and drink, how much we exercise, whether we meditate, where we choose to live and the jobs we choose to do.

And we create aspects of our own reality by whether we choose to believe we will live a long and healthy life, overcoming any illness, or whether we choose to believe we will die young as a result of our genetic inheritance or at the first sign of disease.

The choice is ours. Do we stay stuck in depression and the belief that we are powerless and dependent, or step into autonomy, working on our own or with a therapist, to take control of our health and our future?

I would like to close this chapter with a quotation from the traditions of the Hawaiian Kahuna shamans: *We can choose, to live in the light… or the dark. Most of us live in twilight, with occasional patches of brilliance or shadow. Each thought is a choice.*[62]

## GLOSSARY FOR CHAPTER 3

**Alternative medicine**: alternative and complementary medicine are often bracketed together as CAM. CAM focuses on the whole person and includes physical, emotional, mental and spiritual health.[63]

**Meta-analysis**: a statistical technique for combining the findings from independent studies. Good meta-analyses aim for complete coverage of all relevant studies.

**Neuroplasticity**: the ability of the brain to change structurally and develop new neurons, new synaptic connections and new circuits when responding to environment and experience.

**Nocebo**: a medicine or procedure which harms our health even when there is no pharmacological basis for this.

**Placebo**: as defined in the dictionary, a medicine or procedure prescribed to humour or placate someone without any direct pharmacological effect. My argument is that this is an oxymoron.

**Response expectancy**: what people experience depends on what they expect to experience.

---

62 Chia, Mantak and North, Kris Deva. 2009. *Taoist Shaman: Practices from the Wheel of Life* p.71 Rochester, Vermont, USA: Destiny Books quoting from the Hawaiian Kahuna tradition and taken from North, Kris Deva. 'Calabash of Light'. *Positive Health* 91 (August 2003)

63 https://www.mayoclinic.org

# CHAPTER 4: THE HEMISPHERIC BRAIN AND PERCEPTION

**Which do you think is more important in perception – the functionality of the right-hemisphere of the brain, or the left-hemisphere? Alternatively phrased, are emotions, intuition and creativity more or less important than language, logic and compartmentalisation?**

> *It is our interpretation of observations that transforms a perceptual occurrence into a form compatible with the world we navigate. This interpretation is dependent on our human ability afforded by our brain processes.*[64]
>
> (Karl Pribram)

## Introduction

There are well-documented differences in structure and functionality of the two hemispheres of the brain cortex. In particular whether we perceive and are interoceptive from the

64 Pribram, Karl H. M.D.. 2013. *The Form Within: My Point of View* pp142–143 Westport, CT, USA: Prospecta Press

right- or from the left-hemisphere impacts the way we react to the world.

Neuroscience and psychology are rapidly moving in the direction of the primacy of the right-hemisphere for autonomy and self-regulation. But value in the Western world is often associated with the attributes of the left-hemisphere, such as logic and language, which has a tendency to dissociate from our own bodies, from empathic emotional interaction with others and from recognition of our symbiotic relationship with the planet we live on.

And what exactly is perception? Until his death in 2015, for six decades Karl Pribram was a leading figure on defining perception and how it occurs within the brain, which is very different from, albeit sometimes connected with, the sight that takes place with the eye.

The work of Pribram and other neuroscientists since the 1970s has demonstrated that perception and memory are distributed across the brain in a holographic network within the hippocampus and the synaptodendritic web.

Fourier transformations are a mathematical tool to transform a set of variables from one dimension to another, for instance from spatial co-ordinates to the time domain. Pribram showed that Fourier transformations simultaneously convert the potential world of spectral flux (interferences among waves) to the space-time world of experienced reality, and convert the information we receive in our minds to the physical realm of the brain cells.

But there is very little objective perception, objective memory or objective experienced reality. Everything is subjective, dependent upon our attitudes and intentions, the state we are in at the moment of perception. To help in obtaining the best possible experience in our lives we need to learn that we are capable of changing this state if we so choose.

## Structure and functionality of the two hemispheres of the cortex

In Chapter 1, I introduced how our past impacts the present. Our previous life experiences impact how we interpret and react to what we see around us and the way we respond to events that happen to us.

Relevant to how we perceive what is out there in the world around us is whether we are using the right or the left cortex to observe and process the information received from our senses.

It has long been known that physiologically the left side of the brain controls the right side of the body, and the right side of the brain controls the left side of the body, with the nerves crossing over in the medulla oblongata. But a real understanding of the huge differences in the structure and function of the left and right sides of the cortex is relatively new and derives from the neurobiology made possible by modern brain-imaging techniques.

Iain McGilchrist's epic and highly acclaimed work, *The Master and his Emissary*, describes these differences in great detail. He writes: *There is no such thing as the brain, only the brain according to the right hemisphere and the brain according to the left hemisphere: the two hemispheres that bring everything into being also, inevitably, bring themselves.*[65]

In a condensed form his research shows that in terms of structure, as illustrated in Figure 12:

- Anatomically, the right-hemisphere is longer, wider and generally larger as well as heavier than the left.

---

65 McGilchrist, Iain. 2009. *The Master and his Emissary: The Divided Brain and the Making of the Western World* p.175 New Haven and London: Yale University Press

- There is greater dendritic overlap in the right-hemisphere, that is a greater connectivity between the neurons.
- As previously noted in Chapter 1, white matter in the cortex results from myelination of neuronal axons which greatly speeds up the outgoing transmission of signals between neurons and there is more of this in the right-hemisphere. Areas of the central nervous system that largely consist of cell bodies rather than axons do not appear white, and these areas constitute what is known as the grey matter of the brain, which is more predominant in the left-hemisphere.
- The hemispheres differ in their sensitivity to hormones and to pharmacological agents.
- They depend on different neurotransmitters (the left is more reliant on dopamine and the right is more reliant on noradrenaline).

Figure 12: structure of two brain hemispheres

Right side:

Longer, wider,
larger and heavier

More dendritic overlap,
so greater connectivity

More white matter

Relies more on
noradrenaline

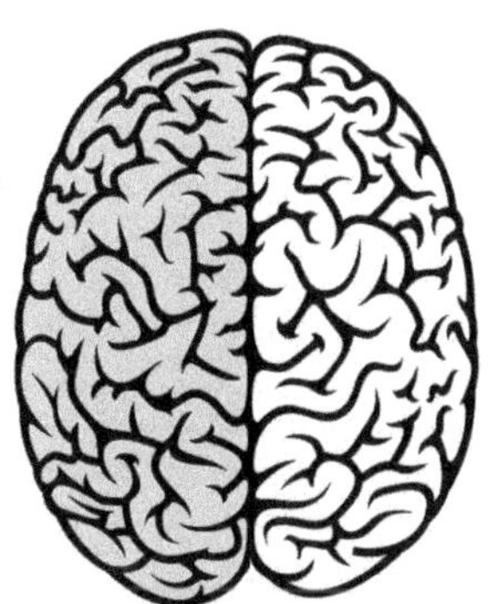

Left side:

Relies more on
dopamine

More grey
matter

In terms of function McGilchrist cites hundreds of different studies, concluding that there is left-brain dominance for local, narrowly focused attention and right-brain dominance for broad, global and flexible attention, a result of the prevalence of grey matter in the left-brain and white matter in the right-brain.

Only the right-hemisphere attends to the peripheral field of vision and the learning of new information or skills. However, once the skills have become familiar they shift to being the concern of the left-hemisphere, which is more efficient in routine situations where things are predictable, but less efficient when assumptions have to be revised.

These different functional attributes are summarised in Table 2.

**Table 2: Different functional attributes of the two hemispheres of the brain**

| Left-Hemisphere | Right-Hemisphere |
| --- | --- |
| Abstract and impersonal | Sees things in context |
| Excels at linear, sequential reasoning and systematic thought | Interested in the personal and in others as individuals |
| Precise and focused | Centre of empathy |
| The centre of language and symbol manipulation | Orbitofrontal cortex is essential to emotional understanding and regulation |
| Appears to see the body as an assemblage of parts, something from which we are relatively detached | Regulates the neuroendocrine interface between the body and the emotions |
| Needs certainty, needs to be correct | Responsible for our sense of our body as something we inhabit |
| Things are explicit, compartmentalised, fragmented and static | Specialises in non-verbal communication |

So whether we perceive things from the right-brain or the left-brain perspective dramatically alters the questions we ask about any situation (What is it?) and hence the answers we receive (How should we act?).

If we are using the left-brain we will be narrowly focused on ourselves and the impact that what we are observing has on us personally. If we are using the right-brain we will have a much more open attention, observing all that is going on in the world around us at large and how that may then impact us. We see ourselves in relation to others as part of a social group, something bigger than ourselves.

I introduced the Mindsight work of Dan Siegel in Chapter 2. As illustrated in Figure 13, he explains that from the body the networks of neurons in the peripheral nervous system send information up the spinal cord to the brainstem and the hypothalamus, (the subcortical area), which sets off an endocrine system reaction. The information is then transmitted further up to the posterior insula where the primary cortical body map is created, especially within the right-hemisphere. The posterior insula firing is then transmitted forward to the right anterior insula where it connects with the anterior cingulate and the medial pre-frontal cortex to make a representation of the posterior image, a metainsular map of the body. This gives us awareness of the internal state of our body, which is known as interoception.[66] This self-awareness allows us self-monitoring and self-regulation, the choice of how to react rather than just being under the autonomic control of the hypothalamus.

As Damasio puts it regarding internal communication (as quoted by Schore): *These nonverbal affective and thereby*

---

66 For further details of this process see Siegel, Daniel J. M.D. 2010. *The Mindful Therapist* pp39–41 and p.59 New York, NY, USA: W.W. Norton & Company, Inc.

*mind-body communications are expressions of the right brain, which is centrally involved in the analysis of direct kinesthetic information received by the subject from his own body, an essential implicit process. This hemisphere, and not the linguistic, analytic left, contains the most comprehensive and integrated map of the body state available to the brain (Damasio, 1994).*[67]

Figure 13: right-brain paths to self-awareness

1. Information comes up brain stem to hypothalamus
2. Hypothalamus then sends information to insula
3. Information then goes to posterior insula
4. Information from the posterior insula then goes to the anterior insula plus the anterior cingulate plus the medial pre-frontal cortex.

This combination of areas gives us self-regulation and self-awareness.

Diffusion tensor imaging technology has demonstrated that we can train ourselves to myelinate our brain in specific areas. The more myelin we can generate in our brains, the greater the neuroplasticity, the ability to change the brain structurally and make new connections and attractor pathways when responding to experience. Myelin is predominant in the right-hemisphere, the source of interoception and self-regulation.

67 Schore, Allan N. 2012. *The Science of the Art of Psychotherapy* pp39–40 New York, USA: W.W. Norton & Company

The more we practise attention to monitoring and then modulating our internal states, the better we become at doing this, increasing our ability to choose using the pre-frontal cortex in response to external events and gaining greater capacity for self-regulation. Thus we are able to create a virtuous circle of mindfulness, myelination, neuroplasticity and choice.

Schore also now teaches that the most significant healing work takes place when both client and therapist are communicating from their right-brains. He writes: *at the most essential level, the intersubjective work of psychotherapy is not defined by what the therapist does for the patient, or says to the patient (left brain focus). Rather, the key mechanism is how to be with the patient, especially during affectively stressful moments (right brain focus).*[68]

During a consultation, if the therapist or doctor is stuck in their own left-brain, they are more likely to be watching the clock, focused on meeting targets, coming across as terse, factual, seeing the current symptoms in a more localised, mechanical way, and less concerned about how they deliver information (including possibly bad news) to the patient. Just within the consultation process they may unconsciously confirm to the patient pre-held feelings of uselessness, unworthiness or of being a hopeless case. Of course if a doctor is in the middle of a complex operation, it is better for the patient if they are in their left-brain, paying close attention to detail, without being distracted by outside thoughts. You want your surgeon to be paying full and localised attention as he or she removes, repairs or replaces your vital organs!

During the consultation process if the therapist or doctor is in touch with their right-brain they will tend to see, hear and understand the patient empathically, as much through non-verbal observation and communication as through discussion.

68 Schore, Allan N. 2012. *The Science of the Art of Psychotherapy* p.44 New York, USA: W.W. Norton & Company

They will be able to assess the patient's wider issues and see the problems they are facing in a systemic context. Even if they prescribe no medication or course of treatment, they may have helped just by their actions to make the patient feel better, giving them hope and through empathy, love. Siegel calls this attunement and it relates to the power of the placebo discussed in Chapter 3.

Equally for the patient/client is it extremely important to be able to engage their own right-hemisphere during the consultation or therapy, as the left-hemisphere will have a tendency to keep on repeating the old stories, or what it knows, possibly from a mechanical or dissociated stance. The left-brain will not be able to acknowledge the feelings and emotions of the whole body and their relationship to the self. It is the right-brain that can see pain and suffering in the complete context of our experiences with compassion and understanding.

So part of the successful results obtained by right-brain focused therapists could be described as real treatment and part of it could be described as placebo psychology. It is unknown how to draw the line between these elements, and even if we could, does it really matter? Surely the key is the healing that the client experiences.

To conclude this section I would like to quote McGilchrist once more: *If I am right, that the story of the Western world is one of increasing left-hemisphere domination, we would not expect insight to be the key note. Instead we would expect a sort of insouciant optimism, the sleepwalker whistling a happy tune as he ambles toward the abyss.*[69]

He also comments: *It is as though, blindly, the left hemisphere pushes on, always along the same track. Evidence of failure does not*

---

69 McGilchrist, Iain. 2009. *The Master and his Emissary: The Divided Brain and the Making of the Western World* p.237 New Haven and London: Yale University Press

*mean that we are going in the wrong direction, only that we have not gone far enough in the direction we are already headed.*[70]

It is time to bring this unhappy period to a close and switch direction, into the new paradigm that is here and available for those who will embrace it.

**Case Study Client E**

Client E is in her mid-thirties with two young children. She also has a demanding job but is suffering from massive anxiety about very simple things, like travelling on the train.

She knows nothing about anatomy and physiology or the structure and function of the brain, yet when I go and hold her head and ask her to visualise what it looks like or feels like in one side and then the other, she immediately gets a vision of a little man in a chair inside the left-hand side. She feels he is 'the controller'. On the right-hand side she feels as if there is a large expansive space. When asked what the right-hand side would like to say to her, the right-hand side says 'I am what matters. The man thinks he's in control but he's not.' (This is such a text-book description of the left-right split that I ask her if she is consciously aware of the anatomy and physiology of the two hemispheres. She most definitely is not.)

I then ask where she feels her fear and anxiety? The solar plexus. When I hold into it and ask solar plexus what it would like to say if it was allowed a voice, it says it just doesn't want to travel at all. She feels as if there is a round, red pain there, like a 'Stop' sign. The left-brain wants to say it will organise

70 McGilchrist, Iain. 2009. *The Master and his Emissary: The Divided Brain and the Making of the Western World* p.235 New Haven and London: Yale University Press

every detail of any travel so it will be safe. The right-brain is not happy with that. It worries that if it relaxes too much it won't be able to spot danger and it needs to do that. The left-brain agrees that spotting danger is not its job.

We agree that we can't get to the source of the fear in the solar plexus within that session, but as a way of progressing until the next time, I put a big stone on the solar plexus where the fear resides. I suggest that when she gets anxious she can get in touch with the fear and then blow it from her body into the stone, then bury it in the earth. She tries that and it feels good for the solar plexus.

Right-brain agrees that she could give the stress to the stone and it would still be alert but without being hyperaroused. Left-brain is also happy with that suggestion.

In later sessions we do further work around the source of the fear and the judgement, but throughout we continue talking to the two hemispheres of the brain which initially are deeply split but are able at least to start a dialogue.

This demonstrates how talking to the body parts reveals splits in the psyche but also how opening a dialogue leads the way to a resolution rather than continuing with constant unconscious repression of one or more parts of ourselves.

## How do vision and perception actually work?

The section above has described the differences in outcome depending on whether we are acting on decisions made by the right-brain or the left-brain. At a more fundamental level, how do our eyes actually see objects, colours, the world around us, and then convert that seeing into a perceptible image in the brain, whether we are observing and processing with the left-brain or the right-brain? How does what is out there travel to the eye, then pass electronically through the optic nerve, to reconfigure as a three-dimensional perception and then a memory in the brain?

A complete answer to this question was one of the life-long driving forces underlying the work of Dr Karl Pribram whom I introduced in Chapter 1. He makes a careful distinction between objects and images. Objects are what are there in four-dimensional space-time reality, and they can be looked at from various perspectives to perceive a range of profiles or images of them within our brains. The implication is that different people, or the same people at different times in their lives, can observe the same object but perceive it differently, interpret it differently, and produce a different image of that object within their brains. Seeing is not the same as perceiving.

When there is little movement of or around an object, then we can use two-dimensional Euclidian geometry, that is geometry on a surface, to portray an image of the object. But when we come to perceive figures that rotate in space and time, higher-order dimensions of geometry become necessary. Early in his career Pribram concluded that: *It is these higher-order descriptions that hold when we look at what is going on in the brain. The retina of our eye is curved, and this curvature is projected onto the cortical surface. Thus, any process in the sensory and brain systems that allows us to perceive an object's movement must be a geodesic: a path around a globe.*[71]

By the 1970s he had concluded that things were more complex and to understand his developing views of perception we need some basic knowledge of holograms and the mathematical concepts of Fourier and Gabor transformations.

71 Pribram, Karl H. M.D. 2013. *The Form Within: My Point of View* p.142 Westport, CT, USA: Prospecta Press

## Holograms, Dennis Gabor and Joseph Fourier

Joseph Fourier lived from 1768 to 1830. His contributions to science have been used extensively throughout physics as well as medicine, and date back at least to 1822 when he developed a method for measuring the interference pattern (known as the spectrum) resulting from waves intersecting. I don't want to introduce any mathematical equations here, but the concept underlying his theorem gives scientists a mathematical way to transform a linear system (time) into wave functions or frequencies and vice versa. As illustrated in Figure 14, in terms of perception Fourier transforms turn out to be crucial in converting waveform potential into observed or experienced reality.

Figure 14: transforming potential to experience

More than a century later in 1947 Dennis Gabor developed the mathematics of holography, which is based on taking an image from our normal world of space-time and spreading it (using a special short time case of the Fourier transformation rule or spread function) over the extent of the recording medium. This transformation enfolds all parts of the image with each other (the intersecting waves) and at the same time the whole is totally enfolded in each part.

Nowadays, whether we understand the mathematics or not, we experience holograms in our lives every day on our bank cards, advertising boards and driving licences. They are three-dimensional images displayed on a two-dimensional surface. They appear to move when you tilt them or walk past them and the special feature of holograms resulting from the enfolding of the image is that even if you smash a hologram into millions of pieces, each tiny piece still incorporates the entire three-dimensional picture represented in the whole structure, totally unlike a conventional jigsaw. Each part of the smashed hologram will show the object from a different perspective as if you are moving around it, but it will include the entire object. In other words, a seemingly small, incomplete and disconnected piece contains within it the entire information of the complete picture.

The construction of a hologram is illustrated in Figure 15. Holograms are made from laser light, which is light of just one single coherent wavelength,[72] where all of the peaks and troughs of the waves are lined up and move (resonate) in sync, which is known as phase conjugation. The laser sends a beam of light to a splitter, which splits the beam into two separate streams. One beam, known as the **object** beam, reflects off the object you want to represent in the hologram and onto a high definition photographic plate. The surface of the object is rough on a microscopic level, so it causes a diffuse reflection, scattering light in every direction. This diffuse reflection is what causes light reflected from every part of the object to reach every part of the holographic plate. The other beam, the **reference** beam, hits the same photographic plate without reflecting off anything other than a mirror.

Since the beams were originally joined together and perfectly in step, the phase conjugation of the individual waves in the two beams creates a spatially and temporally coherent channel of communication when the beams are recombined, showing how the light rays in the object beam

72 coherence describes all the properties of the correlation between the physical quantities of a single wave, or between several waves or wave packets.

have been changed compared to the light rays in the reference beam.

Figure 15: the construction of a hologram

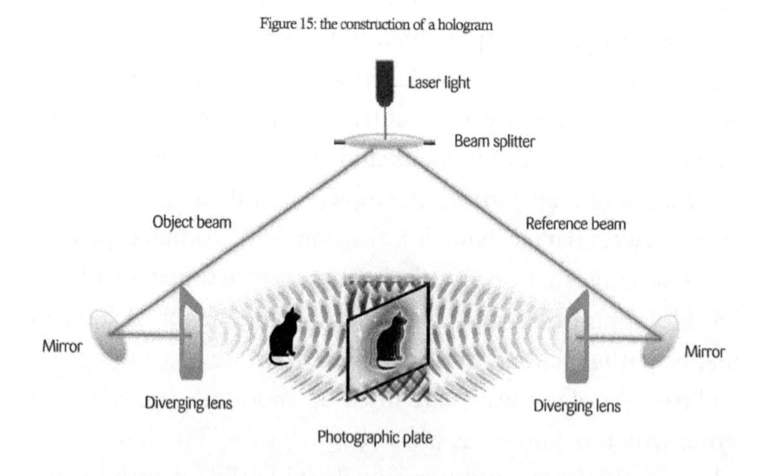


You need the correct light source to see the hologram, but when the appropriate form of light is reflected off the surface of the holographic plate it makes an image. Your brain interprets this as a three-dimensional representation of the object in question. So a hologram is effectively a permanent record of what something looks like, seen from every angle.

## Your brain is a neural hologram

Having made that digression into holography, let's go back to Pribram and his investigation of perception. What he discovered was that objects in the world reflect and refract radiant energy (such as light and heat) which becomes scattered, spectral and holographic. He writes: *The input to our eyes is (in)formed by this spectral, holographic radiant energy. The optics of our eyes (pupil and lens) then perform a Fourier transformation to produce a space-time flow, a moving optical image much as we experience it. At the retina, the beginning of another transformation occurs: the space-time optical image, having been somewhat diffracted by the gelatinous composition of the lens, becomes re-transformed into a quantum-like multidimensional process that is transmitted to the brain.*[73]

This unconscious ability of our eyes, and specifically our retinae, to perform complicated Fourier transformations in at least four-dimensional space-time (a task that most of us would be horrified to be asked to perform at the conscious level!) does not just apply to how we see, but also how we hear (a discovery that pre-dated the optic evidence).

Trying to put this in more accessible language, the visual, auditory and sensing nerves register wave information from objects outside the body. After a Gabor mathematical transformation of these energy waves coming into the body, the electrical oscillations in the brain create a wave interference pattern that gives rise to an image in the brain and thus a memory is encoded in a holographic way across a wide range of cells. The holographic nature of imagery and memory in the physical brain will prove vital to the nonlocal arguments of how we can connect with an external source of consciousness that I introduce in Chapter 6.

The holographic process appears to be highly dependent on the hippocampus which as I described in Chapter 1 is situated in the limbic brain, very close to the amygdala. In the 1970s Professor John O'Keefe demonstrated that the cellular structure of the hippocampus contains webs of fine fibres that allow perception in a way similar to a hologram in the sense that each tiny part of the picture contains the whole, but from a different perspective.

O'Keefe (quoted within Pribram) writes: *One can conclude*

---

73 Pribram, Karl H. M.D. 2013. *The Form Within: My Point of View* pp101–102 Westport, CT, USA: Prospecta Press

*that each hippocampal place cell can enter into the representation of a large number of environments, and conversely, that the representation of any given environment is dependent on the activity of a reasonably large group of neurons.*[74]

This was the start of the work demonstrating that every piece of a long-term memory is distributed over the entire dendritic arbour in a neural hologram, so that each part of the network contains information about the whole event. What Pribram went on to discover was that the image and memory of the external object that the receptive fields of the brain cortex produce is not constant. It changes according to which part of the brain and which side of the brain is being stimulated at the time.

He notes that: *Electrical stimulation of the inferior temporal cortex changes the form of the receptive fields to enhance Gabor information processing – as it occurs in communication processing systems. By contrast, electrical stimulation of the prefrontal cortex changes the form of the receptive fields to enhance Fourier image processing – as it is used in image processing such as PET Scans and fMRI and in making correlations such as in using EFT... Thus both Gabor and Fourier processes are achieved, depending on whether communication and computation or imaging and correlations are being addressed.*[75]

This means that, as shown in Figure 16, when events stimulate the side of the brain (the inferior temporal cortex), you get images of the objects being perceived that are relevant to calculating and communicating. When events stimulate the front of the brain (the pre-frontal cortex), you get images of the objects being perceived that are relevant to visualisation and putting things in context. But the object that is being perceived is the same in both cases – it is your perception that changes depending on the state of mind you are in when you view the same thing.

---

74 Pribram, Karl H. M.D. 2013. *The Form Within: My Point of View* p.292 Westport, CT, USA: Prospecta Press

75 Pribram, Karl H. M.D. 2013. *The Form Within: My Point of View* p.110 Westport, CT, USA: Prospecta Press

Figure 16: brain stimulation and perception

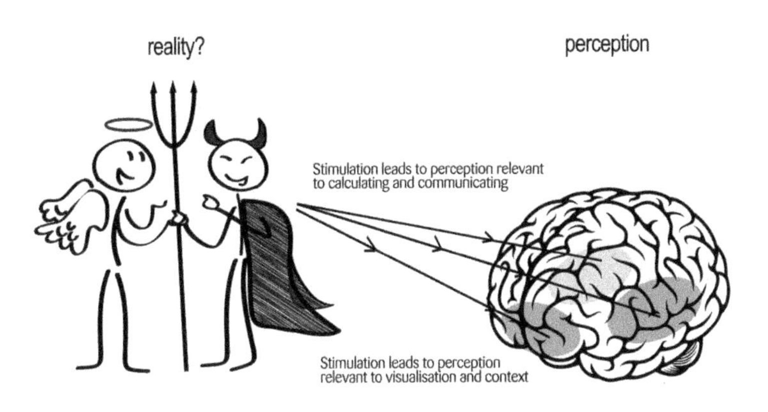


And the state of mind you are in is partly dependent on your conscious intention and partly dependent on how the objects you are receiving information from trigger your neural attractor pathways. If you see a big dog coming towards you, does it remind you of the vicious dog that bit you as a child or does it remind you of your pet that loved you and protected you? One will activate the sympathetic nervous system and the fight and flight hormones while the other will activate the parasympathetic nervous system and your affection and pleasure hormones.

As Pribram writes: *The laws of physics, especially the laws of quantum physics, apparently have their complement in the laws of human perception: the laws of quantum physics have been shown to be dependent on the constraints imposed by the instruments of observation. The laws of human perception have been shown to be dependent on the constraints imposed by processes such as attention, intention and thought organized by the observer's brain.*[76]

Figure 17 is an extension of a diagram used by Pribram to summarise his views of perception.[77]

---

76 Pribram, Karl H. M.D. 2013. *The Form Within: My Point of View* pp 517–518 Westport, CT, USA: Prospecta Press

77 Pribram, Karl H. M.D. 2013. *The Form Within: My Point of View* p.492 Westport, CT, USA: Prospecta Press

At the top is change and communication while at the bottom is inertia and the physics of matter. Communication is associated with attention and intention and can be thought of as an internalised forming of flux, or 'in-formation', but it requires a material medium to manifest. At the other end of the vertical Fourier transform is physical matter or mass which can be described as an 'ex-formation', an externalised, extruded, palpable form of flux.

Figure 17: perception

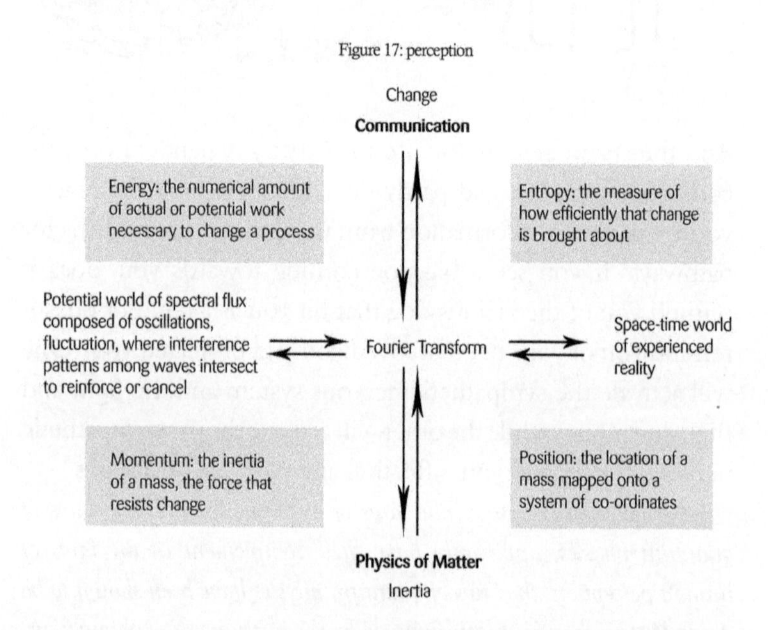


On the left-hand side is uncertainty and the potential world of spectral flux. On the right is conviction or knowledge in the subjective space-time world of experience. Holograms are examples of spectral flux, and they describe potential energy and momentum. Since flux is potential, we cannot measure it until the energy is manifested in space-time. Information and observation lead to the reduction of uncertainty and this transformation between potential and observed again comes about via a Fourier transform.

Pribram explains: *Only through their manifestations in space and time do we get to know of the existence of potentials such as those of energy, of momentum, and of holographic processes. We can know the potential domain only by way of realization in space and time – a dependency between the potential and the world we navigate.*[78]

**Case Study Client F**

Client F works in a law firm in London. He recognises that he is over-worked and stressed and is also concerned about the team members that work for him. He feels sick every time he goes to work and knows he wants to leave his job, but is concerned about the financial implications that would have on his family.

I suggest that we could do an exercise based on perceptual states, viewing his current problem but from different perspectives. We use the possibility of resigning without knowing the future as the crux of the issue and I guide him through a shamanic exercise, viewing this possibility from four different archetypical perceptual states, represented by the qualities of four creatures: serpent, jaguar, humming-bird and eagle. I use drumming, rattling and bells to help him to reach a wider, more open state of consciousness than usual and to help him to engage the right-hemisphere of his brain, outside the logical and rational left-hemisphere.

Serpent is a very grounded and literal place. Everything is as it seems to be. Serpent helps us to walk on this planet in beauty and connection. From the place of serpent he felt

78 Pribram, Karl H. M.D. 2013. *The Form Within: My Point of View* p.496 Westport, CT, USA: Prospecta Press

afraid about leaving his job. But even the worst that could happen wouldn't feel as bad as what he's doing now.

Jaguar is very good at tracking, particularly tracking of emotions and sensations. Jaguar helps us to be fearless and to walk our path without causing harm. He could feel that the best that could happen if he resigned would look and feel amazing.

Hummingbird is joyful and represents the mythic place, the soul's journey, our heart's desire, what is possible in this life. What do we want to say 'yes' to? In the place of hummingbird he imagined talking to the team and the senior partners he would be leaving behind, explaining why he was leaving and trying to make it an amicable and productive departure for everyone. This really surprised him.

Eagle lives in the mountains and helps us to fly high, seeing the higher perspective, the bigger picture, from the level of the super-conscious. Eagle qualities are connected with our very essence. He could see that the fear comes from an experience in his childhood, but he knows that the worst that could happen at this time is that in six months' time he would have to take another job similar to what he is doing, if he hasn't found anything better, but he doesn't really believe that is what would happen.

He leaves feeling much more relaxed, lighter and clearer than when he arrived. He knows what he has to do. The next time I hear from him it is to let me know that he has changed his job to an NGO where he feels he is using his skills but for a much more ethical end purpose. Before he left his old job he voiced to the partners the stress the team are working under and he coached his team on how to work with management in a more constructive and less damaging way going forward as he had visioned from hummingbird.

This shows how we can get stuck in one version of a problem and how the conscious use of different perceptual states can help us to 'think outside the box', particularly seeing the difficult issue as only a small part of a bigger picture.

### Case Study Client G

Client G is a change management consultant. He is twice divorced and now has a new partner. He feels torn between different responsibilities. To some extent he feels he is living a lie and not being authentic in his life. We agree to investigate the word 'truthfulness'.

From the place of serpent he can curl up and lie still for a long time without moving. He also feels as if he has swallowed something big that isn't properly digested.

From the place of jaguar he is very driven to work consecutively with the different colours on the blanket that covers my floor. He finishes on red. Red feels good and feels connected to his place of origin.

From the place of hummingbird he is drawn to the colours green and the blue – they seem to be nurturing colours, he can move easily between them, the land and the sea. He feels very mobile and light.

From the place of eagle he starts swaying around and feels very unstable. He feels as if serpent has to digest what it has eaten and then defecate the rubbish, let go of it all. Eagle wants to gather the blanket up and give all that stuff away, so he rolls it up and puts it in a corner, after which he is capable of looking around in all directions, seeing everything more clearly.

He felt this experience gave him great insight into further work he needs to do, digesting and releasing the past, reconnecting with his ancestors and place of origin, and then visioning a bigger, wider future.

Again this case demonstrates the way our problems can change when we look at them from different perspectives, and use of the archetypes allows us to access archetypical solutions to our issues. The power of fairy tales and myths is often that it permits us to see things in black and white rather than various shades of grey, with much more clear-cut answers to our questions when re-framed in this way.

## Conclusion

The work of leading neurologists and psychotherapists focusing on the primacy of the right-hemisphere for self-awareness and regulation and the escalating recognition of the extent to which myelination and change is possible seem to emphasise the extent to which a paradigm shift towards the bodymind has already been absorbed into clinicians' thinking. However, it raises a question about why is there still such a prevalence of talking therapy, rather than going directly into connection with the body and the emotions (the affects) which are carried in the body in connection with the right-brain?

We also know now that the perception of any specific object or form is subjective and dependent on the way we are moving in relation to it, the environment around us, and our state of mind as we experience it. As illustrated in Figure 18 the upper basal ganglia then go on to convert our perceptions into actions and motivations. And whether we are using our right-brains or our left-brains will determine whether our perceptions are localised or wide-ranging, focused on objects or feelings, communicated to us through language or through the body.

The 'what is it?' primary information received by the amygdala is converted through complex mathematical transformations by the hippocampus into holographic representations, or memories of what we have perceived, then these memories are distributed across many cells with each one containing the whole memory – the holonomic brain.

Figure 18: transforming perceptions into memory and action

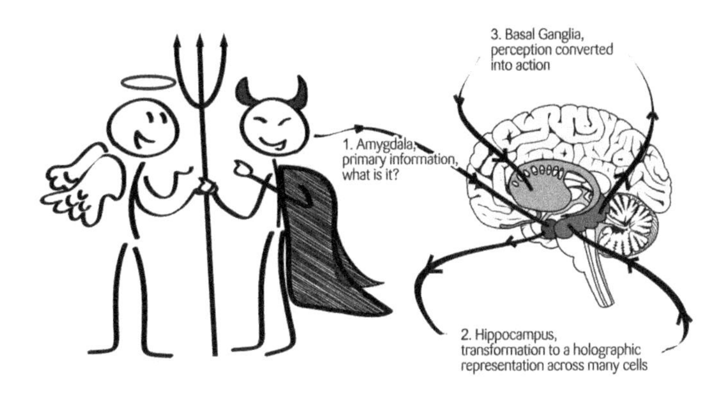


We are capable of a certain amount of personal autonomy and choice about our perceptual states, the actions we decide to take and therefore the memories we go on to form. Variables are not just imposed upon us from the outside, they are the result of our intentions and attention, our level of 'mindfulness' or interoception. The level we work from may appear to be unconscious and outside our control, particularly if our limbic attractors have been programmed by trauma, but work with an empathic, affect- and body-focused therapist can help us to learn to become more conscious as we learn to feel safe in our bodies and allow a greater flow of information to the frontal cortex rather than reacting from the limbic brain.

## GLOSSARY FOR CHAPTER 4

**Enfoldment**: a term coined by physicist David Bohm who believed that all matter is unfolded out of what he described as a holomovement, which is: *vast, rich and in a state of unending flux of enfoldment and unfoldment.*[79]

79 Bohm, David. 1980. *Wholeness and the Implicate Order* p.235 UK: Routledge & Kegan Paul

Bohm considered quantum mechanics to be a process of unfolding and enfolding. He imagined the universe as an infinite sea of space and energy out of which matter could be unfolded, which he called explicating, and enfolded, which he called implicating.

**Fourier transform**: a method for measuring the interference pattern (known as the spectrum) resulting from waves intersecting.

**Gabor transform**: a special short time case of the Fourier transformation rule or spread function.

**Hologram**: three-dimensional images of forms displayed on a two-dimensional surface. The special feature of a hologram resulting from the enfolding of the image is that each tiny piece contains within it the entire three-dimensional picture represented in the whole structure but from a different perspective as if you are moving around the initial form.

**Interoception**: self-awareness of the internal state of our body. It is an iterative process, requiring the interplay between perception of body states and cognitive appraisal of these states to inform response selection.

**Perception**: the brain's internal, subjective interpretation and holographic image of an external form.

**Spectral flux**: a measure of how quickly the power spectrum of a signal is changing.

**Synaptodendritic web**: the web of neuronal connections in the brain that communicates information between axon terminals and dendrites, across the synapses that separate neurons from each other.

**Vision**: the way the optic nerve in the eye collects waves reflecting and refracting from objects in the world around us.

**Wave spectrum**: a mathematical concept used to describe the interference pattern of waves.

# CHAPTER 5: NONLOCALITY

**Do you believe anything travels faster than the speed of light and how do you think microscopic quantum effects impact our macroscopic everyday reality? The answers to these questions will impact your belief in quantum biology and the interaction between brain, mind and consciousness.**

> *If you don't admit many-worlds, there is no way to have a coherent picture.*[80]
>
> (Lev Vaidman)

> *The 'paradox' is only a conflict between reality and your feeling of what reality ought to be.*[81]
>
> (Richard Feynman)

## Introduction

Although quantum physics has been around for almost a century, it is still not well understood outside academia, partly because many of its implications appear to contradict what we

80 New Scientist, May 2010. *Quantum Wonders: Nobody Understands.*
81 New Scientist, May 2010. *Quantum Wonders: Nobody Understands.*

have been schooled to believe and hence what we think we know about the reality we live in. We don't know how much we don't know.

One of the fundamental implications of quantum physics is the existence of nonlocality, what Albert Einstein denounced as 'spooky action at a distance'. Despite Einstein's scepticism, this nonlocality is now a proven and accepted phenomenon within the academic community of physicists. Quantum theory also requires wave-particle duality, uncertainty, and noncausality.

As acceptance of nonlocality grows, our scientific paradigm shifts, and academic evidence for nonlocal effects is emerging rapidly from a multitude of disciplines, including cosmology, evolutionary biology and consciousness research.

The crucial feature is some sort of unified field of coherent information that is generated, conserved, conveyed and links everything together, from the microscopic to the macroscopic. The implications are that, behind the form we experience every day in four-dimensional space-time, is another, potential form or field that enfolds space, time and causality: a nonlocal holographic form.

## Quantum physics and nonlocality

Thus far I have established the interdependence of our physical, mental and emotional health and hence the necessity for an integrated mind-body approach to healing. I now take things a step further and introduce the scientific underpinnings of energy medicine. Once again this takes us into the strange world of quantum physics and nonlocality.

The theories of quantum physics have been around since 1926 when physicist Erwin Schrödinger demonstrated that quantum mechanics permits entangled states. From 1925 to

1927 physicists Niels Bohr and Werner Heisenberg developed what became known as the Copenhagen interpretation of quantum mechanics. According to this, physics can only predict probabilities and the act of measurement affects the system being observed, causing wave functions of probability to collapse to an observed result.

This was followed in 1935 by a paper on noncausal correlations by Einstein, Podolsky and Rosen (known as EPR) which claimed that the Copenhagen interpretation was unsatisfactory and that quantum physics was a flawed theory unless measuring one particle could instantaneously affect others in the system, which would involve information being transmitted faster than light, which was forbidden by the theory of relativity.

Since then additional mathematical theories (in particular Bell's theorem[82]) and the ability to test some of the physical implications of these mathematical predictions in some of the most modern and technologically advanced linear accelerators have proved EPR wrong and quantum physics correct.

The underlying experiment which finally resolved the theoretical argument about the existence or non-existence of nonlocality is illustrated simply in Figure 19. In this experiment two photons of light, known as twins because they are ejected from a single coherent source at the speed of light[83] in opposite directions, are demonstrated to maintain their connection to one another, no matter how far apart they are. So for example

---

82 John S. Bell was a staff member of CERN (the European Organisation for Nuclear Research) whose primary research concerned theoretical high energy physics. In 1964 he published the mathematical paper which transformed the study of quantum mechanics. It showed that *no physical theory which is realistic and also local in a specified sense can agree with all of the statistical implications of quantum mechanics.*

83 To be precise, the speed of light is not a constant. It depends upon the dielectric medium through which it is propagating. The often quoted value of 299,792,458 meters per second is that for a vacuum.

the measurement of the polarisation (direction of spin) of one of the photons determines the polarisation of the other at its distant measurement site. If nothing can travel faster than the speed of light, as postulated by EPR, this measured result would be impossible. Yet it happens. Nonlocality exists.

Figure 19: spooky action at a distance

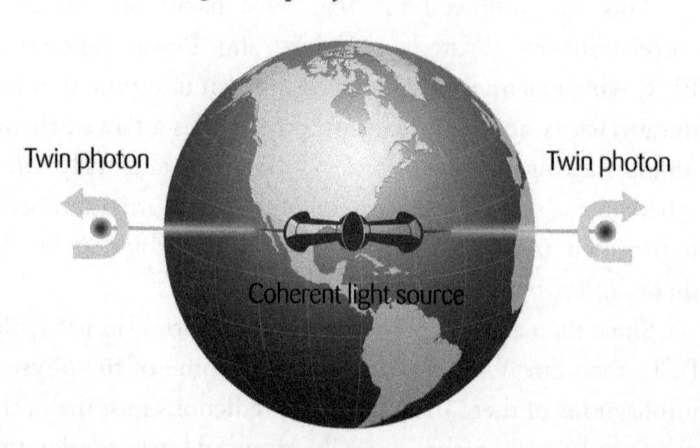


These mathematical theories and their physical implications are beautiful but complex and include many other concepts that often seem to defy what we experience in our everyday lives. The weirdness of the implications of quantum mechanics is one of the reasons why full acceptance of its predictions has not been properly absorbed into our common knowledge base. It was difficult for Einstein to understand, so it is easy to see why it is tough for the rest of us! But just because the conclusions of quantum mechanics are difficult to understand and counter-intuitive to our everyday experience, doesn't mean we can deny their existence, relevance and implications.

As well as requiring nonlocality, quantum theory requires wave-particle duality, uncertainty and noncausality. So what exactly does all this mean and why does it all matter in our everyday lives?

## Wave-particle duality, uncertainty, noncausality and the impact of observation

Complex experiments (many conducted by the Nobel prize-winning physicist Richard Feynman) have demonstrated that everything in this universe (including light, energies and objects) is both a particle and a wave at the same time. These same experiments demonstrated that nothing can be known with certainty until it is observed. As noted by Bohr and Heisenberg in the 1920s, physics can only give you the probability of something happening or any particle being in a particular place at a particular time. Only at the point of observation is the probability function of all possible outcomes of the wave function collapsed into a measurable, actual event.

Even more bizarrely, the act of observation itself impacts the outcome of everything that happens. This applies across the board, from the behaviour of a photon travelling through a slit in a screen, to the placebo/nocebo observation by medical practitioners and therapists of whether someone is healthy or sick, in ways we still don't fully understand.

Much of the evidence for these conclusions is based on a succession of double slit experiments, where particles are fired at a screen with either one or two slits open and a photographic plate behind it.

Much has been written about double slit experiments by many researchers over many years, but the key results, illustrated in Figures 20 to 22 are that:

- If you shine light towards the screen when just one slit is open then a single vertical strip of light is recorded on the photographic plate, indicating that light is a particle.
- If both slits are open, instead of getting two vertical strips

you get a wave interference pattern because of the wave aspect of light.

- When you turn the intensity of the light source down to fire just single photons or single electrons at a time, the result is the same. Conventional reasoning says that with two slits open, each particle must pass through either the left slit or the right slit, producing a single dot on the photographic plate. But this isn't what happens. Instead, somehow when both slits are open, each individual particle effectively knows this and goes through both the left slit and the right slit at the same time, then interacts with itself on the other side to create an interference pattern, just as a wave does.

Figure 20: light as particle and wave

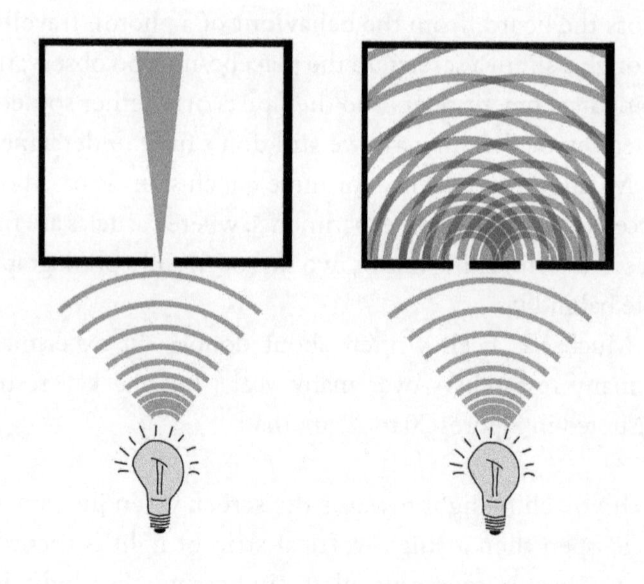

Figure 21: photon as particle and wave

Photon or single
electron light source

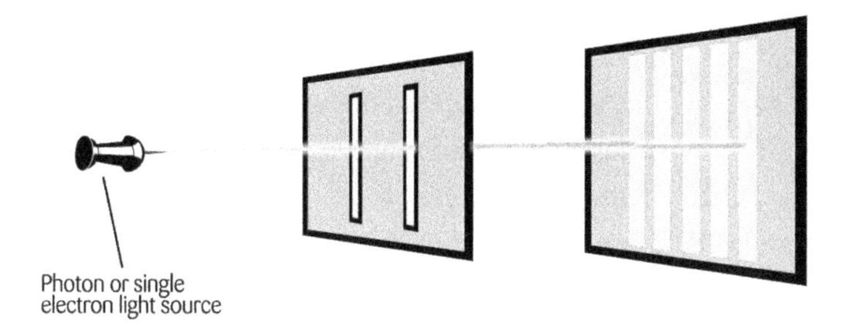

- If you think this is odd so far, the impacts of observation are really strange. Because when you set up a way of observing which slit the electrons go through before they pass through the screen, then even with two slits open the interference pattern disappears! What you get are two parallel strips – what you expected in the first place when you assumed an electron to be just a particle.

Figure 22: impact of an observer

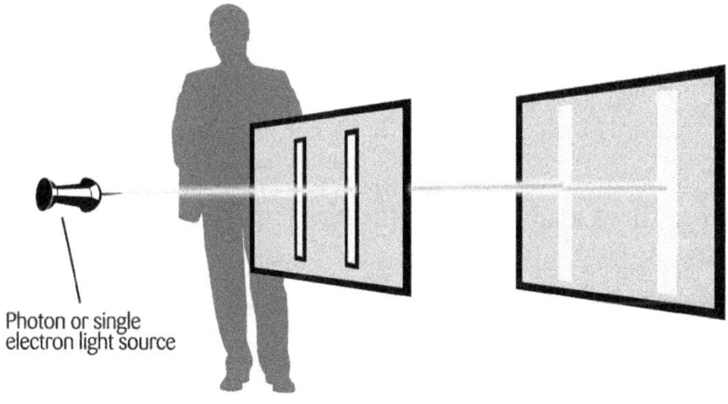

Photon or single
electron light source

The unfortunate but proven conclusion from these experiments is that if you don't observe which slit a particle goes through you will never know the path it took. Indeed perhaps it took both paths. But you will never know exactly what happened in the past if it was not observed. This means the unobserved past is indefinite and there is no exact one-to-one correspondence between cause and effect, so from observing the present we cannot draw any conclusions about what caused the present that we are now observing. This is noncausality.

However, when you observe things, you interfere with and impact the outcome. In mathematical language, everything has a wave function and the wave function tells you the probability of a particle being in a particular place at any given time. When you observe the path the electrons or photons are taking, you force the wave probability function to collapse so that the electrons or photons behave like particles with a specific position in space and time. You have created reality through the act of observation!

The more difficult implication of these experiments is that particles have 'knowledge' of their surroundings, including how many slits are open and whether you are observing them or not. If you are, you influence the form and position they take. But how do they know? And why do they care? These are still unanswered questions.

## Nonlocality and the metaphor of the holographic universe

Much of my recent understanding and knowledge about the expanding academic evidence for nonlocal coherent effects comes from Professor Ervin Laszlo's work. In his long and distinguished career he has been variously professor of philosophy, systems theory and futures studies in the US, Europe and the Far East. He writes: *a new concept of the universe is emerging... In this concept the universe is a highly integrated, coherent system: a 'supermacroscopic quantum system'. Its crucial feature is in-formation that is generated, conserved, and conveyed, and links all its parts...*

*Thanks to the in-formation conserved and conveyed by the A-field,*[84] *the universe is of mind-boggling coherence. All that happens in one place happens also in other places; all that happened at one time happens also at all times after that. Nothing is 'local', limited to where and when it is happening. All things are global, indeed cosmic, for all things are connected, and the memory of all things extends to all places and to all times.*

*This is the concept of the in-formed universe, the view of the world that will hallmark science and society in the coming decades.*[85]

In technical terms, which I am not going to go into in detail here but which are important for the quantum mechanics underlying the in-formed universe, it is not just that nonlocal events are simultaneously correlated (predictably related), as emphasised above by Laszlo, they also appear to be coherent. Very briefly, as shown in Figure 23, to be coherent waves must be of the same amplitude (size), of the same frequency (in phase in time), with a constant spatial phase difference (phase difference is the difference, expressed in degrees or time, between two waves having the same frequency and referenced to the same point in time).

---

84 The A-field is Laszlo's abbreviation for the Akashic Field, in honour of the ancient Sanskrit concept of Akasha, meaning space.

85 Laszlo, Ervin. 2007. *Science and the Akashic Field: An Integral Theory of Everything (Second Edition)* p.80 Rochester, Vermont, USA: Inner Traditions International and Bear & Company, http://www.Innertraditions.com

Figure 23: wave coherence

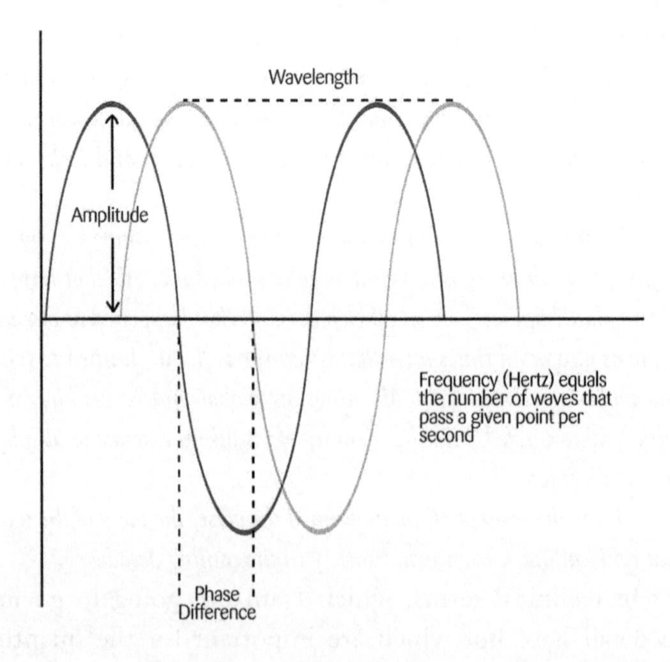


Coherence represents a huge increase in the degree of entanglement compared with simple correlation. In particular wave functions that are coherent, or together form a particular pattern, then carry that pattern as information, forming a quantum hologram in which each part of the hologram contains information about the whole but from a different perspective. Laszlo notes: *it is clear that nonlocal coherence has important implications. It signals that there is not only matter and energy in the universe, but also a more subtle yet real element: an element that connects, and which produces the observed quasi-instant forms of coherence.*

*Identifying this connecting element could solve the puzzles at the forefront of scientific research and point the way toward a more fertile paradigm.*[86]

86 Laszlo, Ervin 2007. *Science and the Akashic Field: An Integral Theory of Everything (Second Edition)* pp60–61 Rochester, Vermont, USA: Inner Traditions International and Bear & Company, http://www.Innertraditions.com

So back to the question of what is this connecting element, this entanglement that exists throughout space and time and is not subject to the restrictions of light speed?

We now need to move on from waves in which the position of any particle is described by a probability function, to fields, which are an even more bizarre concept and yet one whose real-life effects we all live with and accept (even although we cannot scientifically explain them). We are attached to the surface of this planet through its gravitational field. All our electronic devices work through the electromagnetic field. But we cannot directly perceive these fields, we can only perceive their characteristics and their effects. And fields require no medium to exert their remote influence; they occupy what used to be labelled as empty space and are themselves a form of empty space. We are going to get back to how this impacts our everyday lives and our consciousness in the next chapter.

What has been discovered in recent years is that this so-called empty space was actually very unfortunately labelled, as it turns out to be far from empty. At absolute zero, or -273.15 degrees Celsius, it is full of energy, and at the subatomic level it undergoes constant quantum fluctuations that create new quanta seemingly from nothing, which then immediately disappear again. These quantum fluctuations of creation and annihilation are known as the virtual energy sea or zero-point energy. As Laszlo writes: *As scientists now realize, the unified vacuum – now widely known as the unified field – is the originating ground as well as the ultimate destination of all the things that arise and evolve in space and time.*[87]

He continues: *The unified field is a space-filling medium*

87 Laszlo, Ervin. 2009. *The Akashic Experience: Science and the Cosmic Memory Field* p.3 Rochester, Vermont, USA: Inner Traditions International and Bear & Company, http://www.Innertraditions.com

*that underlies the manifest things and processes of the universe. It's a complex and fundamental medium. It carries the universal fields: the electromagnetic, the gravitational, and the strong and weak nuclear fields. It carried the ZPF, the field of zero-point energies. And it's also the element of the cosmos that records, conserves and conveys information. In the latter guise it's the Akashic field, the rediscovered ancient concept of Akasha. A lived connection to this field is the hallmark of the Akashic experience.*[88]

In the subatomic world of nonlocality and entanglement, it turns out not to be that something is travelling faster than the speed of light. It is that everything is encoded and stored as permanently accessible wave functions in nonlocal space.

The analogy that is often used to explain how this works, based on the research of Professor David Bohm, is once again the hologram and it was Bohm who originally coined the term 'the holographic universe'.[89] The implication is that behind the form we experience in the four-dimensional space-time world we navigate, is another potential form that enfolds space, time and causality: a nonlocal holographic form.

But in the holographic form of the cosmos, extending from the micro to the macro, the information is not encoded in a physical medium (as in the holograms on our bank cards) but is stored nonlocally as wave functions in nonlocal space. It is a permanent record of all information which is always and everywhere immediately available. A disturbance of this nonlocal space is seen as the carrier of the information that connects or correlates all different parts nonlocally and instantaneously.

Other names given to the holographic universe are physical

---

88 Laszlo, Ervin. 2009. *The Akashic Experience: Science and the Cosmic Memory Field* p.5 Rochester, Vermont, USA: Inner Traditions International and Bear & Company, http://www.Innertraditions.com

89 Bohm, David. 1980. *Wholeness and the Implicate Order* UK: Routledge & Kegan Paul

space-time, hyperspace, the holofield, the implicate order, the inforealm, the Akashic field, the knowing field or simply the field. Whenever I quote from scientists from different specialisations using any of these terms, they all mean this same thing, and from now on in this book my own preferred label will be the inforealm.

## Conclusion

Nonlocality is a scientifically accepted phenomenon. Everything that exists in the macroscopic world is sourced in the super-small quantum world of subatomic particles and we are surrounded by a field of nonlocal coherent information that appears to transcend space and time. The huge question is whether we can access this nonlocal information field, and potential ways of doing so are covered in the next three chapters.

## GLOSSARY FOR CHAPTER 5

**Akasha**: the ancient Sanskrit concept meaning space.

**Coherence**: waves with the same amplitude, of the same frequency and with a constant spatial phase difference.

**Field**: in classical physics a region of influence in which every point is affected by a force. In quantum physics a region which occupies space, contains energy, and its presence eliminates a true vacuum.

**Inforealm**: the holographic form of the cosmos where information is stored nonlocally as wave functions in nonlocal space. It is also known as physical space-time, hyperspace, the holofield, the implicate order, the Akashic field, the knowing field or simply the field.

**Nonlocality**: entanglement of particles such that

measurement of one impacts another instantaneously, involving information being transmitted at least as fast as the speed of light.

**Wave function**: a mathematical equation that tells you the probability that, at a particular place at any given time, when there is an observer, the resulting measurement will indicate a particle or a wave.

# CHAPTER 6: CONSCIOUSNESS

**Do you think consciousness is held within the physical brain or in some sort of field outside the brain? In other words are you a materialist or a dualist? If the latter do you believe in the emerging field theories of consciousness?**

> *Certainty is the greatest of all illusions: whatever kind of fundamentalism it may underwrite, that of religion or of science, it is what the ancients meant by hubris. The only certainty, it seems to me, is that those who believe they are certainly right are certainly wrong. The difference between scientific materialists and the rest is only this: the intuition of the one is that mechanistic application of reason will reveal everything about the world we inhabit, where the intuition of the others leads them to be less sure.*[90]
>
> (Iain McGilchrist)

## Introduction

For centuries philosophers have argued about the nature

90 McGilchrist, Iain. 2009. *The Master and his Emissary: The Divided Brain and the Making of the Western World* p.460 New Haven and London: Yale University Press

of consciousness whilst scientists have usually ignored the question of consciousness, handing that debate over to their non-scientific colleagues. In recent decades however consciousness has come back onto the scientific agenda and is being investigated by many sources and disciplines.

Physicists in collaboration with medical doctors are now focusing on whether the human brain is actually just a transmitter to, and receiver from, an external nonlocal field of consciousness, rather than being the source of consciousness. A number of theories have been put forward suggesting mechanisms by which this could operate, but they tend to introduce additional metaphysical assumptions on the morality of the inforealm so they appear to suggest a solution to one debate while introducing another.

Other exponents of the medical profession focus on experimental evidence accumulating from the study of near-death experiences which suggests that people are capable of consciousness beyond death and of connection with the inforealm during these expanded states of consciousness. There is preliminary evidence that this is mediated by the endogenously produced molecule di-methyl-tryptamine.

And for a nonlocal consciousness to be consciously useful to us, we would need to be able to access it at will, which historically has been the realm of the shaman (someone who intentionally induces altered states of consciousness for the exploration of the human condition), not something regarded as the right of every human being.

**The nonlocal mind**

Everything presented so far about the internal bodymind connection through the brain, the nervous system and the endocrine system is now accepted within twenty-first century medicine. And everything presented so far about the nonlocal universe is accepted within twenty-first century science. These theories may not be entirely right, we may in due course find they were incomplete or even incorrect, and they may be difficult for non-scientists to fully comprehend, but within academia they are not currently controversial.

In this chapter I am heading into more speculative territory regarding how the microscopic nonlocal quantum inforealm within our physical bodymind might be able to relate to the macroscopic nonlocal quantum inforealm surrounding us and comprising this world we live in. To do this I am going to draw heavily on the work of the cardiac surgeon Pim Van Lommel, M.D. as well as physicist Roger Penrose, anaesthetist Stuart Hameroff and neurobiologist Herms Romijn, all recipients of many academic degrees and prizes for their work as they pioneered the new scientific approaches to nonlocal consciousness.

**What is the source of consciousness?**

As Pribram developed his holonomic theory of memory within the brain he wrote: *If quantum laws operate at every scale, then despite their weirdness, these laws should have an explanation at an everyday scale of inquiry.*[91]

When we explore the connections between the nonlocal cosmic inforealm and our daily lives here on earth, we quickly get drawn into the age-old questions:

- What exactly is consciousness and where does it come from?

91 Pribram, Karl H. M.D. 2013. *The Form Within: My Point of View* p.108 Westport, CT, USA: Prospecta Press

- Is it internal, an attribute of the human brain, or external, an attribute of a cosmic force around us (however you want to label that)?

Materialists have argued that it is purely a mechanistic function of the brain, while external theories have often been associated with a divine or religious source. The new science suggests that the source may be cosmic without invoking the metaphysical.

I quote once more from Laszlo: *There is no need to ascribe nonlocal coherence, the remarkable space- and time-transcending connection of everything with everything else, to the action of divine will, or to forces above or beyond the natural world. Nonlocal coherence is a bona fide scientific phenomenon, just as real and understandable as light, electromagnetism, mass and gravitation.*[92]

**The science of the brain as a receiving and transmitting interface from an external source of consciousness**

William James (1842 – 1910) was professor of psychology and of philosophy at Harvard University, and is considered to be one of the greatest American thinkers. He provided a new model of the self and consciousness back in the Ingersoll lecture at Harvard in 1898. There he introduced the idea that thought is a transmissive function of the brain. He writes: *Just how the process of transmission may be carried on, is indeed unimaginable… Consciousness in this process does not have to be generated de novo in a vast number of places. It exists already, behind the scenes, coeval with the world.*[93]

92 Laszlo, Ervin. 2007. *Science and the Akashic Field: An Integral Theory of Everything (Second Edition)* p.157 Rochester, Vermont, USA: Inner Traditions International and Bear & Company, http://www.Innertraditions.com

93 https://www.uky.edu/~eushe2/Pajares/jimmortal.html

The model of the brain and the body functioning as an interface for an external, independent, non-material consciousness – James' process of transmission – has been gaining ground as physicists' understanding of nonlocality has increased in parallel with brain-imaging techniques, giving neuroscientists access to the microscopic, quantum nature of our cells.

In this new, scientific class of models of nonlocal consciousness, the brain has the function of being both a receiver and a transmitter. It has a facilitating as well as a producing role and it enables us to connect with and experience a consciousness which is nonlocal and functions as the origin or basis of everything, including the material world.

The modern metaphors used to describe this process are often the television or the internet. In the case of television representing the brain, programmes are being broadcast across the world all the time, twenty-four hours a day, seven days a week. But we may not even have a television in our homes, and if we do it may be turned off. We are not watching anything, but this doesn't mean the programmes aren't being broadcast 'out there'. When we switch the TV on, we then need to decide which particular programme to watch, how we are going to 'tune in'.

In the case of a computer representing the brain, there is now a huge amount of information stored globally on millions of servers worldwide that represent the internet. But we may not own a computer and so we can't access the internet. Or we may own a computer but only use it to do things like word processing or accounts or storing photographs. We may not have internet access. Beyond that, if we do have internet access, what answers we get depends on what questions we ask. But all the information is always there. Whether we choose to access it or not and then what we choose to access is up to us, and that choice in turn impacts our life experience.

## Model 1: Roger Penrose and Stuart Hameroff

Since the early 1990s the quantum physicist Sir Roger Penrose has teamed up with the anaesthetist Dr Stuart Hameroff to investigate consciousness. They are among the leading proponents of the theory that the brain is just the receiver and transmitter between the physical body and a nonlocal, independent consciousness.

It is now well established that within the brain, the axon of each neuron has a skeletal structure (the cytoskeleton) formed from a system of long, rigid but hollow, cylindrical protein beams known as microtubules. These are formed from the lateral linking of long polymerised strings of proteins known as alpha and beta tubulin as shown in Figure 24. These microtubules join together to form the microtrabecular network.

Figure 24: Microtubles

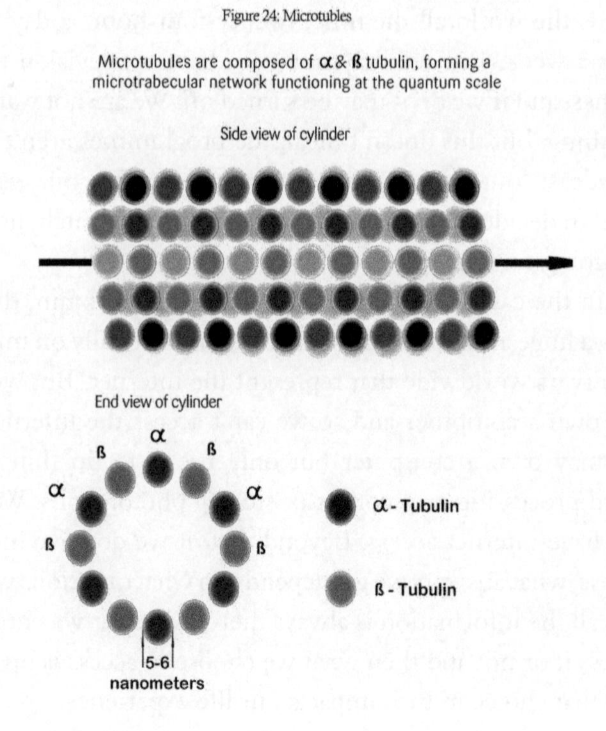

Penrose and Hameroff developed the hypothesis that it is the resonance of these microtubules that is the physical body's link with consciousness – the mechanism by which the information in the external holographic consciousness is downloaded into the brain. Hameroff gives his thinking in great detail in an online paper, *Quantum computation in Brain microtubules? The Penrose-Hameroff "Orch OR" model of consciousness*[94] where Orch OR stands for orchestrated objective reduction.

For their model of consciousness to work, it requires quantum coherent states and quantum computation at the neuronal level within the brain. They argue that this is possible because there are approximately 10 to the power 18 microtubules within the human brain and the filaments are just five-to-six nanometers in diameter, so the giant microtrabecular network is functioning at close to the super-small quantum size.

While microtubules were traditionally considered to be purely structural components, recent evidence has demonstrated that they contain extraordinarily fast mechanical signalling and communication functions. They seem to switch on and off in the nanosecond scale. Each biological cell contains approximately 10 to the power 7 tubulins, and nanosecond switching predicts roughly 10 to the power 16 operations per second, per neuron. Also, recent research has confirmed that microtubules are transient and are frequently rebuilt, in some cells several times an hour, raising the question of how they can possibly store information when they are in such constant flux? It seems far more plausible that they are just the resonators not the storage units.

A recent paradigm within postquantum physics is signal nonlocality, which means that a change in the state of one system induces an immediate change in an entangled

---

94 http://www.quantumconsciousness.org/personal.html

system without even passing on any information. Ede Frecska, M.D., Chief of Psychiatry at the National Institute of Psychiatry and Neurology in Budapest explains: *Signal nonlocality is purely correlational; it doesn't involve information transfer exceeding the speed of light. Therefore, Einstein's principle is not violated... Just as special relativity is a limiting case of general relativity, so is classical quantum mechanics with signal locality a limiting case of postquantum theory with signal nonlocality. The latter is exactly what is implicit in the microtubule model of quantum consciousness.*[95]

In the online paper mentioned previously, Hameroff notes that: *In a panpsychist view consistent with modern physics, Planck scale*[96]*spin networks encode proto-conscious experience as well as Platonic values. Particular configurations of quantum spin geometry convey particular varieties of proto-conscious experience, meaning and aesthetics. The proposed Orch OR events occur in the brain, extending downward to processes in an experiential Planck scale medium. The basic idea is that consciousness involves brain activities coupled to self-organizing ripples in fundamental reality...*

*Potential possibilities interact and then abruptly self-collapse, a slight quake in spacetime geometry. As quantum state reductions are irreversible, cascades of Orch OR events present a forward flow of subjective time and "stream of consciousness".*[97]

This theory introduces the assumption that the quantum field around us (what Hameroff describes as the Planck scale spin networks) actually contains a moral code, the subjective

---

95 Frecska, Ede, M.D.. 2007. The Shaman's Journey, Supernatural or Natural? A Neuro-Ontological Interpretation of Spiritual Experiences, p.190 in *Inner Paths to Outer Space* by Strassman, Rick, M.D., Wojtowicz, Slawek, M.D., Luna, Luis Eduardo, PhD, and Frecska, Ede, M.D. Rochester, Vermont, USA: Inner Traditions International and Bear & Company, http://www.Innertraditions.com

96 The Planck length is 1.61619926 × 10-35 metres

97 http://www.quantumconsciousness.org/personal.html

Platonic values of truth, good and beauty. Somehow these are fundamental qualities, all of which are accessible in the field of potential possibility, which collapses to a particular outcome when we consciously observe it.

The Penrose-Hameroff model of biological quantum computation requires quantum coherent states within the brain. Cosmologist Max Tegmark[98] and others have argued that the warm temperature of the brain will prevent the material organisation necessary for quantum computation because of the phenomenon called heat decoherence. Decoherence is the loss of coherence and hence the loss of information from a system. Heat decoherence exists when warming something up causes the emission of phonons which knock the waves out of their coherent phasing.

An extended model suggested by physicists Edward Witten and Alexei Kitaev to get around this problem of heat decoherence, is based on something known as quantum weaving, because quantum weaving in the microtrabecular network may potentially eliminate the problem of decoherence. Knots can store information and according to Witten and Kitaev as paraphrased by Frecska: *a braided system of quantum particles can perform quantum computation. Using quantum particles with just the right properties, braiding can efficiently carry out any quantum computation in superfast time. Further, while traditional qubits are prone to decoherence, braiding is robust... data stored on a quantum braid can survive all kinds of disturbance.*[99]

---

98 Tegmark, Max. 2000. Importance of Quantum Decoherence in Brain Processes in *Physical Review E61: Statistical Physics, Plasmas, Fluids, and Related Interdisciplinary Topics* pp4194-4206

99 Frecska, Ede, M.D. 2007. How Can Shamans Talk with Plants and Animals?, pp219–220 in *Inner Paths to Outer Space* by Strassman, Rick, M.D., Wojtowicz, Slawek, M.D., Luna, Luis Eduardo, PhD, and Frecska, Ede, M.D.. Rochester, Vermont, USA: Inner Traditions International and Bear & Company, http://www.Innertraditions.com

This theory goes on to suggest that a vast braided loop network may enable an organism to resonate with the world around it, resulting in a phenomenon described as topological consciousness.

As an alternative argument against the doubts raised by Tegmark, recent work compiled together and reported by the quantum biologists Jim Al-Khalili and Johnjoe McFadden has discovered a wealth of quantum tunnelling within a huge array of living cells, ranging from plants to enzymes to the genes encoded within our DNA. Somehow decoherence is being held at bay within the warm temperatures of the body, against all expectations. The biological systems have evolved to maintain coherence even at temperatures that would normally be expected to cause decoherence. This evidence removes the objection raised by Tegmark et al to the Penrose-Hameroff model.

Al-Khalili and McFadden write: *it was only a decade or so ago that most scientists dismissed the idea that tunnelling and other delicate quantum phenomena could be taking place in biology. The fact that they have been found in these habitats suggests that life takes special measures to capture advantages provided by the quantum world to make its cells work. But what measures? How does life keep that energy of quantum behaviour, decoherence, at bay? This is one of the biggest mysteries of quantum biology.*[100]

A few pages later in their book they write: *Quantum coherence is normally expected to be very short-lived unless the quantum system can be isolated from its surroundings (fewer jostling particles) and/or cooled to a very low temperature (much less jostling) to preserve the delicate coherence…*[101]

---

100 Al-Khalili, Jim and McFadden, Johnjoe. 2014. *Life on the Edge: The Coming of Age of Quantum Biology* pp138–139 London, UK: Bantam Press. Reproduced by permission of The Random House Group Ltd.

101 Al-Khalili, Jim and McFadden, Johnjoe. 2014. *Life on the Edge: The Coming of Age of Quantum Biology* p.164 London, UK: Bantam Press. Reproduced by permission of The Random House Group Ltd.

*However, we now know that down at the molecular level, many important biological processes can indeed be very fast (of the order of trillionths of a second) and can also be confined to short atomic distances – just the sort of length and timescales where quantum processes like tunnelling can have an effect. Thus, although decoherence can never be entirely prevented, it may be kept at bay for just long enough to be biologically useful.*[102]

The massive speed and tiny size of the structures within the microtrabecular network would appear to fit these criteria for coherence within the living organism.

## Model 2: Herms Romijn

Herms Romijn is a neurobiologist who hypothesises a link between consciousness and the brain mediated by virtual photons as the carriers. He defines consciousness as: *those subjective experiences that, as a result of attention, have expanded to a certain degree of complexity such that they contain an aspect of time (when?), space (where?), and/or self (it is me who is aware of).*[103]

So first of all, what is a virtual photon? It can most simply be described as a disturbance in the real electromagnetic field, leading to an attraction or repulsion between two photons. So virtual photons transfer forces through the field. Romijn proposed that the fleeting patterns of electromagnetic fields in the brain, spread across the dendritic neuronal network, record our experiences such as pain and pleasure, or perceived colours. He goes on to propose that since these electromagnetic

102 Al-Khalili, Jim and McFadden, Johnjoe. 2014. *Life on the Edge: The Coming of Age of Quantum Biology* p.165 London, UK: Bantam Press. Reproduced by permission of The Random House Group Ltd.

103 Romijn, Herms. 2002. *Journal of Consciousness Studies, Volume 9, Number 1, 1 January 2002,* pp61–81(21) Imprint Academic

fields contain virtual photons: *it is the highly ordered patterns of virtual photons that encode for subjective (conscious) experiences.*[104]

He proceeds to argue that subjective conscious experience itself is coded into the virtual photons which are omnipresent in the universe. So consciousness: *did not emerge during evolution only after neuronal networks had been formed able to generate electric and/or magnetic fields of sufficient complexity but, rather, that subjectivity already existed in a very elementary form as a fundamental property of the omnipresent virtual photons, i.e., of matter. The contribution of neuronal networks to consciousness was to generate highly ordered patterns of germs of subjectivity (virtual photons), so allowing complex subjective (conscious) experiences.*[105]

## New assumptions within these models

Models 1 and 2 both propose mechanisms based on quantum physics by which the brain could be connected to the inforealm, but both introduce a metaphysical and untestable assumption. In the Penrose-Hameroff model this assumption is that Planck scale spin networks encode Platonic values, i.e. assigning some sort of morality to the networks of consciousness. In the Romijn model the assumption is that subjectivity (which he equates to consciousness) is encoded into virtual photons as a fundamental property of the cosmos.

Although these assumptions may be regarded as unsatisfactory, at least the models start to provide possible scientific explanations of how our physical minds can interact with a nonlocal inforealm, whether you want to ascribe moral values to that or not. And although these theories may seem

104 Romijn, Herms. 2002. *Journal of Consciousness Studies, Volume 9, Number 1, 1 January 2002,* pp61–81(21) Imprint Academic

105 Romijn, Herms. 2002. *Journal of Consciousness Studies, Volume 9, Number 1, 1 January 2002,* pp61–81(21) Imprint Academic

highly abstract, their recent proliferation and the debates they have raised indicates the interest that consciousness is now attracting within science, having been ostracised to the realm of the metaphysical in the 19th and 20th centuries.

If it is true that there is a nonlocal consciousness containing all information, of which we are always a part, what difference does that make to our lives unless we can choose to access it consciously, rather than it operating in the background without our knowledge?

### The experimental evidence of the brain as a receiving and transmitting interface from an external source of consciousness

Van Lommel and his team have been leading medical investigations into near-death experiences (NDEs) of their own patients and others since 1986. During their NDEs many of these patients appeared to be able to engage with an enhanced and nonlocal consciousness, which among other things frequently allowed them to communicate with the dead, or experience a sense of unconditional love and acceptance, or contact a form of ultimate and universal knowledge and wisdom. These results applied equally regardless of the prior beliefs of the patients, their sex, race or religion.

In his 2010 book *Consciousness Beyond Life: The Science of the Near-Death Experience* Van Lommel summarises his findings over 20 years and concludes: *An NDE is both an existential crisis and an intense learning experience. People are transformed by the glimpse of a dimension where time and space play no role, where past and future can be viewed, where they feel complete and healed, and where infinite wisdom and unconditional love can be experienced... After an NDE, people realize that everything and everybody are connected, that every thought has an impact on oneself and others, and that our consciousness survives physical death. The realization that everything is nonlocally connected changes both scientific theories and our image of mankind and the world.*[106]

Van Lommel researched many scientific models for an explanation of the near-death experiences he logged so carefully from his case studies. His conclusions after years of study help to explain the possible interface between what we normally experience and what we are capable of experiencing. He writes: *Complete and endless consciousness is everywhere in a dimension that is not tied to time or place, where past, present, and future all exist and are accessible at the same time. This endless consciousness is always in and around us… The brain and the body merely function as an interface or relay station to receive part of our total consciousness and part of our memories into our waking consciousness. Nonlocal consciousness encompasses much more than our waking consciousness.*[107]

He went on to try to explain this duality of consciousness between waking and nonlocal as analogous to the dual particle-wave aspects of light, noting: *The physical aspect of our consciousness in the material world, which we experience as waking consciousness and which can be compared to the particle aspect of light, stems from the wave aspect of the 'complete' and 'endless' consciousness created by collapse of the wave function in nonlocal space. This particle aspect, the physical effect of our waking consciousness, is observable and demonstrable in the brain… whereas consciousness in nonlocal space is not directly demonstrable on (quantum) theoretical grounds: everything that is visible emanates from the invisible.*[108]

---

106 Van Lommel, Pim, M.D. 2010. *Consciousness Beyond Life: The Science of the Near-Death Experience* p.329 New York, NY, USA: Harper Collins Publishers

107 Van Lommel, Pim, M.D. 2010. *Consciousness Beyond Life: The Science of the Near-Death Experience* p.xvii New York, NY, USA: Harper Collins Publishers

108 Van Lommel, Pim, M.D. 2010. *Consciousness Beyond Life: The Science of the Near-Death Experience* pp248–249 New York, NY, USA: Harper Collins Publishers

Figure 25: wave particle duality of consciousness

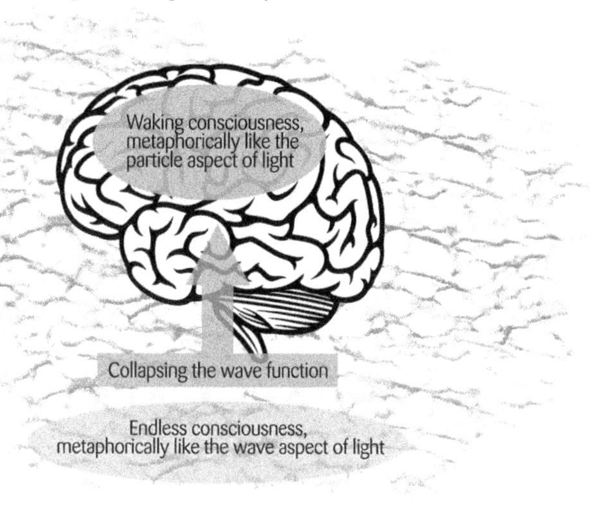


When we are dying, the functions of the brain that are dependent on electromagnetic fields are disrupted and somehow we are able to access an expanded consciousness: *Life allows us to make the transition from nonlocal space to our physical world, space-time. The oxygen deficiency brought on by the stopping of the heart temporarily suspends brain function, causing the electromagnetic fields of our neurons and other cells to disappear and the interface between consciousness and our physical body to be disrupted. This creates the conditions for experiencing the endless and enhanced consciousness outside the body (the wave aspect of consciousness) known as an NDE: the experience of a continuity of consciousness independent of the body.*[109]

The molecule di-methyl-tryptamine (DMT) is hallucinogenic and is produced in large quantities during the process of dying. This DMT is hypothesised to play

109 Van Lommel, Pim, M.D. 2010. *Consciousness Beyond Life: The Science of the Near-Death Experience* p.251 New York, NY, USA: Harper Collins Publishers

an important role in the experience of an expanded consciousness during an NDE. Dr Rick Strassman is one of the few scientists in recent years to have been given permission to carry out research on DMT, which I will discuss further in the next chapter. His work points out that DMT can access the brain from the pineal gland via the cerebrospinal fluid and a simple process of diffusion without entering the bloodstream. Hence if it is produced in the endocrine system at the time of an NDE it can impact the consciousness we have in the brain by attaching to specific receptors through the lipoprotein networks even although we are declared dead in terms of our heart function and hence circulation of blood.[110]

### How can we use our nonlocal consciousness more effectively?

The key to a truly expanded consciousness (way beyond mindfulness or interoception) within our waking lives is to be able to access the nonlocal consciousness without an NDE. If we could access the holographic universe, the inforealm, at will then we could gain information about any part of the cosmos through space and time.

So how do we learn to become like the metaphorical switched-on TV that is tuned into the most interesting programmes, or the connected laptop asking the cloud the most useful questions for our own lives and our impact on this planet we live on? More scientifically this question can be posed as, if our physical brains are capable of being receivers

---

110 Strassman, Rick, M.D. 2000. *DMT: The Spirit Molecule* p.79 Rochester, Vermont, USA: Inner Traditions International and Bear & Company, http://www.Innertraditions.com

and transmitters of a consciousness which is stored in the holographic universe, enfolded as waveforms in the quantum zero-point energy field, how do we learn to resonate with the waveforms of information that will be of most benefit to us?

That is the topic of the next chapter and takes us into the realm of the mystics, shamans and users of hallucinogenics who intentionally induce altered states of consciousness for the exploration of the human condition.

## Conclusion

Science and medicine have resumed interest in consciousness. There is mounting experiential medical evidence that, in altered states of consciousness such as near-death experiences, people can retain consciousness despite total loss of heart or brain function and can access the inforealm, a consciousness external to the physical body.

There are a number of theories emerging from physicists in collaboration with doctors regarding how the microtrabecular networks of our brains might act as receivers and transmitters, allowing us to access an external omniscient and omnipresent consciousness.

This leaves open the question of whether and how this external consciousness embodies any moral values. It leads on to whether and how we can intentionally engage with this external consciousness.

## GLOSSARY FOR CHAPTER 6

**Heat decoherence**: quantum decoherence is the loss of quantum coherence of the wave functions of a system and hence the loss of information from the system. Heat decoherence exists when warming a material up causes the emission of phonons and then photons which knock the wave functions of the material out of their coherent phasing.

**Microtrabecular network**: the network in the brain linking microtubules consisting of long polymerised strings of proteins known as alpha and beta tubulin.

**Panpsychism**: the doctrine that mind is a fundamental feature of the world which exists throughout the universe.

**Phonon**: a definite discrete unit or quantum of vibrational mechanical energy, just as a photon is a quantum of electromagnetic or light energy.

**Psychonaut**: someone who intentionally induces altered states of consciousness for the exploration of the human condition.

**Resonance**: connection between two systems such that one drives the other to oscillate at a particular frequency without any direct physical interaction. Resonant systems can be used to generate vibrations of a specific frequency or pick out specific frequencies from a complex vibration containing many frequencies.

**Virtual photon**: a disturbance in the real electromagnetic field, leading to an attraction or repulsion between two photons. A disturbance that transfers forces through the field.

# CHAPTER 7: PSYCHEDELICS AND THEIR INTERFACE WITH CONSCIOUSNESS

**Do you think psychedelic compounds are helpful or dangerous and if so in what circumstances? Do you support further research into these chemicals that interact with neurotransmitters to assist people suffering from disorders such as PTSD, addiction, cluster headaches and depression, as well as those facing death as a result of a terminal illness?**

*The list of freedoms we enjoy today that were not enjoyed by our ancestors is indeed a long and impressive one. It is therefore exceedingly strange that Western civilization in the 21st century enjoys no real freedom of consciousness.*

*There can be no more intimate and elemental part of the individual than his or her own consciousness. At the deepest level, our consciousness is what we are – to the extent that if we are not sovereign over our own consciousness, then we cannot in any meaningful sense be sovereign over anything else either. So it has to be highly significant that, far from encouraging freedom of consciousness, our societies in fact violently deny our right to sovereignty in this intensely personal area and have effectively outlawed all states of consciousness other than those on a very narrowly defined and officially approved list.*[111]

(Graham Hancock)

## Introduction

For the inforealm, this scientifically proven field of information, to be truly useful to us, we have to be able to access it at will, to collect information that will help us in our lives. We potentially may be able to do this by sending questions out to the field at the right frequency and then tuning into and downloading the coherent answers that are available within the inforealm.

There are many ways in which people throughout the ages believe they have achieved access to the inforealm, sometimes intentionally, including meditation, breathwork, participating in trance dance, listening to bi-neural sound and taking hallucinogens. Many others believe they have achieved this unintentionally through spontaneous out-of-body experiences, NDEs and what they describe as 'alien' abduction.

The people who have consistently been able to journey intentionally outside four-dimensional space-time, sometimes aided by hallucinogens, sometimes not, have been the shamans, the healers who have existed in many tribes around the planet. For centuries Westerners did not believe their stories, but new research into hallucinogens is backing their claims.

---

111 Hancock, Graham, 2015. *The Divine Spark: Psychedelics, Consciousness and the Birth of Civilization* p.3 London, UK: Hay House, Inc.

## Altered states of consciousness

I hope I have presented enough evidence in the previous chapter to suggest that many serious scientists and doctors now believe that the brain is both a receiver and transmitter, at least of information and most likely of consciousness itself, interacting somehow (quite how still being the subject of research and debate) with a nonlocal field of information (and possibly of consciousness).

For many people who have experienced alternative states of consciousness (ASCs) at one time or another in their lives, science is finally groping towards an acceptance, understanding and even validation of what they have experienced, but which in the past they have frequently kept quiet about for fear of being labelled as delusional or even psychotic.

So is it possible for all of us to gain this access, as and when we choose? Increasingly the answer emerging from research centres such as the Monroe Institute,[112] the Multidisciplinary Association for Psychedelic Studies (MAPS),[113] the Beckley Foundation,[114] the Council on Spiritual Practices in conjunction with John Hopkins University,[115] the Heffter Research Institute[116] and the Institute of Noetic Sciences (IONS)[117] is being acknowledged as yes.

As already mentioned, some of the traditional ways of gaining access have been meditation, ecstatic dance, shamanic drumming and journeying, as well as the use of psychedelics. The keys to activating the ability to resonate consciously with the inforealm by the use of any or all of these methods so that

112 https://www.monroeinstitute.org/
113 http://www.maps.org/
114 http://www.beckleyfoundation.org/
115 http://www.csp.org/practices/entheogens/entheogens.html
116 http://www.heffter.org/
117 http://www.noetic.org/

we can use it to improve our health and happiness appear to be first the presence in the brain of the molecule di-methyl-tryptamine (DMT) and secondly the so-called junk DNA which accounts for more than 95 per cent of our total DNA.

## The role of DMT in accessing nonlocal consciousness

Looking at the first key, DMT, it is a tryptamine molecule. All of the tryptamine family contain a nucleus of tryptamine itself, a derivative of tryptophan which is an amino acid naturally present in our diet. Nuts, seeds, oats, beans, lentils, tofu, cheese, red meat, chicken, turkey, fish and eggs are particularly high in tryptophan. When we ingest sufficient tryptophan, the brain is able to synthesise the neurotransmitter known as serotonin which goes on to have a wide-ranging effect on multiple brain functions, including control of certain physiological systems (such as the cardiovascular and endocrine systems), temperature regulation, emotional, cognitive, and sensory functions.

In the following diagrams the unmarked balls represent carbon and there are some additional hydrogen atoms which are not shown for clarity of comparison between the molecules.

Figure 26: Tryptamine

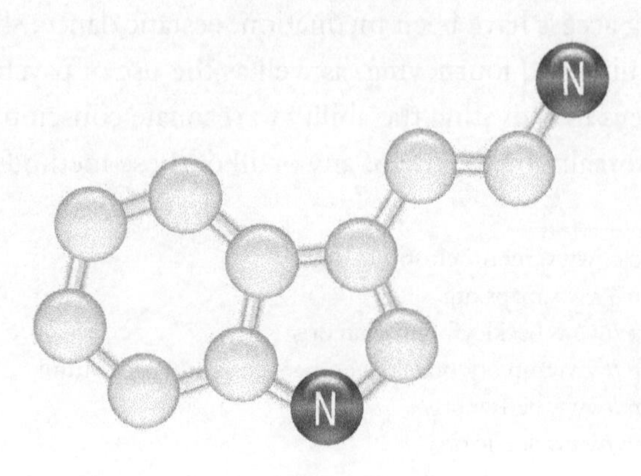

Serotonin is 5-hydroxy-tryptamine (5-HT), which is tryptamine with one extra oxygen atom added. 10 carbon, 2 nitrogen, 1 oxygen. It was discovered in 1948 and labelled as the first known neurotransmitter.

Figure 27: Serotonin

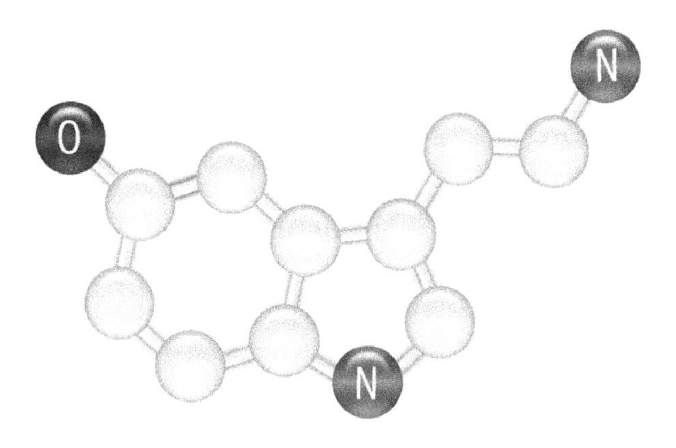


DMT adds two methyl groups (each methyl group contains one carbon and three hydrogen atoms, $CH_3$) to the tryptamine molecule and so contains 10 carbon, 2 nitrogen, 2 methyl groups.

Figure 28: Di-methyl-tryptamine

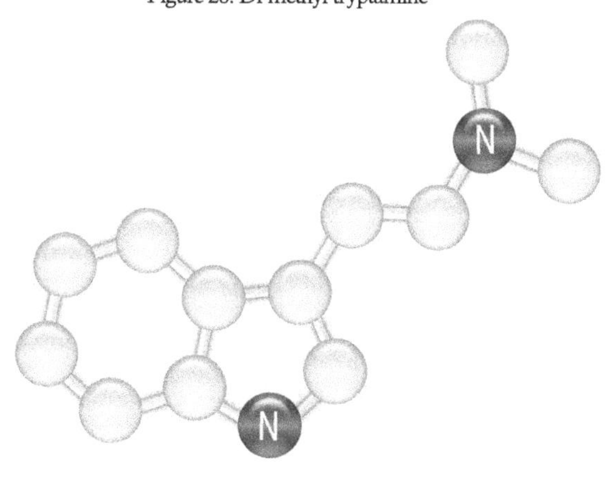

Other famous hallucinogenic substances are also tryptamines. For instance psilocybin (found in the stereotypical magic mushrooms) is DMT plus one phosphorus and four oxygen. Ibogaine (found in plants of the Apocynaceae family) as well as the synthetically produced LSD both have tryptamine cores.

DMT is a beta-carboline produced naturally in the pineal gland (as is serotonin) when sufficiently stimulated by the adreno-corticotropic hormones cortisol, adrenaline and noradrenaline. As well as being produced endogenously within the body, it is found in large quantities in nature, especially in plants growing in South America and Mexico. Its psychoactive relatives psilocybin and mescaline are found extensively in mushrooms and cacti respectively.

It is carried around the body by the bloodstream and, as well as binding to the serotonin receptors in the brain, it is found in the lungs, the liver and the eyes.

Because it results from stimulation by the adreno-corticotropic hormones, during incidences of major psychological or physical stress when the body releases large quantities of these hormones, these in turn activate the production of a large amount of DMT. In particular during the process of dying (which for many people is the ultimate experience of stress), large quantities of DMT are thought to be released through the death of cells in the pineal gland.

When the pineal gland produces DMT it also produces a monoamine oxidase inhibiting (MAOI) molecule called harmine which is capable of blocking the enzymatic breakdown of DMT, allowing the DMT to cross the brain-blood barrier and attach to serotonin receptors in the central nervous system. This crossing of the brain-blood barrier is very unusual. There are cells that line the brain's blood vessels that prevent most blood-borne chemicals from moving into the brain. Other examples of molecules that are allowed through from the blood into the brain are glucose and some amino acids that the brain cannot synthesise internally. But why does the brain expend the energy necessary to block the breakdown of DMT in the bloodstream, hence allowing it across the barrier? As yet we don't have an answer to this question.

Because of the unique position of the pineal gland, DMT can also diffuse from it directly into the brain by way of the cerebrospinal fluid, without first having to enter the blood circulation and cross the blood-brain barrier, so it does not require the heart to be functioning and the blood to be circulating in order to enter the brain. This is of particular significance to the fact that DMT may be present in the brain in near-death experiences when the heart has stopped.

Within the brain there are more than 20 different types of serotonin receptors and they exist in high concentrations on nerve cells in brain areas regulating a host of important psychological and physical processes, including cardiovascular and hormonal regulation, as well as sleep, feeding, mood, perception and motor control. Researchers are now concerned with determining which of these serotonin receptors different psychedelics attach to, to help classify which of serotonin's effects might also be capable of being caused by these psychedelics, and it seems as if DMT attaches to the same subtypes of serotonin receptor as do other classical psychedelics such as LSD: that is the 5-HT2A and 5-HT1A sites. When this attachment occurs it immediately causes changes in perception and mood.

After the discovery of the psychedelic properties of LSD in 1943 by the Swiss Chemist Albert Hofmann there was huge excitement in the psychiatric community and the contemporary field of 'biological psychiatry' was born. Over 25 years, until psychedelic substances were made illegal, nearly 700 studies with LSD and other psychedelic drugs were conducted. Serotonin and LSD were found to compete for uptake receptors in the brain and, because of the connection between these exact receptors and so many psychological and physical processes, the research suggested that LSD has a remarkable medical potential across a wide range of problems.

Combined with psychotherapy it was shown to be successful in helping previously untreatable patients suffering from obsessions and compulsions, post-traumatic stress, eating disorders, anxiety, depression, alcoholism, and heroin dependence. It was also demonstrated to safely reduce the anxiety and pain of terminally ill patients. As reported by Strassman: *Some therapists believed that a transformative, mystical, or spiritual experience was responsible for many of these 'miraculous' responses to psychedelic psychotherapy.*[118]

However, the increasing use of psychedelics in the 1960s was also highly associated with a rapidly escalating counter-culture which questioned the establishment and its values. As a result, there was a political backlash and over the objections of nearly every scientist in the field at the time, in 1970 the United States Congress passed a law making LSD and other psychedelics illegal. So the endogenously produced DMT was categorised as a Class A drug, along with manufactured LSD, and human studies with these drugs were terminated until 1990. This despite the extremely positive results of clinical trials over 25 years pointing to the potential of these drugs to improve the lives of millions of people[119] as well as the massive breakthroughs reported through the use of psychedelic psychotherapy.[120]

---

118 Strassman, Rick, M.D. 2000. *DMT: The Spirit Molecule* p.25 Rochester, Vermont, USA: Inner Traditions International and Bear & Company, http://www.Innertraditions.com

119 Hoffer, Abram and Osmond, Humphrey. 1967. *The Hallucinogens* New York: Academic Press

120 Pahnke, Walter N., Kurland, Albert A., Unger, Sanford, Savage, Charles and Grof, Stanislav. 1970. The Experimental Use of Psychedelic (LSD) Psychotherapy in *Journal of the American Medical Association* 212 1856–1863

As Strassman wrote in 2001: *Many of today's most respected North American and European psychiatric researchers, in both academics and industry, now chairmen of major university departments and presidents of national psychiatric organizations, began their professional lives investigating psychedelic drugs. The most powerful members of their profession discovered that science, data, and reason were incapable of defending their research against the enactment of repressive laws fuelled by opinion, emotion, and the media.*[121]

## DMT case studies

This is now beginning to change and after his extraordinary efforts (documented in detail in *DMT: The Spirit Molecule*) Strassman was given permission to run case studies again in the United States with people who had already declared themselves to be (illegal) users of LSD, or DMT administered exogenously, either through drinking plant based liquids containing DMT plus an MAOI, or through smoking DMT vapour.

During the five years of his studies he administered approximately 400 doses of manufactured, human grade, pure DMT dissolved in saltwater to 60 human volunteers at the University of New Mexico's School of Medicine in Albuquerque. These doses were injected directly into the bloodstream because taken orally DMT has an extremely short lifespan. When it reaches the gut and liver it is quickly broken down by monoamine oxidase enzymes. As noted above, when it is produced endogenously it is accompanied by harmine which is a monoamine oxidase inhibitor (MAOI), allowing it

121 Strassman, Rick, M.D. 2000. *DMT: The Spirit Molecule* p.28 Rochester, Vermont, USA: Inner Traditions International and Bear & Company, http://www.Innertraditions.com

to exist in the body for longer without being broken down and hence it can travel and attach to the brain receptors.

For the trials Strassman did not give his patients MAOIs in conjunction with the DMT, meaning that even though it was injected into the bloodstream and hence went directly to the brain without going through the digestive system as it normally does if taken orally, its impact was short-lived and extraordinarily intense. He notes that effects began within seconds and the peak of the response was around two minutes after the injections, with participants feeling as if they were coming down from the peak at around five minutes.

Strassman was astonished and even somewhat overwhelmed by the results of his work. He categorised the responses into three classes:

1. Personal experiences, limited to the volunteer's own mental and physical processes within their psychology or their relationship to their body.
2. Invisible experiences, involving encounters with seemingly solid and freestanding realities co-existing with this one.
3. Transpersonal experiences in which near-death and spiritual-mystical themes emerge.

In particular Strassman was surprised by the results that at least half of the volunteers 'made contact' with other beings in one form or another, category 2 above. He writes: *Research subjects used expressions like 'entities,' 'beings,' 'aliens,' 'guides,' and 'helpers' to describe them. The 'life-forms' looked like clowns, reptiles, mantises, bees, spiders, cacti, and stick figures.*[122]

---

122 Strassman, Rick, M.D. 2000. *DMT: The Spirit Molecule* p.185 Rochester, Vermont, USA: Inner Traditions International and Bear & Company, http://www.Innertraditions.com

He goes on to note that this is not a typical reaction to other psychedelics. The meetings with 'them', other beings in a non-material world, appear to happen only with DMT.

With regard to the category 3 experiences he writes: *DMT reproduces many of the features of an enlightenment experience, including timelessness; ineffability; coexistence of opposites; contact and merging with a supremely powerful, wise, and loving presence, sometimes experienced as a white light; the certainty that consciousness continues after death of the body; and a first-hand knowledge of the basic 'facts' of creation and consciousness.*[123]

Back in 2001 he was led to conclude that this may be possible because DMT may alter the characteristics of our brains so that we are able to perceive what physicists call dark matter and dark energy, or the 95 per cent of the universe that is known to exist but that at present remains invisible and which we are aware of only by its gravitational effects. In the language I have been using so far I would rephrase it, that DMT may alter the characteristics of our brains to allow us to resonate at a frequency that connects us with the inforealm.

## Shamanic use of DMT

Strassman's volunteers were following a long historic precedent of taking DMT exogenously. The shamans from Central and South America particularly have been ingesting and journeying with DMT for centuries and they get it to work by combining the DMT-containing plants, diplopterys cabrerana or psychotria viridis, with the MAOI tetrahydroharmine in the vine banisteriopsis caapi. This allows the DMT swallowed

123 Strassman, Rick, M.D. 2000. *DMT: The Spirit Molecule* p.246 Rochester, Vermont, USA: Inner Traditions International and Bear & Company, http://www.Innertraditions.com

orally to exist in the digestive system long enough for it to be transported through the intestinal wall and liver into the bloodstream, making it available for the central nervous system when it crosses the blood-brain barrier.

The shamans claim the drink containing this potent combination, known as ayahuasca, allows them to communicate with the plant world, the animal world and the spirit world. For these shamans, meeting up with other entities, as reported by Strassman's volunteers, is entirely anticipated!

Indeed there is mounting evidence, summarised by Graham Hancock in *Supernatural: Meetings with the Ancient Teachers of Mankind*, that shamans have been working with such psychedelics throughout the world since pre-historic times, given the evidence of the cave paintings throughout Europe and Africa, which we are only now able to contextualise as typical responses to hallucinogenic experiences. He writes: *There is a phenomenon here, and whether we call it 'shamanism' or something else, it is in fact a universal phenomenon with very distinctive, recognisable and eerily consistent characteristics amongst the San, the Ungus, and scores of other peoples and cultures throughout history and on all inhabited continents. These prominent universal characteristics are based upon the neurological capacity of all humans (by means of a range of techniques varying from rhythmic dancing to the ingestion of hallucinogenic drugs) to enter altered states of consciousness, to experience hallucinations in those altered states that are interpreted as supernatural contacts with a spirit world or otherworld... and to use these contacts to bring back to this world what are believed to be healing powers, control over the weather, control over the movements of animals and other useful benefits.*[124]

Anthropologist Dr Jeremy Narby was one of the first

---

124 Hancock, Graham. 2005. *Supernatural: Meetings with the Ancient Teachers of Mankind* p.180 London, UK: Century. Reproduced by permission of The Random House Group Ltd.

Westerners to work seriously with ayahuasca and the Ashaninca Indians in the Peruvian Amazon. He discovered they had huge knowledge about the healing properties of thousands of plants, individually and in combination, and he kept being told that this knowledge came from the plants themselves, particularly during ayahuasca ceremonies.

As he writes in *The Cosmic Serpent*: *So here are people without electron microscopes who choose, among some 80,000 Amazonian plant species, the leaves of a bush containing a hallucinogenic brain hormone, which they combine with a vine containing substances that inactivate an enzyme of the digestive tract, which would otherwise block the hallucinogenic effect. And they do this to modify their consciousness.*

*It is as if they knew about the molecular properties of plants and the art of combining them, and when one asks them how they know these things, they say their knowledge comes directly from hallucinogenic plants.*[125]

Narby himself experimented with ayahuasca and became convinced that it really does allow those drinking it to receive information at least from other living things containing DNA. He then dedicated the next few years of his life to seeking the scientific explanation for how this could be possible. His research chronicles the multitude of indigenous peoples around the globe whose cosmological myths are based on the serpent or the dragon, sometimes an individual creature, but more often a twinned or double serpent, sometimes with wings, which can represent a variety of myths. He gradually connected the twin serpents of mythology to the double helix of DNA and the second key to accessing nonlocal consciousness at will.

125 Narby, Jeremy. 1999. *The Cosmic Serpent, DNA and the Origins of Knowledge* pp10–11 New York, NY, USA: Jeremy P. Tarcher/Putnam

## The role of DNA in accessing nonlocal consciousness

Human DNA is a huge molecule with a double-helix structure. Each strand of the helix is a polynucleotide containing a long succession of nucleotides and in turn each of these is composed of a nitrogen-containing nucleobase plus a sugar and a phosphate group. There are four different nucleobases known as C, G, A, T and it is the sequence of these nucleobases that encode our biological information.

Genes contain our hereditary information within the DNA. They instruct each cell on its function whether it is bone, blood, muscle, nerve and so on. Each gene produces a different protein formed of amino acids and it is estimated that the body contains more than 100,000 different proteins.

In the early years of the twenty-first century it came as a great shock to scientists to discover that human DNA contains less than 25,000 genes (estimates had been that there would be at least 120,000 genes). And despite the advances made by the genome project we have discovered that less than five per cent of DNA encodes proteins (which we initially considered to be the only useful function). Until recently it was unclear what the remaining 95 per cent is for, and therefore it was misleadingly and unhelpfully labelled junk DNA.

The National Human Genome Research Institute is continuing to fund the ENCODE project: The Encyclopedia of DNA Elements[126] to investigate the entire DNA sequence. In an interview with Scientific American, published on 1 October 2012, Ewan Birney, lead analysis co-ordinator for the ENCODE project said of junk DNA: *I really think this phrase does need to be totally expunged from the lexicon.*[127] It is now more

126 https://www.genome.gov/10005107/encode-project/#al-1

127 https://www.scientificamerican.com/article/hidden-treasures-in-junk-dna/

appropriately referred to as non-coding DNA. The project has discovered that many regions of the human genome that do not contain protein-coding genes are used for regulation of the genes, switching them on and off. As a result they appear to be closely associated with health and disease.[128]

What is also being uncovered is that the more complex an organism is and the more advanced its development, the higher its percentage of non-coding DNA. So perhaps this non-coding DNA is actually related to our evolution in some way?

In the 1990s Narby reached the conclusion that DNA is at the origin of shamanic knowledge and that the shamans around the world induce neurological changes that allow them to pick up information from the DNA present in the cells of all living things. His favoured explanation for this was linked to the crystal properties of DNA. These are two-fold.

In the protein-encoding genes (the five per cent of the DNA that we believe we know the function of), the four nucleobases sit on top of each other in the order dictated by the genetic text, giving it an aperiodic crystal structure,[129] which allows it to trap and transport electrons with efficiency as well as emitting photons at ultra-weak levels. This photon emission has a high degree of coherence, meaning that it gives the sensation of bright colours, a luminescence and an impression of holographic depth.

He suggests that: *the molecules of nicotine or dimethyltryptamine, contained in tobacco or ayahuasca, activate their respective receptors, which set off a cascade of electrochemical reactions inside the neurones,*

128 https://www.genome.gov/27549810/2012-release-encode-data-describes-function-of-human-genome/2012-release-encode-data-describes-function-of-human-genome/

129 In a periodic crystal structure there is consistent pattern of molecules within the crystal which has a lattice structure. Each cell could potentially stack exactly on top of any other cell. In an aperiodic crystal the symmetry of each cell is lacking, they cannot stack.

*leading to the stimulation of DNA and more particularly to its emission of visible waves, which shamans perceive as 'hallucinations.'*[130]

At the same time, in part of the non-coding DNA, the four nucleobases form a regular arrangement of atoms, a periodic crystal structure, which by analogy with quartz, can potentially pick up as many photons as it emits. As he speculates: *The variation in the length of the repeat sequences, (some of which contain up to 300 bases) would help pick up different frequencies and could thereby constitute a possible function and new function for a part of 'junk' DNA.*[131]

So the non-coding DNA is potentially the receiver and the transmitter of information to and from the inforealm, while the genes could provide the hallucinations that accompany this transmission and receiving.

More recent work has confirmed that living cells emit a stream of pulsating, very low intensity coherent light in the form of biophotons. The source of these biophotons appears to be DNA and their purpose seems to be intracellular communication, known as bioinformation. Bioscientists such as Marco Bischof and R. Van Wijk believe that because DNA is the probable source for the creation of a coherent field of photons, it could function as the interface between nonlocal space and the living organism.[132,133]

Returning to the work of Van Lommel, he speculates that: *Consciousness is the nonlocal repository of all past experience. The reception of information from nonlocal space rests on our free will (intention), attention, and the state of our (waking) consciousness. In all*

---

130 Narby, Jeremy. 1999. *The Cosmic Serpent, DNA and the Origins of Knowledge* p.127 New York, NY, USA: Jeremy P. Tarcher/Putnam

131 Narby, Jeremy. 1999. *The Cosmic Serpent, DNA and the Origins of Knowledge* p.130 New York, NY, USA: Jeremy P. Tarcher/Putnam

132 Bischof, M. March 2005. Biophotons – the Light in Our Cells in *Journal of Optometric Phototherapy* 1–5

133 Van Wijk, R. 2001. Bio-photons and Bio-communication in *Journal of Scientific Exploration* 15, no 2 183–197

*probability, our person-specific DNA has given the different manifestations of our consciousness, such as waking consciousness and the individual subconscious, their different places of resonance, both in the brain and in other cell systems... There is also a universal or collective human consciousness that links each individual human being with everything in existence or everything that ever was or will be, and this happens via the universal-human DNA with a shared access code.*[134]

## Renaissance in psychedelic drug research

Since the work of Strassman there has been a renaissance in clinical psychedelic drug research, including studies on the impacts of LSD, MDMA, and psilocybin. Some of the leading centres for this work are the Multidisciplinary Association for Psychedelic Studies (MAPS),[135] the Beckley Foundation,[136] the Council on Spiritual Practices in conjunction with John Hopkins University[137] and the Heffter Research Institute.[138] All of them are currently supporting research with psychedelics as treatments for a variety of medical disorders, including addiction, post-traumatic stress disorder and cluster headaches, with great success.

These institutions are investigating how psychedelics interact with the brain using the latest brain-imaging technologies of functional magnetic resonance imaging (fMRI) which gives information about the changes in blood flow that result from the brain's metabolic activity and magnetoencephalography (MEG) which records magnetic

134 Van Lommel, Pim, M.D. 2010 *Consciousness Beyond Life: The Science of the Near-Death Experience* pp279–280 New York, NY, USA: Harper Collins Publishers

135 http://www.maps.org/

136 http://www.beckleyfoundation.org/

137 http://www.csp.org/practices/entheogens/entheogens.html

138 http://www.heffter.org/

field changes produced by electrical currents. There is a wealth of information on their websites about the ongoing studies and opportunities to participate in them. As the Beckley Foundation states: *by changing consciousness, we learn more about normal consciousness.*[139]

Amongst the findings from these brain scans to date are that psychedelics destabilise the Default Mode Network (DMN) region of the brain, shown in Figure 29, which is critically involved in high-level cognitive functions such as those that give us our sense of possessing an intact sense of self. Returning to the anatomy presented in Chapter 1, the DMN includes the posterior cingulate cortex, the medial pre-frontal cortex, the anterior temporal pole, the thalamus, the hippocampus and more. This network is typically overactive in depression but its activity is reduced or even deactivated by psilocybin and ayahuasca.

Figure 29: default mode network

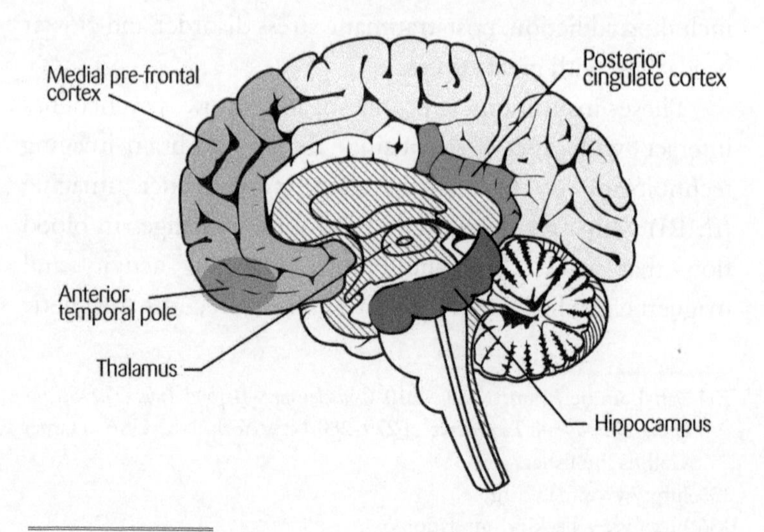


139 http://www.beckleyfoundation.org/wp-content/uploads/2013/05/A3-science-leaflet-130410.pdf

Speaking at the Psychedelic Science conference in 2013, Amanda Feilding of the Beckley Foundation said: *All the data showed reductions in blood flow and neural activity to this important network, and the degree of the reduction correlated with the subjective effects of psychedelic experience. That is, more intense subjective experiences correlated with larger decreases in blood flow to the Default Mode Network. We also found that the centres of the network became less connected with each other and with other brain regions.*[140]

The DMN is particularly active when we are engaged in inwardly directed activities such as introspection, day-dreaming and recollecting memories. It appears to control the distribution of blood in the brain and hence the neural activity of the brain, which effectively censors what is allowed to enter consciousness. Somehow, when psychedelics reduce its activity, there is less censoring and judging and we can communicate better with things outside us – including the inforealm. So the expanded consciousness that we get through psychedelics in many ways is the opposite of the waking consciousness that we achieve through normal interoception or mindfulness.

Feilding continues: *Psilocybin acts by constricting the flow of blood to the Default Mode Network, and thereby decreasing its controlling and repressive activity. Thus, sensory and emotional impulses, which would normally be repressed, reach consciousness, and users experience a spontaneous, unconstrained mode of thinking – a more fluid and plastic state of consciousness. This state more readily allows access to areas of the brain normally kept repressed, e.g. traumatic memories or spiritual awareness…*

*By facilitating the access to repressed memories, even those which have, for much of a lifetime, been closed off from conscious thought, the psychedelics facilitate the washing out of toxic memories, which can free the person from their unconscious grip…*

140 http://www.beckleyfoundation.org/2013/05/amanda-feildings-talk-at-psychedelic-science-2013/

*This would explain why the psychedelics are conducive, not only to accessing repressed memories and alleviating depression, but also to experiencing mystical states, to enhanced creativity, and to seeing the unity and interconnectedness of all things and our place in the greater whole.*[141]

With regard to DMT Strassman says: *The spirit molecule is neither good nor bad, beneficial nor harmful, in and of itself. Rather, set and setting establish the context and the quality of the experiences to which DMT leads us. Who we are and what we bring to the sessions and to our lives ultimately mean more than the drug experience itself.*[142]

The work by Feilding quoted above with regard to psilocybin again emphasises the necessity of using psychedelics in a favourable setting. For optimal effect we need to feel safe as we access those repressed memories and have someone tracking our experience and whether we need guidance (in the indigenous experience this would usually be through music or movement) to emerge from the toxic memories to connection with the wider dimensions of consciousness.

## Psychedelics as entheogens

When psychedelics are used in ceremony, they are known as entheogens, deriving from the Greek for substances which evoke the divine within. And the key to most reliably achieving Strassman's third type of experience with psychedelics seems to be using the plant medicines within a conducive setting, and in particular within a ritualistic ceremony with an experienced

141 http://www.beckleyfoundation.org/2013/05/amanda-feildings-talk-at-psychedelic-science-2013/

142 Strassman, Rick, M.D.. 2000. *DMT: The Spirit Molecule* p.327 Rochester, Vermont, USA: Inner Traditions International and Bear & Company, http://www.Innertraditions.com

shaman or therapist holding the space safely for those who are journeying. In this setting the psychedelics are not recreational drugs, they are ceremonial teachers.

The great hope of those who experiment with these psychedelics is that they can be introduced widely enough in the world within safe, held spaces, to bring healing and hope to the millions suffering from the effects of trauma and the fear of death. Beyond that their use more widely could even encourage humanity to stop inflicting the catastrophic damage we are causing to each other and this planet by connecting people with the oneness within and the oneness all around us in all living things. When we connect with each other in this way we want to make love, not war. We want to live in peace and not create a state of fear. The plants teach us of our interconnectedness with at least everything containing DNA and the need to live in symbiosis. The earth has great capacity to regenerate itself over time, and if we can reconnect with our symbiosis with every living thing, recognising that we don't own the earth, rather we are part of the earth, then we can start to take steps to protect it.

Although entheogens can be a helpful fast-track to cosmic consciousness for many, it is also true that they are not necessary for everyone and there are reports from thousands of people around the world who find it possible to journey and communicate with the inforealm without the use of exogenous chemicals and without the trauma of an NDE. These experiences may come from out-of-body visions, meditation, trance dance, lucid dreaming, breathwork, constellations therapy, regression therapy, working with sound such as hemi-sync, drumming, gonging, crystal bowls or chanting and many more sources. These are the people who can potentially release DMT endogenously, although the historical ban on research has prevented proper testing of this hypothesis.

In whichever way these individuals have managed to

achieve it, they do seem to have succeeded in allowing their brains to resonate at a frequency that allows transmission and reception of information to and from the inforealm, as and when they choose.

For instance Sri Aurobindo is considered to be one of the greatest of Indian philosophers. Although he died in 1950 his teachings were the foundation of the community at Auroville in Tamil Nadu, India, which continues to grow and evolve today and is largely inhabited by Westerners seeking a different way of being in the world. He wrote in terms that were totally outside the scientific knowledge of his day, and yet which seem to fit in very well with today's knowledge of nonlocality: *The individual is not limited to the physical body – it is only the external consciousness which feels like that. As soon as one gets over this feeling of limitation, one can feel first the inner consciousness which is connected with the body, but does not belong to it, afterwards the planes of consciousness above the body, also a consciousness surrounding the body, but part of oneself, part of the individual being, through which one is in contact with the cosmic forces and with other beings. Each man has his own personal consciousness entrenched in his body and gets into touch with his surroundings only through his body and senses and the mind using the senses. Yet all the time the universal forces are pouring into him without his knowing it. He is aware only of thoughts, feelings, etc., that rise to the surface and these he takes for his own. Really they come from outside in mind waves, vital waves, waves of feeling and sensation, etc. which take particular form in him and rise to the surface after they have got inside.*[143]

Psychologists Ede Frecska and Levente Moro along with anthropologist Hank Wesselman, in a joint article, say much the same thing but using more modern and scientific

143 Aurobindo, Sri. 2001. *A Greater Psychology* pp363–364 Pondicherry, India: Sri Aurobindo Ashram Publications Department

language. They describe how in normal waking consciousness, we are mostly focused on the more reliable 'local' signals coming from the physical perceptual organs so we pay little attention to the nonlocal signals bombarding the quantum array antennae. However: *In integrative forms of ASCs (altered states of consciousness) (e.g., meditation and contemplation), coping, planning, and task-solving functions are put into the background along with the agent (ego) bearing those functions. Thus, a chance appears for fragments of 'nonlocal' information – present already in subcellular networks – to be projected and transferred into the neuroaxonal network and to be experienced also by the ego.*[144]

For indigenous people around the world throughout the ages, the shaman has been the tribe's access to the inforealm, both in cultures where the shamans use plant medicine and in cultures where they are able to journey without ingesting psychedelics.

Today, alternative therapies are largely focused on allowing this access to everyone, so that we may all experience oneness with the planet we live on, the greater cosmos that surrounds us, and all those we encounter in our lives, asking for the wisdom we need to bring in healing to ourselves and all those that we can resonate with as we consciously engage with the inforealm.

**Case studies**

In the Appendices I describe some of my own work in the Amazonian jungle working with the plant medicine, but to illustrate the types of experiences that are frequent after drinking ayahuasca, I give two short descriptions below.

144 Frecska, Ede, Moro, Levente and Wesselman, Hank. The Soul Cluster: Reconsideration of a Millennia-Old Concept in Hancock, Graham. 2015. *The Divine Spark: Psychedelics, Consciousness and the Birth of Civilization* p.266 London, UK: Hay House, Inc.

**Example 1**

During the ceremony I get visions of amazingly beautiful patterns with a strong theme of rainbow lights, sometimes vertical and sometimes horizontal. There are lots of spiralling black tunnels with rainbow lights spinning around them and inviting me in. Near the beginning there is a string of people passing by in modern Western clothes and business suits. Some of them seem to have gifts for me but I don't know what. And I don't recognise any of them, they are just grey men in grey suits.

The best part is when the shaman is singing the icaros directly to me and I get a huge kinesthetic sense of transference of power into my hands. It's amazing, as if he is gifting me something very special. Then when he puts his hands behind my shoulders and brings them up over my head, it is as if a rainbow is suffusing up from the shoulders, through my head and out the crown. It's very beautiful and afterwards I start to get a vision of a vertical column of rainbow light and there's a wise being in the middle of it.

Towards the end of the ceremony I get a sense of sitting under the earth – I think in the roots of Remokaspi (one of the Master trees), and it feels very safe there. Then a little later I get the vision of a huge tree going right up into the stars. What I need to take out for the world seems to be that the trees do commune with the inforealm.

**Example 2**

At the beginning of the ceremony as the medicine is entering my system, I ask for whatever information would be helpful for me to better understand my clients. I get exactly what I asked for but not in the way I had anticipated!

To begin with there is a show of amazingly fast green and white lights with a bit of blue. Everything is moving so very fast and it seems to be trying to show me the energy patterns that everything is made of. I feel bad that I am not a neuroscientist or a biologist so I can't really make sense of what they are trying to show me, although the energy is beautiful.

After that for a while the experience is very dark – one person is vomiting repeatedly and some very heavy energy seems to be coming out of him. Another person next to me has transformed into a frightening tiger. The shaman is prowling around the room as a jaguar. Two others in the ceremony seem to be having a very difficult time and I seem to be experiencing everyone's fear and anger and darkness. I feel it is over-whelming but on the other hand I don't want the whole thing to stop, I just want the dark energy to stop because I want to get to the beautiful lights that I usually experience. I ask for it to change and Mother Ayahuasca tells me off because she is giving me exactly what I had asked for: a better understanding of the fear and suffering of my clients. I say I understand that and apologise for having set that intention without thinking properly what it might involve.

After that the experience changes and the message and teaching seem to be all about having humility and compassion. I say I understand that message, but ask please that I may only share in my clients' pain when I am actually working with them, not all the time. It is too much pain and suffering if I have it continuously.

Then I start to get beautiful visions travelling up and up, sometimes into the stars, sometimes into the trees, sometimes into many different worlds. In the other worlds I can see myself as eagle flying over different places, but I don't feel embodied in eagle, I am not eagle,

I am only observing eagle. The only time I really get to be eagle is when the shaman is singing to me and he tells me he is going to transform himself. He seems to become my father eagle and he takes me up and holds me while he is flying to let me feel what it's like. Then he drops me, so I have to fly or I will die! At that point I do really feel as if I am eagle for some time.

Finally there are lots and lots of tunnels and a couple of times I manage to go out and out and out through them into what seems like an infinite universe. How far can I go? The possibilities feel endless and unlimited. It is a very intense experience and I feel as if it is lasting for a long time, although the ceremony had only lasted about three hours when I am able to look at my watch again.

**Conclusion**

While recognition that we can access the inforealm opens huge possibilities, it also hands us huge responsibilities. Everything we say or think gets stored in the holographic records of the universe. It is potentially available for others to access, throughout space and time. It may have ripples in space-time that we need to be mindful of, for ourselves and others.

I would like to conclude this chapter with a quote from the painter and sculptress Martina Hoffman, which sums up the significance that every one of us has when we acknowledge our interconnectedness through the inforealm: *With every thought, feeling, and action being an integral part of the Web, we directly influence how it vibrates, contracts, expands, and ever changes. In this ancient cosmology, all beings and all that is are intimately connected. To know and see all that is as an important part of the whole, and us not just at the mercy of the Gods but rather as an individualized reflection of the "One" provides us a precious gift and opportunity: to become instrumental in the creation of our reality, hopefully conscious cocreators for our planetary existence as well as aware guardians for our planet.*[145]

## GLOSSARY FOR CHAPTER 7

**Ayahuasca**: factually the ayahuasca plant is the vine banisteriopsis caapi which contains a monoamine oxidase inhibitor, but frequently the drink they serve in ceremonies in South America, which includes DMT – containing plants, diplopterys cabrerana or psychotria viridis, is the brew known as ayahuasca.

**Beta-carboline**: beta-carboline is an alkaloid (it contains mostly nitrogen atoms) and consists of a pyridine ring that is fused to an indole skeleton. Pyridine is used in the in vitro synthesis of DNA and the indole skeleton is an intercellular signal molecule which can be produced by bacteria as a degradation product of the amino acid tryptophan. It is closely associated with the neurotransmitters melatonin and serotonin.

**Entheogen**: psychedelics used in ceremony, which in the correct setting can become substances that evoke the divine within.

**Icaro**: a sacred song that calls in various spirit guides (plants or animals or wise beings) from a different dimension.

**Psychedelic**: a hallucinatory drug that can produce a mental state characterised by a profound sense of intensified sensory perception.

**Psychonaut**: someone who intentionally induces altered

145 Hoffman, Martina. How Expanding Consciousness and our Connection to Spirit Might Help the Survival of Life on Planet Earth in Hancock, Graham. 2015. *The Divine Spark: Psychedelics, Consciousness and the Birth of Civilization* pp72–73 London, UK: Hay House, Inc.

states of consciousness for the exploration of the human condition.

**Symbiosis**: the interaction between two different organisms living in close physical association, typically to the advantage of both.

**Tryptamine**: a neurotransmitter that contains one amino group that is connected to an aromatic ring by a two-carbon chain and contains an indole ring structure.

# CHAPTER 8 – SHAMANIC HEALING

**What do you think shamanic healing involves and is it genuinely effective? And do you believe that the shamans have had access for centuries to information which more advanced civilisations are only now re-discovering?**

> *The shaman, a mystical, priestly, and political figure emerging during the Upper Paleolithic period and perhaps going back to Neanderthal times, can be described not only as a specialist in the human soul but also as a generalist whose sacred and social functions can cover an extraordinarily wide range of activities. Shamans are healers, seers, and visionaries who have mastered death. They are in communication with the world of gods and spirits. Their bodies can be left behind whilst they fly to unearthly realms. They are poets and singers. They dance and create works of art. They are not only spiritual leaders but also judges and politicians, the repositories of the knowledge of the culture's history, both sacred and secular. They are familiar with cosmic as well as physical geography; the ways of plants, animals, and the elements are known to them. They are psychologists, entertainers, and food finders. Above all,*

*however, shamans are technicians of the sacred and masters of ecstasy.*[146]

(Joan Halifax)

## Introduction

The tradition of shamanic healing is ancient and global, and is founded on the principal of the shaman being able to enter an altered state of consciousness, either endogenously or exogenously induced, to retrieve information of value to the community.

This chapter describes a little about the cosmology and methodology of the Q'ero shamans of the Peruvian Andes, and the plant medicine of the Shipibo shamans of the Amazon, the lineages that I have trained with most extensively.

I briefly describe some of the techniques and processes that you might encounter if you visit a shamanic practitioner and how these may help you to connect with the inforealm and receive intense and rapid healing, whether what ails you is physical, mental or emotional. Further detail about the processes used by the Q'ero lineage is in Appendix 1 where I also compare the principles at work with those used in modern psychotherapy and trauma therapy.

I conclude with a discussion of ritual and suggest that one of the reasons rituals are so important and successful in assisting healing is their role in communicating information received by the right-brain from the inforealm, to the left-brain for use in our everyday lives.

---

146 Halifax, Joan, PhD. 1991. *Shamanic Voices: a survey of visionary narratives.* pp3–4 New York, NY, USA: Viking Penguin

## The role of the shaman

The description by Joan Halifax that opens this chapter seems to encapsulate the extraordinary role that shamans have played around the globe for thousands of years. They are still revered in many cultures, but the Judeo-Christianity tradition condemned them along with women and witches!

Of course it is true that with power comes responsibility, and within the shamanic communities there is a clear distinction between those working for healing, when asked to by individuals or the community (known in South America as the curanderos), and those interfering in the lives of others or even casting curses for financial benefit to themselves (known in South America as the brujos, or sorcerers).

Shamanic traditions around the world have honoured many of the same principles, although with cultural differences, often based on the type of land tribes were living on. Above all the shamans have been masters of the rituals and ceremonies which have allowed them (and sometimes others) to enter altered states of consciousness. The academic theologian Mark Seelig suggests: *Wise women and men in tribal cultures have preserved the sacred art of holding ceremony and have passed on the wisdom and tools to us so that we can now study this art and learn what it means to live in harmony with all sentient beings and with the universe.*[147]

I am going to briefly describe the two shamanic traditions that I am most familiar with, but their principles are almost universal.

---

147 Seelig, Mark. 2015. Communion with the Goddess: Three Weeks of Ayahuasca in Brazil p.189 in *The Divine Spark: Psychedelics, Consciousness and the Birth of Civilization,* edited by Hancock, Graham. 2015. London, UK: Hay House, Inc.

## Q'ero shamans: Masters of the living universe of energy

In Peru the Q'ero people have legends of how, when the Conquistadors arrived, a number of their ancestors went up into the high Andes and disappeared from society for over 400 years. Even today the Q'ero villages are remote, located at an altitude of over 4,400 metres above sea level and home to less than 2,000 people. They have been visited by few Westerners and they are most definitely not on the normal Andean tourist trail around Cusco and Machu Picchu.

The Q'ero shamans were right to leave for the sanctuary of the high mountains to preserve themselves and their skills, because historians now believe that, between 1527 and 1572, almost 90 per cent of the inhabitants of the Inca Empire lost their lives as a result of diseases, civil war, conquest, and colonisation.

The legend continues that in the 1950s a number of the Q'ero shamans came down from their villages at the time of the annual full moon Qoyllur Riti or star festival in the glaciers of the Andes, which takes place when the Pleiades constellation reappears in the Southern Hemisphere. The crowd parted as these elders dressed in their ancient costumes with the emblem of the sun on their ponchos re-emerged from the high mountains. They were real, not just mythical! They said it was time for them to share their knowledge with the world. My teacher Alberto Villoldo is one of those that they chose to spread their traditions globally.

I want to give a very brief overview of the traditions of the Q'ero here, to illustrate how these ancient teachings appear to integrate so well with the modern science of the interconnected inforealm where everything we say and do has an impact. Note too that, while I am describing things in the words of the Q'ero, shamanic traditions the world over hold many similar beliefs.

In the Q'ero tradition the only commandment is to live a life of Ayni, which approximates 'give and take' or 'exchange with the universe'. This is a kind of cosmic law, which is both part of everyday life and part of a supernatural order. It's about living in right relation with ourselves, others and all of creation. If we are intimately connected in balance with everything and everyone around us, then we are in rhythm with the natural flow of things. Life then requires much less effort to accomplish much more.

The *kausay pacha* is the energy of the living universe and they believe it expresses itself in two fundamental types of energy: sami and hucha.

1. Sami is the refined or ordered energy of the natural world in its pristine state; the breath of life of our creator; and sami helps us achieve harmony and be in effortless connection with the cosmos. This could be interpreted as the cosmic consciousness.
2. Hucha is heavy or disordered energy; and hucha is produced only by human beings. We create hucha with jealousy, envy and anger. This could be interpreted as our egocentric brain.

The three ways of living are yankay (or llankay), munay and yachay.

1. Yankay is action, associated with the second chakra. It is expressed through service and physical work and it manifests as personal power and physical strength achieved through self-discipline. It represents a right way of living that is ecologically sound and promotes the welfare of others.
2. Munay is love, associated with the heart. It is expressed through natural beauty and tranquility and it manifests

through kindness and love, incorporating empathy and selflessness. To the Q'ero beauty and love are inseparable. When you have these in your heart, you are peaceful.

3. Yachay is thinking, associated with the third eye. It is expressed through using the power of the intellect, learning and knowing and it manifests in the superior consciousness arrived at through the proper cultivation of the principles of munay and yankay.

The higher shamans are called *alto mesayoq* (literally translated as high mesa carriers, where the mesa is the shaman's healing kit). They believe that they work and communicate directly with the living beings of the *kausay pacha*, especially with the *Tekse Apus*, which are:

Pachamama (Cosmic Mother), Wiraqocha (Cosmic Father), Taita Inti (Father Sun), Taita Waira (Father Wind), Mama Qocha (Mother Water), Mama Killa (Mother Moon), Mama Ch'aska (Mother Stars) as well as honouring the wisdom teachers from all traditions including figures such as Jesus Christ, Buddha, Isis, Osiris, Shakti and Shiva.

The relationship of an *alto mesayoq* with the Tekse Apus is reciprocal – they talk to each other and exchange knowledge. Through his or her dialogue with the Tekse Apus and the upper world, the alto mesayoq can access the very fabric of space-time where he or she is able to impact the kausay pacha.

If you compare these ancient beliefs with the emerging science of the inforealm they are remarkably similar. The shamans work with a universal energy that is in all living things and can enter a state of consciousness where they are both able to connect and communicate with this energy. At the advanced stages they are able to shift things and change things, using their interaction with the living energy to become co-creators of the world they inhabit.

At the same time *yankay, munay* and *yachay* represent the

physical, emotional and mental/spiritual aspects of the way we live our lives, which incorporate living in harmony with the land, having compassion for others and connecting with the wider energy field or inforealm.

## Shipibo shamans: Masters of plant medicine

Many of the shamanic cultures have used psychedelics through the ages, but not all of them, and the Q'ero are among those who have journeyed and communicated with the inforealm without the use of plant medicine.

Another shamanic community that I have worked with personally on a number of occasions are the Shipibo people, who live in the Amazon jungle, based around Pucallpa and Iquitos in Peru. What always leaves me in awe after working with them is their vast knowledge of Amazonian plants and how to use them for healing physical, mental and emotional illnesses. They are experts in knowing whether to use bark, leaves, roots or a combination thereof and how to prepare concoctions for internal consumption or external application. This knowledge of the curing powers of the forest plants and animals and preparation of remedies is being lost, both because the forests are being cut down and because the wisdom keepers are dying out, as it requires a rigorous and dedicated life to acquire their immense knowledge.

This knowledge comes from an apprentice working under a maestro and dieting with the various trees and plants. Such diets may last between two weeks and three months on each occasion. There is an initiation period of connecting with the plant followed by continuous follow-ups. During these times the shaman will be on a heavily restricted intake of food, with no fat, sugar, meat, spices or salt. This is to purify the physical system. Simultaneously they may smoke the leaves of the plant or tree they are working with, or drink juice made from the sap, bark, leaves or roots. They may even be living out in the forest beside the trees or plants they are working with, cooking on an open fire and sleeping in a hammock slung in the branches of the tree. The intention is to allow their body to take in the energy of the plant. As they do this they become increasingly able to communicate with it and use its wisdom to assist others.

These constant diets take a toll on the shaman and require very strict discipline and self-control. This is one of the reasons why the number of true *curanderos* is dying out. Their knowledge can only be gained experientially.

The Shipibo are also masters of psychedelic medicine, including the DMT-based ayahuasca brew, but also tobacco and toe (a Datura plant containing atropine and scopolamine). As they and their clients engage in healing ceremonies, the shamans sing icaros, sacred songs that call in various spirit guides such as plants, animals or wise beings from a different dimension. The shamans get diagnostic and healing information from these guides that may be applied to the client physically after the ceremony, while the spirit guides also transmit healing to the client at a deep energetic level during the ceremony.

I have written about some of my experiences with the plant medicine in Appendix 2, and I have felt healers from many life-forms and energy-forms working in my body and mind. If you have never taken psychedelics these stories may seem outrageous but nothing will ever cause you to change your mind except personal experience.

Referring back to two of Strassman's points detailed in Chapter 6, first he was surprised by the number of the volunteers in his DMT case studies that experienced 'others', entities which appeared solid and free-standing and as real as anything in this dimension, but that were from a different, co-existing dimension or reality than this one that we usually inhabit. However, the shamans call in these 'others' in every single ceremony. Secondly Strassman noted the significance of set and setting for the outcome of a psychedelic experience. This is important as psychedelics get their bad reputation in society because this is not understood by people taking these sacred compounds.

The Shipibo shamans are very specific about both. Their ceremonies are held in a specially built sacred space and before drinking the medicine they purify everyone in the room with herbs and tobacco, then bless the medicine, asking for help with a specific intention for the journey in mind. During the ceremony the shamans track the journeys of every participant. People are not on their own; the shaman is with them holding a safe and sacred space as they call for help, wisdom and guidance from the creatures and energies of the inforealm.

## Shamanic healing in the Western world

If you want shamanic healing in the Western world there are now a number of practitioners advertising their services, including myself. As with any other therapist, it is advisable to check someone's qualifications, but also to meet them and see whether they can create that safe, trusted space (the temenos) that will provide the best possible healing environment for you, the client.

A variety of different healing services may be offered by shamanic practitioners and one fundamental difference that you might want to consider before making an appointment is that, in some lineages the shaman will journey for the client to collect the knowledge required from the inforealm, while in other lineages the shaman will lead the client on their own journey. You may have a strong preference one way or the other and it is something that you might want to discuss with the shaman before making an appointment. I personally offer both options at different times, with different procedures, but even if I journey for my client I never interpret the information I receive at the archetypical or mythical level. What it means to the client is for them to decide.

Full information about some of the common shamanic healing practices is found in Appendix 1, along with a discussion about their parallels with modern psychotherapy and trauma therapy, and a variety of case studies, so here I will just list them briefly.

1. Cleansing of heavy energy attached to the client. This may have been sent intentionally by others in the form of psychic daggers or curses, or less intentionally through negative words, thoughts, or strong negative feelings.

   In the Western world many people believe in the power of prayer and blessings, so it should not be surprising to learn that the opposite side of the coin, ill-wishing, is equally powerful. All the work in previous chapters about our ability to transmit and download to and from the inforealm suggests it is possible for an energetic impact to be transmitted nonlocally. Thus we should all try to be careful what we say and think about others and indeed most of us have likely, in ignorance, stepped into accidental 'sorcery' at some point, often without real intention or recognition of the damage we are causing.
2. Soul retrieval. Another service common to many shamanic traditions is to help the client to retrieve a part of their soul that they have lost. This work seems to fit in very closely with the theory underlying much of modern trauma therapy, namely that traumatic dissociation results in a psychological split of the psyche with certain parts being hidden away for a person's own safety. The intention

is to re-integrate this long lost part and the qualities it represented safely back into the psyche. These are often the lost qualities of childhood such as innocence, joy, beauty, freedom and playfulness.

3. Releasing limiting beliefs. This exercise may be appropriate if clients have a repeating pattern in their life or feel they are blocked or stuck, usually without knowing the source of their self-sabotaging behaviour. Journeying back using the breath, the body may be able to access the source of the self-limiting belief which may come from conditioning by parents, teachers, religious leaders or even peers, or it may be a belief we have adopted to please others. When we see the source we can recognise that it is not our own truth and indeed it is only a subjective opinion, not 'the truth'. As a result we may be able to immediately open a new limbic attractor pathway that will serve us better going forward and which can be strengthened through carrying the work into our real lives using affirmations, mantras and rituals.
4. Conscious dying or death and rebirth within life. This process is used for resolving unfinished business with those approaching death, often bringing in real healing for these clients and their families. It can also be used for people who want a fresh start, a metaphorical death and rebirth, to completely let go of the past and bring in a new beginning. It represents a closure to the old ways of being and a step into a new path, a new direction, with new beliefs, perspectives and intentions.
5. Working with the ancestors. Another type of work that is frequently done by the shamanic practitioner is with the familial ancestors, or in a smaller community, even with the whole tribe. This recognises that the client does not live in isolation, they are part of a system. I will cover this type of work in more detail in Chapter 10.

## The importance of ritual

Within shamanic healing there may be rituals with fire, power animals, spirit guides or with the land. The power of these rituals to help people has been demonstrated throughout the ages by the continuation of the shamanic traditions in many parts of the world as well as by the mounting evidence from scientifically validated studies in the Western world. Yet at this time many of us have lost touch with the ancient rituals and ceremonies that used to form a pillar of our communities. We might even ridicule them, as we denounce spirit in the name of science.

To me, rituals can be extremely important in two different ways.

Category 1: Rituals that help us to connect with the inforealm. Rituals can be important tools in allowing us to resonate with and access the inforealm, assisting the right-brain in its wide-ranging intuitive, empathic, emotional, non-verbal activities, and loosening the hold of the Default Mode Network, or the censoring and judging area of the brain.

When we want to get into the correct brainwave state to optimally ask for and receive information from the inforealm, it is important to set the scene, creating a safe and sacred space for our work in which we clearly state our intentions. For this work, the more any ritual resonates with the individual performing it, the stronger the outward transmission of biophotons will be, making the reception and download of information from the mythical and energetic levels easier and more successful.

So, if you are going to engage in a ritual it is important to collect the right tools, dress up, get all the necessary bits and pieces together. Engage with it in your mind, your body, your clothes, your actions, your thoughts. Be fully in it. You are honouring something sacred and often ancient with the ritual, creating an energy field that beams out and connects nonlocally in the inforealm, resonating with all those who have done the same ritual in the past, calling in the ancestors, calling for help from the wider nonlocal consciousness.

Category 2: Rituals that help us to connect the right-brain and left-brain. Rituals can act as powerful transmission and anchoring methods between the energetic and the physical, or the right- and the left-brain. To manifest the mythical and archetypical information we receive from our journeying (which arrives into the right-brain) into our daily, four-dimensional lives, requires that the information is communicated to the narrowly focused, verbal, compartmentalised and organising left-brain.

As already discussed in Chapters 1 and 2, it is well known from modern neurobiology that we see what we believe, rather than believing what we see, and we experience what we expect to experience, not what is actually happening in the present moment, because we have formed neural attractor pathways that, like muscles, become stronger the more often we exercise them.

Rituals can set the scene for changing our perceptual state, taking us out of our usual stories and belief systems into a more ancient world of archetypes and myths, thus helping us to engage the neuroplastic potential of the brain to change and form new attractor pathways. Remember from the work of Pribram and Siegel described in Chapter 4, that when we see the same thing but from a different perspective or a different state of mind, we activate different parts of the cortex and apply different mathematical transformations to the space-time flux of information emanating from that which we observe, resulting in a different form, a different memory within the brain.

Thus ritual can help us to reprogramme the limbic attractors of our brains, creating new neural pathways and new forms and memories outside the old stories, helping to embody what we have received in our right-brains from the cosmic consciousness into the four-dimensional, logical, left-brain of everyday waking reality.

## Specific rituals for our lives

Some of the rituals that I work with regularly and which include elements of both categories 1 and 2 above are:

1. Letting go of that which no longer serves us by blowing and releasing it into a stone and giving it to Mother Earth, or blowing it into a stick and giving it to a fire. This is first an observation and acknowledgement of the problem and second an intention to release it and not carry this wound or burden any more. The former helps us to change our perceptual state and activate the pre-frontal cortex. The physical action helps us to envisage the heavy energy leaving our bodies, which may well have a placebo effect while the breathing also helps us to switch the nervous system from the sympathetic to the parasympathetic mode, and visioning the heavy energy being absorbed by the earth or the fire helps to reprogramme the neural network, forming a new perception in the brain.
2. Acknowledging gifts and lessons we have received from people who may be leaving our lives in one way or another, then releasing that person with a ceremony, while retaining and integrating the gifts and lessons. This is an acceptance of non-attachment, i.e. acknowledgement of choice and autonomy from the consciousness of the pre-frontal cortex. It is also a closure of the past with gratitude and blessings rather than with ill-thoughts or psychic daggers, which may involve a reprogramming of the neural network. The closure may be in the inforealm,

especially if the people involved are already dead, but then a physical ceremony can help to bring the change that takes place at the mythical level in the inforealm into our waking, left-brain reality.

3. Respecting people's fate and not trying to carry it for them – leaving them their dignity and their choices, which may involve giving back a burden which you have tried to carry for them. Accessing what you are carrying on behalf of another, perhaps on behalf of the ancestral lineage, may initially need to be done through a combination of shamanic bodywork and right-brain connection with the inforealm. This may facilitate downloading information from the ancestors, or even a mythical conversation with the living, followed by a change of perception and a reprogramming of the neural network.
4. Including and acknowledging a person who has been excluded from the family system (excluded people are often those who have borne illegitimate children, suicides, mentally ill, perpetrators). Once more this starts with a connection with, and conversation in, the inforealm, followed by a change of perception and reprogramming of the neural network regarding our stories and limiting beliefs.
5. Acknowledging a quality that would assist us in our lives or the qualities of a split soul part that we are re-integrating into our psyche, bringing those qualities into the energy field through one of the body's energy centres through repeated ritual. Again the information may come from a journey in nonlocal consciousness, but it is brought into everyday, four-dimensional reality through rituals such as mantras, mudras, the writing of affirmations or visual stimuli such as art work or even texts sent to our own mobile phones, which gradually reprogramme the neural networks.

6. Using a fire ceremony. This ritual has been and continues to be of huge significance to shamans around the world, who believe that we can give things to the fire for closure; take things from the fire in renewal; feed our energies from the fire, and connect across space and time through the fire. This is why shamans hold global vigil fire ceremonies, when fires are lit and tended across the world simultaneously, usually for a minimum of 48 hours and perhaps for as much as a week. These global vigil fires create a strong transmission signal of our intentions or prayers for change and healing, visioning the world we would like to bring into existence as co-creators of the reality we live in and acknowledging that these intentions create a cosmic, resonating, coherent wave form held in the field. This signal is accessible to others seeking change and gradually creates a greater awareness of our interconnectedness and symbiosis with the planet we are living on.

**How shamanic healing works**

I hope that the examples of shamanic practices that I have given above demonstrate that shamanic healing works in at least three ways.

1. Undoubtedly an important part of the transformations that people often experience after shamanic healing is the result of the psychological placebo effect of an empathic therapist, who listens to the client with body and mind, in a safe space, without judgement, and with a set of tools that they assure the client will help resolve their issues. This is now accepted good medical practice.
2. In addition the shamanic practitioner presents a different worldview to the patient, demonstrating that their

conditioned beliefs are just that, beliefs and not knowledge, coming from other human beings, so different opinions and perspectives are possible. This can assist the patient in recognising that it is possible to reprogramme their neural networks, increase myelination and step into a different set of responses to events in the world with greater consciousness and autonomy. Again this is accepted good medical practice.

3. Finally, the intention of shamanic or other nonlocal healing work, including the ingestion of plant medicine, is frequently to glean information from the cosmic consciousness or inforealm, the omniscient and omnipresent energy field. This downloaded and experiential information may bring greater peace, joy, connectedness and a sense of purpose to the client. It seems in practice that it may also bring healing to the deceased and the family system, but more of this in Chapter 10. In the West a huge proportion of disease stems from stress and a sense of alienation (both from communities of people and from the planet we live on), so when the shamanic practitioner helps to reconnect people with some form of spirit, greater consciousness or oneness, they often help to alleviate that alienation and lack of purpose.

Frequently the journeying gives the client external tools, perhaps power animals, spirit guides, or wise beings (usually known as saints or angels in the Judeo-Christian traditions), to communicate with and who offer wisdom and guidance. And the journeying may even help the client to download changes into their DNA at the cellular level using the knowledge of the optimal template of health which is held at the quantum level in the nonlocal inforealm.

As Ede Frecska M.D. puts it: *Shamans are the masters, though not the only ones, of nonlocal realms. In the shamanic state they shift their consciousness from the neuroaxonal mode to the subneural one, enter the quantum hologram stored in the very intricate network of the subcellular systems of their body and journey there. They are in and out at the same time. I suppose that it is the nonlocal correlations that make the out-of-body experience possible. After navigating through nonlocal realms within the quantum hologram, shamans are able to bring information into the local aspect of the universe by mastering nonlocal connections. In essence, they manipulate nonlocal correlations and their conversion into local information, which may involve the transfer of direct-intuitive-nonlocal experience pertinent for healing to the level of cognitive symbolic processing.*[148]

The nonlocal aspect of shamanic healing, number 3 in the list above, is still not fully accepted within Western medical practice, but it is gradually receiving validation. However, even if this last part of 'how it works' is a step too far for you, the first two routes to the efficacy of shamanic healing should not be discounted and demonstrate the validity of shamanic practitioners being added to the list of complementary therapists receiving state and insurance company funding.

## Conclusion

I would love to encourage everyone to experience an altered state of consciousness at least once in their lives, for only then will you truly believe in your own ability to receive

148 Frecska, Ede, M.D. The Shaman's Journey, Supernatural or Natural? A Neuro-Ontological Interpretation of Spiritual Experiences p. 203 in Strassman, Rick, M.D., Wojtowicz, Slawek, M.D., Luna, Luis Eduardo, PhD., and Frecska, Ede, M.D.. 2007 *Inner Paths to Outer Space.* Rochester, Vermont, USA: Inner Traditions International and Bear & Company, http://www.Innertraditions.com

information from the inforealm, which is what shamanic practitioners do daily in their work with clients. For different people an altered state can best be accessed in different ways, whether it is through plant medicine, drumming, dancing, meditation, hypnosis, breathwork, re-birthing or visiting a shamanic practitioner or retreat centre. Some people initially may doubt if they can do this, but it seems that it is everyone's birth-right and we all have the innate ability. I will provide more evidence for this statement in the next chapter, when discussing our potential to step into the field to communicate with the deceased. For now however I will close this chapter with a quotation from Graham Hancock.

He writes: *Although the precise ways in which this capacity is used in different societies and cultures may vary from place to place and epoch to epoch, it is the capacity itself that is fundamental. Many people never in their whole lives exercise it. Some only do so rarely in private and individual settings – whether through the use of drugs, deep meditation or other techniques. What marks shamans out is simply that they exercise this capacity to alter consciousness more frequently than others, that they do so on behalf of their community, and that they build up high levels of skill, familiarity and confidence in navigating the hallucinatory spirit world and negotiating with the supernatural beings who they are convinced inhabit it.*[149]

## GLOSSARY FOR CHAPTER 8

**Affirmation**: a written or spoken statement, usually a positive declaration about ourselves that we want to reinforce through building a new attractor pathway in the brain.

149 Hancock, Graham. 2005. *Supernatural: Meetings with the Ancient Teachers of Mankind.* pp180–181 London, UK: Century. Reproduced by permission of The Random House Group Limited

Affirmations are frequently written many times a day to ensure that the change we desire is fully manifested.

**Ayni**: exchange with the universe. Living in ayni is about living in right relation with ourselves, others and all of creation. It is a kind of cosmic law, which is both a part of everyday life and a part of a supernatural order.

**Mantra**: generally a transformative sacred word or sound that is repeated over and over to aid concentration in meditation.

**Mudra**: a symbolic hand gesture that is used in meditation with specific intentions to channel the body's energy flow in particular ways.

**Psychic dagger**: energetic ill-wishes sent with the intention of harming the target person.

**Ritual**: a process that helps us to enter an altered state of consciousness, often a ceremony that has been passed down the generations of our lineage.

**Shamanic journeying**: consciously intending to access nonlocal realms through what is known as a journey, often involving visualisation to either an upper or a lower world. This may involve the assistance of power animals, plant helpers or guides from another realm.

**Soul retrieval**: journeying to find a part of the psyche or soul that was split off for its own safety and protection at the time of a trauma. This can be from the current life or a past life. Ideally the lost part returns to be re-integrated.

**Temenos**: a protected physical and emotional space in which the transforming work of healing takes place through learning and teaching.

# CHAPTER 9: WHAT DO YOU THINK HAPPENS AT DEATH?

**When your physical body dies do you believe that 'you' become extinct, do you reincarnate in a different form, does your individual consciousness continue in some other dimension, or does your individual consciousness in some way re-join a collective consciousness in a different dimension or within an omniscient and omnipresent field of energy?**

> *It is hard to avoid the conclusion that the essence of our endless consciousness predates our birth and our body and will survive death independently of our body in a nonlocal space where time and distance play no role. There is no beginning, and there will never be an end to our consciousness. In view of this, we should seriously consider the possibility that death, like birth, may be a mere passing from one state of consciousness into another. During life, the body functions like an interface and facilitates the reception of some aspects of our enhanced consciousness; junk DNA and DMT may play a role in this process.*[150]
>
> (Pim Van Lommel)

150 Van Lommel, Pim, M.D. 2010. *Consciousness Beyond Life: The Science of the Near-Death Experience* p.307 New York, NY, USA: Harper Collins Publishers

## Introduction

The question of the existence or otherwise of a soul, a continuing energy of some sort that survives the death of the physical body here on earth, has been one of the main questions of philosophical, religious and metaphysical debate for as long as there has been a human consciousness, an observer of the mind.

All the world's major religions teach that there is an eternal soul, although there has been a huge discrepancy in beliefs about what happens to it upon leaving the physical body, from heaven/hell, to reincarnation or union with the void.

There is now mounting experiential evidence and a growing belief that there is a soul or spirit that continues beyond the grave from those who are not religious practitioners of any sort, but have survived near-death experiences (NDEs), those who believe they have revisited past lives, and those who believe they have managed to connect with the dead via the inforealm through a multitude of channels. The belief in this form of a soul comes from very different bedrock to religious faith. It comes from personal experience that has no other explanation.

## Experience instils knowing rather than belief

My journey into altered states of consciousness and quest for an explanation of what is really happening there started with an experience that my logical, atheist left-brain could not explain. The initial catalyst was a reference I came across to the American 'Psychic Spying' or 'Remote Viewing' (RV) programme that started at the Stanford Research Institute (SRI), California, in 1973. The programme was conceived within and funded by the US Department of Defence and staffed largely by highly decorated military officers from 1975 until 1995. It taught these officers the skill of 'seeing' what was going on at a place and time removed from their physical bodies and over time it was known in the intelligence community as Scangate, Grillflame, Centerlane, Starburst and Stargate.[151]

The apparently impossible feats accomplished within the programme attracted my attention and deep curiosity since it was conducted within the military establishment; not the sort of people usually associated with New Age psychology! Furthermore, the research was conducted at the renowned SRI, under the control of a group of well-established scientists, well used to conducting experiments using a repeatable, verifiable protocol.

Intrigued, I read the published works of various members of the remote viewing team, *Psychic Warrior* by David Morehouse[152], *Mind Trek* by Joe McMoneagle, *The Seventh Sense* by Lyn Buchanan[153] and *Limitless Mind* by Russell Targ[154].

The more I read the more convincing it became. These people have repeatedly produced accurate and verifiable descriptions and drawings, of people, places and events located at a remote place or time. There are hundreds of examples accumulated over many years in a huge variety of circumstances, within the RV programme run by the military and after that, in the private enterprises that the remote viewers

151 Details of the CIA assessment of Stargate are provided in McMoneagle, Joseph. 1993. *Mind Trek, Exploring Consciousness, Time and Space Through Remote Viewing*. Chapter 7. Charlottesville, VA, USA: Hampton Roads

152 Morehouse, David. 2000. *Psychic Warrior, the true story of the CIA's paranormal espionage programme.* UK: Clairview

153 Buchanan, Lyn. 2003. *The Seventh Sense, The Secrets of Remote Viewing as Told by a 'Psychic Spy' for the U.S. Military* New York, NY, USA: Paraview Pocket Books

154 Targ, Russell. 2004. *Limitless Mind, a guide to remote viewing and transformation of consciousness* Novato, CA, USA: New World Library

have set up, as well as in experiments conducted for television and film crews.

If this can be done, then the mind or spirit must be able to travel outside the physical body and through time. My rational brain recoiled at this, but the evidence presented in a scientific, lucid and rational manner seemed to be incontrovertible. There was only one thing for it; I had to find out for myself.

That was how I ended up attending a remote viewing course and while my physical body was sitting in a room in Wales, using the prescriptive and methodical Co-ordinate Remote Viewing technique developed at SRI I was able to accurately view sites that had been given to me only as a six number target. I could get a sense of the scale, colours, materials and use of the target locations I was being sent to view. I am aware that there are many things about that statement that seem impossible and if it had not happened to me I would not have believed it, but it did happen, I couldn't deny my own experience and that was the start of my journey.

Since then I have had many experiences while in altered states of consciousness that, as they are happening, have appeared to be totally real.

I have received advice from external entities about what to do in my life, all of which has proven to be very wise.

I have received information about past-life soul contracts that I have made and their sources, which has given me great insight into certain ways I had been acting in my life and this information then allowed me the choice of changing how I live.

I have seen aspects of previous lives and how I am carrying those wounds and patterns into this life. Again this insight has allowed me to make choices about changing who I am now, in this life.

I have communicated with deceased people that I know

absolutely nothing about and the information received appears to be incredibly accurate.

I have journeyed into the information field for clients and received information about the core wounds they carry and their limiting beliefs which has proven to be very accurate.

And I appear to have been visited by etheric essences of plants, animals and also wise beings that have tried to communicate their knowledge to me.

These personal experiences which initially at least were completely outside my belief system, hence totally unanticipated and unsought, have given me what I would describe as a state of knowing, beyond belief, of the existence of a soul, of reincarnation and of entities that live in other dimensions that are as real as we are, but I don't expect my experiences to convince you. Only your own personal experiences with altered states of consciousness can achieve that.

Sri Aurobindo, the great Indian philosopher introduced in Chapter 7, writes: *If the intellect is our highest possible instrument and there is no other means of arriving at supraphysical Truth, then a wise and large Agnosticism must be our ultimate attitude... It is only if there is a greater consciousness beyond Mind and that consciousness is accessible to us that we can know and enter into the ultimate Reality. Intellectual speculation, logical reasoning as to whether there is or is not such a greater consciousness cannot carry us very far. What we need is a way to get the experience of it, to reach it, enter into it, live in it. If we can get that, intellectual speculation and reasoning must fall necessarily into a very secondary place and even lose their reason for existence.*[155]

In 1945 Aldous Huxley used the term 'the perennial philosophy' to describe the four fundamental factors he perceived as being present in all the major wisdom traditions

155 Aurobindo, Sri. 2001. *A Greater Psychology* pp182–183 Pondicherry, India: Sri Aurobindo Ashram Publications Department

and religions of the world. In his book of the same name[156] he writes that one of these fundamental factors is that human beings are capable of realising the existence of the divine through their own consciousness, by a direct intuition, superior to reasoning. This immediate knowledge unites the knower with that which is known.

**Where does science stand on the existence of the soul?**

From the scientific perspective, whether or not we have souls that continue beyond physical death continues to be an unresolved question with even those that teach the principles and implications of nonlocality and the emerging theories of a holonomic mind and an entangled universe being unclear and divided on the answer.

Another of the fundamental factors identified by Huxley as part of the perennial philosophy is that humans possess a dual nature, a temporary ego and an eternal self, which is the spark of divinity within the soul. This eternal self is the manifestation of a divine individualised consciousness within the greater consciousness which is the fundamental building block of the universe.

The Christian and Islamic religions teach that, after death from the human physical form, this eternal self or soul will enter a different dimension (i.e. paradise/heaven or hell) depending on our actions in human form, while Judaism teaches that the soul will return to the divine source and Buddhism and Hinduism firmly espouse reincarnation and the related concept of karma.[157]

156 Huxley, Aldous. 1945. *The Perennial Philosophy* USA: Harper and Row

157 Karma can be summed up as 'what goes around comes around'. Your own fate in future existences will be determined by your actions in this and previous states of existence.

Many of the scientists embracing the implications of nonlocality would agree with, and argue the logic of, a continuing energy or consciousness, but not necessarily reincarnation and certainly not judgement. If anything they appear on balance to be closer to the Judaic concept of our energy (soul if you choose to use this word), returning to a greater source, whether or not that is considered to be divine.

David Jay Brown is a famous psychonaut and prolific interviewer of the great and the good. He asked a number of the scientific leaders in the field of nonlocality for their views on what happens to consciousness after death.

Dennis McKenna is one of the world's leading ethnopharmacologists and co-founder of the Heffter Research Institute: Research at the Frontiers of the Mind. He has undoubtedly had more hallucinogenic experiences than most. He answered: *Is the brain more like a generator or a detector? The brain could be like a radio antennae, essentially, and you change the channel… If that's true, then that's not even the correct way to interpret the question. Maybe asking if consciousness persists after death is like asking, does the electromagnetic spectrum persist after you break the radio and send it to the trash heap? Of course it does, because it has nothing to do with the individual radio receiver. It's still out there. So if you choose to believe that – and I don't think we really know yet what it is – then I think there's every possibility that in some sense consciousness does persist after death, or some nucleus, or a kernel of individual consciousness re-emerges into the universal mind or whatever you want to call it.*[158]

The question underpinning this comment is whether the holonomic, or external to the brain, models of consciousness are indeed accurate i.e. is the brain a transmitter and receiver for the mind rather than being synonymous with the mind? This reverts

---

158 Brown, David Jay. 2013. *The New Science of Psychedelics: At the Nexus of Culture, Consciousness and Spirituality* pp238–239 Rochester, Vermont, USA: Inner Traditions International and Bear & Company, http://www.Innertraditions.com

back to the various models of consciousness that I posed in Chapter 7 and which are at the forefront of neurological research.

Asking the late Edgar Dean Mitchell, founder of the Institute of Noetic Sciences, the same question about what happens to consciousness after death, Mitchell replied: *The most advanced modelling we can do at the moment, I believe, is called quantum holography... Essentially it says that the historical events of all matter are preserved in its quantum holographic record, and it's preserved nonlocally, which means it is useful or usable by future generations... this supports the idea that information is there available to us at the psychic or subjective level, and it's rooted in this quantum holographic phenomena. But this does not suggest that consciousness can exist independently of the living system. It merely says the information is available to the living system... It seems to be responsible not only for psychic abilities, as we understand them, but also the basis of why we have perception at all. So the modelling, so far, suggests that information about existence is preserved following life. We haven't yet been able to account for discarnate consciousness. I don't know how to account for that or how to model that.*[159]

Mitchell died in February 2016 and I am certain there will be people who worked with him over the years at the Institute of Noetic Sciences that will be attempting to contact him in the inforealm, so I look forward to hearing of that work as it emerges into the public domain.

## Evidence on past lives and after – death communication

As with other areas of 'psi' research[160], as a cursory search

159 Brown, David Jay. 2013. *The New Science of Psychedelics: At the Nexus of Culture, Consciousness and Spirituality* pp257–258 Rochester, Vermont, USA: Inner Traditions International and Bear & Company, http://www.Innertraditions.com

160 Research into experiences that appear to transcend the usual boundaries of space and time.

of Amazon books will reveal, there are many studies now published attempting to verify the existence of past lives, using the very specific memories of young children about times before they were born, as well as the accounts of adults about past-life connections with others that they meet in their lives today. Some well-regarded examples of past-life regression by analysts include the works of Roger Woolger and Brian Weiss.[161]

I have trained in past-life regression therapy and in my healing practice with my clients, many of them appear to connect with a past life as they track back to the core wound underlying the belief or life contract that is holding them back and adversely impacting their lives today. They certainly believe they are connecting with a karmic past and the knowledge they gain by visiting this previous life can be of significant assistance in their current lives. Even if you do not believe that this is real, that the information comes only from either the imagination or the deep unconscious memories of the brain, the placebo effect is undeniable. Several examples of the impact this work can have on clients are in the case studies at the end of this chapter.

There are of course many metaphysical teachings on death and rebirth and the continuation of an individuated consciousness from both the Buddhist and Hindu traditions. These insights are usually attained after long and arduous meditation, which one could argue allowed these teachers to connect with the inforealm via the endogenous release of DMT in their state of deep meditational trance.

However, all these personal experiences do not necessarily

161 Woolger, Roger J. 1987. *Other Lives, Other Selves: A Jungian psychotherapist discovers past lives* London, UK: Aquarian/HarperCollins and Weiss, Brian, Dr. 1988. *Many Lives, Many Masters: The true story of a prominent psychiatrist, his young patient and the past-life therapy that changed both their lives* USA: Simon and Schuster Inc.

convince scientists and even Laszlo, who has been such an important figure in spreading knowledge about the Akashic field or inforealm, cautions: *There is a wide array of evidence for past-life experiences, but the evidence does not guarantee a correct interpretation. Spiritually disposed persons tend to assume that these experiences are from a previous life, yet this is merely one interpretation. The interpretation that is more consistent with what we know of the in-formed universe is that our brain becomes tuned to the holographic record of another person in the vacuum. 'Past life experiences' signify the retrieval of information from the A-field, rather than the incarnation of the spirit or soul of a dead person.*[162]

This is in accordance with Mitchell's response earlier in the chapter, that quantum holography suggests the storage of all information nonlocally, in a form that can be accessed psychically. But even if we can access information nonlocally, it leaves open the question of whether we are accessing information about some sort of personal or karmic consciousness, or whether it is from some person or event that resonates with us, or is coherent with our brainwave transmission and reception for whatever reason.

Although in the previous quote Laszlo is agnostic about the existence of past lives, he also notes that: *The level and intensity of the transmission of information varies in accordance with the degree of conjugation between the wavefields. It is the most direct and hence evident when the wavefield of one hologram is highly conjugate with the wavefield of another. Lesser conjugation means weaker resonance and lesser effect.*

*Normally the most direct and evident resonance occurs between our brain and the hologram we ourselves have created. This is the basis of long-term memory. When we remember a thing, a person, or an event*

---

162 Laszlo, Ervin. 2007. *Science and the Akashic Field: An Integral Theory of Everything (Second Edition)* p.124 Rochester, Vermont, USA: Inner Traditions International and Bear & Company, http://www.Innertraditions.com

*from many years ago, or have an intuition that we have already seen or experienced something... we do not address the memory stores in our brain: we 'recall' the information from the hologram that records our experiences.*[163]

This seems to suggest that we can most easily tune into the holographic records of what we ourselves have stored in the inforealm. That is the information with the strongest resonance. So this seems to leave open the possibility that we are connecting with a past life. Or maybe not. Maybe we are tuning into something/someone that desperately needs attention – a strong transmission or cry for help from the inforealm. An obvious alternative is that we tune into a strong signal from the records of our family or our community, the tribe or the society we live in. Thought forms and belief systems have an energetic signature, as do all religions, philosophies, sciences, lineages and cultures. When we visit past lives maybe they are not our own, maybe they belong to the ancestors or others that we are energetically entangled with. Either way, whatever it appears to be that we are connecting with, and however we are connecting with it, such processes appear to be capable of bringing healing to the client in the current space and time and also, potentially, to the souls of those we connect with.

That is the hypothesis that is also coming through strongly from the work of psychotherapist Allan Botkin, head of the Center for Grief and Traumatic Loss in Libertyville, Illinois. He and his colleagues have successfully induced after-death communication in well over three thousand patients using Eye Movement Desensitization and Reprocessing therapy (EMDR).

---

163 Laszlo, Ervin. 2007. *Science and the Akashic Field: An Integral Theory of Everything (Second Edition)* pp115–116 Rochester, Vermont, USA: Inner Traditions International and Bear & Company, http://www.Innertraditions.com

Botkin's most recent research in combination with many practitioners of his method around the world, demonstrates that induced after-death communication (IADC) works for seventy-nine per cent of the people who try the specific EMDR process that has that intention[164]. He notes that: *We now know that a patient's beliefs have no effect on the outcome. It works equally well for the devoutly religious, the highly spiritual, agnostics, and atheists. It works for patients experiencing normal bereavement and those suffering from horrendous traumatic grief. It works for patients with recent losses as well as for those who have suffered a loss many decades in the past. In short, it appears to work with nearly everyone, nearly all of the time.*[165]

I should make it clear that initially ADCs were not what Botkin and his team were intending to achieve – they were simply looking for grief resolution. Initially he was shocked by what his patients were experiencing and initially the communications appeared to be largely for the benefit of the living clients, but as this work has evolved, there has been increasing evidence of benefit also to the dead, particularly through forgiveness: *Regardless of the gravity of the traumas the deceased inflicted, however, the patients consistently describe the deceased as being deeply remorseful and apologetic, taking responsibility for their actions and asking for forgiveness. In every case, the patient forgives the deceased and, in every case, the anger dramatically decreases from that moment.*[166]

Very much in line with my own beliefs, Botkin considers these IADC experiences to be highly valuable even if we can't

---

164 Figure communicated in correspondence to me.

165 Botkin, Allan L. PsyD and Hogan, R. Craig, PhD. 2005, 2014. *Induced After-Death Communication: A New Therapy for Healing Grief and Trauma* ppxx-xxi Charlottesville, VA, USA: Hampton Roads Publishing, c/o Red Wheel/ Weiser, LLC Newburyport, MA, www.redwheelweiser.com

166 Botkin, Allan L. PsyD and Hogan, R. Craig, PhD. 2005, 2014. *Induced After-Death Communication: A New Therapy for Healing Grief and Trauma* p.131 Charlottesville, VA, USA: Hampton Roads Publishing, c/o Red Wheel/ Weiser, LLC Newburyport, MA, www.redwheelweiser.com

fully explain how they work: *For now at least, it doesn't matter what I believe or what the other psychotherapists using IADC therapy believe... We look at the results of the methods and apply them as they are appropriate and efficacious for our patients... Our beliefs are simply irrelevant to its use.*[167]

**Case Study Client H**

Client H works in the medical profession. He feels empty inside despite appearing to the outside world to be successful, with a good job and a wife and family. He has been trying to do some shamanic journeying on his own but finds it difficult to go down into the earth, the lower world. It brings up fear but he doesn't know why, although he is also afraid of going into caves.

We decide to journey for the root of his fear and using the breath as I hold his head he quickly gets visions of a man working a field, ploughing. Other men come along and demand food but he has nothing to give them. They go to his house where his wife and two daughters are and again demand food. There is nothing to give them so the men get angry. Then there is a gap in the story and the next thing the man remembers is waking up inside a wooden box. He can't move and has been buried alive. He tries to get out but can't breathe or escape and he dies in the box underground. When the dead man's spirit has left the physical body and moved into an altered state of consciousness a beautiful girl appears to him. She says she represents freedom.

167 Botkin, Allan L. PsyD and Hogan, R. Craig, PhD. 2005, 2014. *Induced After-Death Communication: A New Therapy for Healing Grief and Trauma* p.190 Charlottesville, VA, USA: Hampton Roads Publishing, c/o Red Wheel/ Weiser, LLC Newburyport MA, www.redwheelweiser.com

I ask him in this lifetime what is it that he has never been free to do or say? He has never been allowed to say no. Who told him or taught him that?

He immediately flips to another past life, this time as a fifteen-year-old boy, captured and thrown in front of a rich man. The boy is not allowed to look at the man, he must look only down at the ground. He is not allowed to say no, he must always do as he is told. The boy escapes and runs away, he runs and runs but there is nowhere to go. Men on horses come after him and recapture him and he is hanged in the town square.

We come back to this life and he is astonished at the array of images that came so easily. He did not believe he could do this. We then practised saying no, verbally and physically, pushing things away with his hands and feet as I bring them towards him. It is fascinating to him as he always says yes, and feels extremely uncomfortable saying no. But now he has a new affirmation: it is safe for me to say no, now I can say no.

From then on he loses his fear of journeying into the lower world and also he is able to use his intuition in his work much more effectively and trust the images he gets, as well as being able to manage his time better by saying no when necessary.

This demonstrates how experience can change our belief systems more than any amount of reading or studying and also how practising new words or a new way of being can very quickly lead to change in our day-to-day lives.

**Case Study Client I**

Client I feels very heavy. She self-sabotages and feels chronically tired. She has a fear of not being good enough.

On the table we go back to the core wound. Initially she sees an incident in school when she was just four years old. Then she goes back further and she visits what appears to her to be a past life. She was a man, with bare feet and robes like a monk, in a very simple room. She didn't feel it was a prison, it was a choice. I ask her to use the breath to go back to the time before he was a monk, why didn't he feel good enough? She receives the information that he hated looking in the mirror – he had been disfigured in a fire. We breathe forward to the end of that man's life and he died in his room, the others in the order took care of his body and he had found peace in his spiritual practice.

From the place beyond death he wants to communicate to her in this life that she should enjoy her looks and her body and not be ashamed of them. She should enjoy life and be proud of herself. She tells him she is sorry for what he suffered but she is glad he had found peace.

Back in this lifetime I ask her to look at herself in the mirror. She looks and sees herself and can say that she is good enough and even recognise that she is amazing. She loves the session and leaves resolved to go out and buy some beautiful lingerie and pamper her body.

This is an example of how the information we receive in the form of archetypical stories can instantaneously lead to a huge 'a-ha!' moment of understanding about what has been keeping us stuck, with a resultant change in our belief systems about what we are capable of.

**Case Study Client J**

Client J feels as if she has had an enormously blessed life and she has a wide range of professional skills and a successful career within a large organisation. However, she is in a somewhat controlling relationship with a man that reminds her of her father and feels fear about setting up her own business. She lies on the table and I put two rocks on her solar plexus, the fear centre. One to represent her father (deceased) and one to represent her partner. She calls in her father first and using the stone as a physical representation she gives him back his fear, his judgement, his keeping himself small. He accepts it and apologises – he says he understands more now and is grateful to be able to have this conversation with her.

She then goes to the stone connected with her partner. She feels tightness in the throat and is having difficulty breathing. She finds herself in the life of a young servant girl in a kitchen. The girl was illegitimate, her father was master of the house and her mother was a servant. Her mother died when she was a very young child but her father took her in and fed her and gave her somewhere to live, but only as a lowly servant. An older woman in the kitchen beat her around the head and damaged her neck, after which work became even more painful and she died young and totally alone. In the spirit world she calls in her mother who apologises. The girl apologises too. She had blamed her mother for her misfortunes in life but realised it was not her mother's fault. She can see from the spirit world that her body was buried without ceremony in unconsecrated ground.

Back in this life she realises she has carried cooking and cleaning, hunched over with pain in her neck and upper back, into this world. She allows her partner to control her at home. She has derived her self-worth from what she has done for others, not what she has achieved for herself. She sees that she does not need to carry this pattern any longer.

She leaves to go home to her garden to get a stone which she will bury somewhere beautiful with a prayer to honour the past life she had seen and then she is going to look for a retreat centre that she can go to on her own for a few days to take care of herself without looking after anyone else.

This demonstrates the way in which rocks on the body can help us to embody what we have been carrying and the power of the ritual of releasing them physically. It also shows how physical pain can result from a very old family pattern which can be released once the source is recognised.

## Conclusion

The belief in a soul that continues beyond physical death is intrinsic to all the major metaphysical philosophies and now that consciousness is back on the agenda as a valid topic for scientific investigation, there is mounting scientific evidence from near-death experiences that a consciousness extends beyond death.

There are case studies of people who appear to have knowledge of past lives that is verifiable and unknowable without a psychic effect and several billion people across the world believe in reincarnation. Thousands of people have had past-life regressions which they find meaningful and helpful in living their lives today and thousands more have been in communication with the deceased through ADCs.

In the three case studies I have written above, the client is able to journey easily to what appear to be past lives that they know nothing of. They receive images that help them to understand the sources of fears and limitations that they face every day in their lives and they see that they do not need to hang on to these old patterns. Choice becomes an option and a different way of behaving becomes clear.

Maybe the images are not of past lives. Maybe they come

from the deep unconscious memory in the form of archetypes and fairy tales, so that we can understand the story? Maybe they are not our own past lives, but things that have happened to our ancestors that are now embedded at a cellular level into our conditioning? Perhaps something completely different and unknown is going on!

What does seem evident from these and hundreds of other examples that I could give from my own experience and the experiences of my clients is that this work allows an instantaneous release from the old attractors and the ability to step into new and more constructive belief systems that are appropriate for our current lives. People feel they understand the cause of their problems, they get a real sense of why their limiting beliefs are outdated, and they can see a different way forward.

However, this is an area where people are unlikely to be convinced unless they have some sort of personal experience which gives them a form of knowing, which is what happened in my own case.

Laszlo's preferred label for the inforealm is the Akashic Field and as he writes: *The recognition that the Akashic experience is a real and fundamental part of human experience has unparalleled importance for our time. When more people grasp the fact that they can have, and are perhaps already having, Akashic experiences, they will open their mind to them, and the experiences will occur more and more frequently, and to more and more people. A more evolved consciousness will spread in the world.*[168]

I encourage you to get out there and have an Akashic experience!

---

168 Laszlo, Ervin. 2009. *The Akashic Experience: Science and the Cosmic Memory Field* pp7–8 Rochester, Vermont, USA: Inner Traditions International and Bear & Company, http://www.Innertraditions.com

# GLOSSARY FOR CHAPTER 9

**Ethnopharmacology**: a study of ethnic groups and their use of drugs, usually linked to plant use.

**Karma**: your own fate in future existences will be determined by your actions in this and previous states of existence.

**Psi research**: research into experiences that appear to transcend the usual boundaries of space and time.

# CHAPTER 10: FAMILY SYSTEMS AND ANCESTRAL PAIN

**Do you think it is possible to carry emotional or physical pain on behalf of another member of the family system that you are in whether they are dead or alive? In other words are we energetically entangled with our ancestors?**

> *There may be a powerful impact in a constellation when we become aware that some of the pain we are suffering actually belongs to someone else in the past, but has not yet been laid to rest. We are not responding to actual experiences in our own lives: we seem to be trying to be of service to those in the past, attempting to bring peace to their souls.*[169]
>
> (Jakob Schneider)

## Introduction

Shamanic cultures have always looked at the individual in the context of the family, community or tribe, but looking beyond

169 Schneider, Jakob Robert. 2007. *Family Constellations: Basic Principles and Procedures* p.13 Heidelberg, Germany: Carl-Auer-Systeme

the individual to their social conditioning and family system is relatively new in Western psychology.

What is emerging forcefully is that we carry massive amounts of conditioning from our families and the societies in which we are raised. This can cause problems for the growing numbers of people who are displaced from their ancestral homes and feel split between the expectations of their ancestors and the expectations of the societies in which they live.

People who are excluded by families continue to have an impact within the family system – we cannot just ignore those whose behaviour we don't like! We often behave in ways that don't feel true to ourselves, because we are trying to please others in the family system, either consciously or unconsciously. And out of love we often try to rescue others in the family. We would rather suffer ourselves than see them suffering. But this can leave us feeling depleted, angry and unfulfilled, leading to depression and other forms of disease.

In this chapter I look at some of the modern theories of systemic entanglement and also some innovative approaches to helping entire family systems, which may involve working with the dead as well as the living.

## The impact of our ancestry

Cultural differences are well recognised and have been the source of much exploitation, fear and racism for many centuries. Throughout the ages there have been migrations, and the USA of course was known as the melting pot of cultures. But today there is enormous international movement of people at an unprecedented scale, leaving billions outside the cultural environment of their ancestors, and without any family support network.

*Outliers*[170] by Malcolm Gladwell gives some great examples of the impact of ancestral conditioning on our health and behaviour. In Roseto, Pennsylvania, USA, where the entire town were all immigrants from the Roseto Valfortore region of Italy, they maintained the traditions of their ancestors for many years and astounded scientists by their health and longevity. After years of research the conclusion was that they prospered because of the sense of community, and when that started to crumble their health and longevity started to normalise to the levels found in the rest of the USA.

Another example he gives is the way Northerners and Southerners in the United States of America react differently to perceived aggression, purely based on where they were brought up. He reports the results of a psychological experiment run at the University of Michigan in the early 1990s.[171] A group of young men from the northern part of the USA and a group of young men from the South were faced with the same set-up and reacted totally differently in terms of their cortisol and testosterone levels. The conclusion the psychologists running the experiment reached was that your cultural ancestry continues to impact your behaviour for hundreds of years.

Gladwell writes: *Cultural legacies are powerful forces. They have deep roots and long lives. They persist, generation after generation, virtually intact, even as the economic and social and demographic conditions that spawned them have vanished, and they play such a role in directing attitudes and behaviour that we cannot make sense of our world without them.*[172]

---

170 Gladwell, Malcolm. 2008. *Outliers: The Story of Success* London, England: Allen Lane

171 Nisbett, Richard E. and Cohen, Dov. 1996. *Culture of Honor: The Psychology of Violence in the South* Boulder, Colorado: Westview Press, Inc.

172 Gladwell, Malcolm. 2008. *Outliers: The Story of Success* p.175 London, England: Allen Lane

Now many people are feeling split, dislocated and without a home. They live in a society with a set of expectations very different from those of the ancestors. They want to honour the latter, but cannot do so and also fit into the place they now live. They feel they don't know where they belong and need a way to move on while still honouring their ancestors.

Both shamanic healing and family constellations aim to provide tools and techniques that allow this evolution, and in the process they often appear to benefit the ancestors and others in the family as well as the direct client.

## The theory of family systems and family constellations

The constellations framework of family systems stems from the 1980s and the incredibly brave and insightful work of Bert Hellinger. It considers the client not in isolation, but as a part of a whole system. It looks at the client in the wider context of the lineage and its dark secrets, the skeletons in the cupboard which cannot be discussed, the family members who have been ostracised and excluded. These excluded family members often include people who have been perpetrators, committing crimes or abuse. They may include those who were deemed sinful, such as mothers carrying illegitimate children, those having affairs, sex workers, or those who had an abortion, or the souls of those who were aborted and are never spoken of or acknowledged. They may also include those who were institutionalised for madness or who committed suicide.

I was fortunate enough to train with Albrecht Mahr, a close colleague of Hellinger, and as he explained it to us, there are three different aspects of conscience:

- Personal conscience, which guarantees or endangers belonging to the group. Personal conscience is not an absolute truth, it is a mechanism to regulate belonging. I have a clear conscience means I conform with my group's values. It is nothing to do with morality! One of the most difficult tasks is to evolve beyond the group's values while still paying respect to the tribe.

- The collective or systemic conscience of the group, associated with the completeness of the group. This is not an individually felt conscience, people only feel the effects of it, often unconsciously, because it takes care of and safeguards the completeness of a system. It ensures inclusion of all members and does not allow the exclusion of anybody who rightly belongs to the system. It is extremely important to note that collective conscience again does not provide absolute moral orientation. It balances the integral wholeness of social groups, often by means of seemingly 'immoral' behaviour by its members.
- Third there is integral or spiritual conscience. This level of conscience becomes extremely inclusive, the dynamic is 'it wants us to realise it'. This appears to be the conscience that causes us at crucial moments to ask about our purpose and there is a sickness, termed meta pathology, which is the suffering of not responding to that call.

It is the second of these, the collective or systemic conscience of the group, that causes us to carry things on behalf of others in the system. If someone has been thrown out of the family and kept secret, the constellations framework reveals time after time that another family member tends to take on their characteristics and their pain to ensure they have a place, a representation in the system. Only when we can move to action from our integral or spiritual conscience are we truly free of the burdens of the ancestors.

At the core of the constellations framework is the concept of entanglement. As Jakob Schneider, a German constellations therapist whose quote opens this chapter, describes it: *Entanglement is what brings someone, without knowledge or choice, to repeat or blindly enter into the fate of another person in the family or group system.*[173]

This seems to take place because: *when a person in a family system has been excluded or denied an equal right to belong, or when someone's fate has been kept a secret, (perhaps a suicide), the group conscience co-opts someone else, usually someone born later, to represent the excluded family member.*

*This person is involved without conscious awareness and certainly has not consciously chosen to take on this task…*

*It is as though the function is to maintain an awareness, empathy, and respect for the excluded member's fate, and to bring those aspects back into the community of the group. An equal right of all members of the group to belong, regardless of their fate, serves to preserve the unity of the group so necessary for survival.*[174]

Franz Ruppert is a renowned therapist specialising in trauma and particularly with regard to traumatised families he introduces the term symbiotic system trauma. He describes how you can only have a healthy relationship with another after you have a healthy relationship with yourself. If there is symbiotic entanglement with another person, you get tied up in that person's relationships and traumas and you are not free to have a relationship with yourself, or then another.

Symbiotic system trauma is inter-generational trauma carried in the system, associated with a perpetrator(s). The culture of the family is to re-enact the abuse and it frequently also involves a culture of silence in which it is forbidden to talk about the trauma within the system.

---

173 Schneider, Jakob Robert. 2007. *Family Constellations: Basic Principles and Procedures* p.36 Heidelberg, Germany: Carl-Auer-Systeme

174 Schneider, Jakob Robert. 2007. *Family Constellations: Basic Principles and Procedures* p.43 Heidelberg, Germany: Carl-Auer-Systeme

Trans-generational trauma occurs when what happened to the ancestors could not be digested and so it continues to have an energetic impact. So for instance a woman who believes she was abused by her father may be carrying that perceived abuse on behalf of her grandmother. It is very hard to distinguish the difference which is why we need to step outside any judgement. Her father may not be a perpetrator even if she believes he was, particularly if those memories have surfaced from the unconscious mind during therapy of some kind. Somehow the grandmother needs to be seen and allowed to speak, so that her suffering can be acknowledged and handed back where it belongs rather than being carried by the client in the present.

Ruppert writes: *Every time I have worked with psychotic clients I have found confirmation for an approach based on the concept of the transgenerational transfer of unresolved trauma: i.e. behind all psychotic and schizophrenic forms of behaviour and experiences there are split-off traumatic events within the family, which the person concerned has taken on in their symbiotic entanglement with their mother, grandmother or other person from an earlier generation.*[175]

## The practice of family constellations

Traditionally family constellation work is carried out in a group of between 10 and 30 people, who are most frequently complete strangers and do not know each other's stories prior to the workshop. Everyone sits in a circle and the facilitator asks the client he is about to work with for a very brief description of the issue they would like to deal with. Then the client chooses representatives for themselves and for all

175 Ruppert, Franz. 2012. *Symbiosis & Autonomy, Symbiotic Trauma and Love Beyond Entanglements* p.168 Steyning, UK: Green Balloon Publishing

necessary members of the family, living or dead, or perhaps people they have wronged, from the witnesses sitting in the circle. These representatives are positioned within the circle where they are asked to step into what Hellinger labels the Knowing Field.

At that point the chosen members of the group, known as the representatives, start to gain resonance with those they are representing. I know this may sound impossible, as there has not even been any induction into an altered state of consciousness, but the experimental and experiential data base from this work in the knowing field over the last thirty plus years is now huge.[176] Exactly how it works is still unclear, but I have participated in and witnessed dozens of such constellations. Somehow people start to adopt bodily postures and feel the physical sensations pertaining to those they are representing. Complete strangers start to react to each other, perhaps with love or hate or anger or grief. The scene evolves and sometimes representatives for other people need to be added, sometimes representatives for qualities need to be called in, such as fear or abandonment.

Frequently the client is deeply affected by what they are witnessing. They see the family patterns playing out in a way that seems unbelievable given the participants' prior lack of knowledge. And gradually new information that the client was unaware of will start to emerge. Perhaps one of the representatives says someone is missing and they call in that person, never acknowledged by the family. Perhaps a quality is missing and needs to be added. Perhaps an ancestor wants to talk about how the family is misrepresenting them.

Schneider writes: *When there are deceased family members*

---

176 For just one book citing many references, see Franke, Ursula. 2003. *The River Never Looks Back. Historical and Practical Foundations of Bert Hellinger's Family Constellations* Heidelberg, Germany: Carl-Auer-Systeme Verlag

*who are not yet at peace in the family soul, and therefore continue to affect the living as if they were still alive, the constellation work often resembles a shamanic ritual. Through the representatives, the living and the dead are able to meet, but it also seems to be that the dead can touch others who are dead. Such encounters seem to release the dead from haunting the living in their search for peace. It allows love to flow in the hearts of the living and, insofar as we can say such a thing, love also flows between the dead and from the dead to the living.*[177]

Mahr is now working extensively in Rwanda, with both the victims and perpetrators of the genocide that took place there. He notes that a collective problem arises when a whole group is conditioned to think of themselves as victims of another group, for example the Africans and slavery, or Jews and the Holocaust. He has found through experience that constellations are a way to get to the true essence of the people who have been victims of genocide and other atrocities. Although that was perhaps their story in life, after death they may no longer want to be remembered in that way. It is then very important for the living to release the stories of the ancestors and to acknowledge that, no matter how much suffering there has been, the tribe has survived, and the ancestors may want us to honour them by living fully, as they could not, rather than hanging onto judgement and hatred on their behalf.

The incredible power of this work is that it is bringing healing not only directly to the client, but also to all those, living and deceased, that are called into the circle, working outside space and time.

---

177 Schneider, Jakob Robert. 2007. *Family Constellations: Basic Principles and Procedures* p.66 Heidelberg, Germany: Carl-Auer-Systeme

### Case Study Client K

Client K engages in self-sabotage and keeps having to go back to her mother for money. Her mother seems to enjoy having her children still depend on her and there is a sense that in the family love and money are very entangled. We set up a small constellation with a representative for the client, a representative for her mother and a representative for money. The representative for money reports that they want to float away, and starts to move towards the edge of the circle. The representative for the client follows money and brings it back to the centre. She wants to dance with money but money now feels rooted and immobile. The representative for mother is initially anxious as she watches but then moves away and faces out of the circle.

Then we bring in a representative for grandmother. She wants to cling on to money. It's not allowed to move. Money then felt as if it was rationed like food in the war. Mother comes back into the circle and asks grandmother to let money go, but grandmother doesn't want to hear any of that. She doesn't have anything else. Money at this point sits down on the floor beside grandmother, wrapping their arms around her. They seem to be completely entangled. The representatives for the client and mother try to help money stand up again, but it feels manipulated, it doesn't like everyone pulling it around.

I ask money how it would feel if it were allowed to grow? That would feel good. I ask grandmother how it would be if she could keep some of money for herself but let some go to other members of the family? It has grown now so that there is enough to go around. That feels ok for grandmother as long as she still has a piece of money to hold onto.

Money now gets up and wants to play and move around

everyone in the circle – it can flow and dance and play, but it doesn't like to be abused and manipulated.

The representatives for mother and client finish by honouring grandmother and reassuring her that although there wasn't enough for everyone in the past, there is now.

The next time I hear from the client she has landed a job that for the first time in many years allows her to pay her own way in the world and stop depending on the family for cash. Her mother is able to go on holiday and do some of the things she has always wanted to. She can afford that now as she is no longer subsidising her daughter.

This is an example of how someone can step into a representation that they know absolutely nothing about and yet immediately portray very accurately what has been happening in the family. It also demonstrates that somehow what happens in the constellation can lead to a deep change in the family dynamics and way of being in the world.

## Using shamanic practices for systemic healing

The practice of family constellations has only been around since the 1980s, but shamans have had techniques to work with a person in the context of their tribe for centuries.

Francesca Mason Boring is a Native American healer who relatively recently discovered the psychotherapeutic approach of constellations. She writes: *As a Shoshone and bicultural woman, I have a sense that many of the links that modern people yearn for in the quest for a shaman are available in the therapeutic discipline of Family Constellation... The phenomenological approach in Constellation work utilizes the worldview that the shaman integrated with ease. It involves a way of seeing solutions using information beyond our normal objective reality. This phenomenological way of working does not involve client assessment, treatment plan, and intervention. Rather, it involves waiting, listening, and allowing an organic healing movement that comes from a field beyond the cognitive mind.*[178]

She adds: *These outside forces, and the participation of ancestors, were something that Native people usually talked about only among themselves, because those conversations about ancestors were among the kind of concepts that many Native people had been beaten and humiliated for.*

*The concept of being connected to ancestors, and the dead, had been one of those areas defined as "savage". After a European psychotherapist, Bert Hellinger, started talking about it, some of the white world no longer thought it "primitive".*[179]

In my own shamanic training I was taught a particular way of working in which the client can connect with their dead ancestors to get a greater understanding of their lives, or receive messages or gifts. I have seen cases where there has been great hatred or anger at an ancestor who was perceived as a perpetrator, but when the client steps into their shoes, they can start to forgive because they get a much deeper understanding of why that person acted as they did. I have also seen cases where there has been no knowledge about an ancestor, but when the client steps into their shoes, the secrets start to be revealed. This acknowledgement of their pain and suffering and of their place in the family system seems to bring relief to the dead, as well as giving understanding and closure to the living, allowing them to move on.

In a fusion of my shamanic toolbox with the techniques

---

178 Mason Boring, Francesca. 2012. *Connecting to Our Ancestral Past: Healing through Family Constellations, Ceremony, and Ritual* pp19–20 Berkeley, California USA: North Atlantic Books Reprinted from *ReVision* 32, no. 2 (2011); see www.revisionspublishing.org

179 Mason Boring, Francesca. 2012. *Connecting to Our Ancestral Past: Healing through Family Constellations, Ceremony, and Ritual*, pp13–14 Berkeley, California, USA: North Atlantic Books

I learned from constellations, I have developed a way of working with individual clients who appear to be carrying burdens or limiting beliefs on behalf of either the living or the dead. For instance the limiting belief may centre on a lack of abundance, about not being allowed to speak, about not being good enough, or about working 24/7 or you will face dire consequences, including potential starvation. The burdens may also be taken on when children have been forced into a role-reversal situation where they are caring for/carrying the parent from a very early age, or where they become de facto mothers/fathers to their siblings.

In this way of working I put stones on the client's body to represent the block or the burden. To whom does the block or burden belong, what do the stones represent? The client can usually identify what they are carrying quite easily when they feel the physical presence of the stones. I ask how it serves them to continue to carry the burden and whether they choose to continue to carry it having identified the source? From the knowing field we can then energetically call the person it belongs to into the room, whether living or dead, and the client can explain why they no longer want to carry it for them.

What frequently emerges is that the other is willing and even happy to take the burden back, particularly if they are deceased. They do not want their descendants to carry their suffering or limitations. The client is able to acknowledge the ancestors and what they had to do to survive, but recognises that today they live in a different place and time and can choose a different way of life.

However, there are times when the person to whom the pain or belief belongs is not willing to take it back. In that case the client still has the choice of whether to carry it, or alternatively drop it to the earth.

Sometimes the client feels they are stronger than the person they are carrying the burden for, so they want to continue to carry it out of love, but in that case I introduce a discussion about the victim/rescuer/perpetrator triangle. When we continually try to rescue someone, we tend to keep them as victims. Helping is different from rescuing and rescuing robs the other of their autonomy. We all deserve choice, and while others may not like the choices we make, they are not entitled to make our choices for us, but rescuing often tends to unconsciously impose our choices on others. Choices made with the best of intentions, but still without allowing the other their rightful autonomy. This usually results in a huge 'a-ha!' moment for the client and they are then able to hand back what belongs to another, often with surprising expressions of gratitude during the session and subsequent changes in the behaviour of the other after the session.

**Case Study Client L**

Client L comes from East Europe and is highly skilled. She speaks three languages fluently, has a university degree and worked in a good professional job back at home and then elsewhere in Europe, but in London she is working as a waitress and feels completely lost and scared.

The story that emerges is that she has always been the rescuer in the family. Even as a child she was mother to her mother, and sorted her mother out after her father's suicide, including moving her to a new country, finding her a new home and a job. She has also been mother to her younger brothers, although one of them has already asked her to use their actual names and not call them 'the kids' any more.

I put stones on her body to represent the weight she is carrying for others. What would it be like to give it back? Can she hand them back their power? She has great difficulty doing that. If she does that, who is she then? But on the other hand it would take a huge weight off her if she doesn't need to carry them anymore. She feels that all the weight is on the solar plexus. If she takes the weight off the solar plexus she will be able to feel her heart and she is afraid of that. At the moment her heart is cut off. At this point in the session she becomes very upset but eventually calms down and is able to look at herself in the mirror and see that she is free to do what she wants for herself. She drops the stones on the floor, recognising that carrying the family has given her a sense of identity – she thought it was for them, but actually it was for herself.

The next time she comes to see me she reports that her relationships with her brothers are much better. She has stopped interfering in their lives and feels really good about it. Also her mother has become much more independent.

Since then she has moved to another country, away from her birth family, has a new long-term relationship of her own, and has trained to become a therapist.

This is an example of how the rocks representing almost anything can help clients to connect with what they have been carrying consciously or unconsciously. Giving them back or dropping them helps the client to embody the change that is needed and even although others are not consciously aware of what has happened in the therapy session, their behaviour changes as a result of the work done there.

**Case Study Client M**

Client M comes from a West African background and historically her family lived near one of the major slave ports. Her mother is very controlling and doesn't want to let go of her daughter, my client, who is engaged to be married. We start to work on the table and I ask her to call in her mother from the knowing field. The client speaks to her mother about how she wants to move forward in her own adult life. The mother is terrified of losing her. The client then feels her deceased grandmother entering the space. She had suffered from terrible physical abuse as a child and then became a very violent mother. We ask grandmother if she has a message. Yes – she is proud of the client and wants her to move on. Can grandmother assist mother? No, she can't do that, but then the image of a great aunt comes in. She is willing to assist.

The client performs a short ritualistic ceremony to honour the ancestors and tell them that she lives here in the West now, in the 21st century. They came from a culture of pain and violence but it stops now. She finishes the session by turning to the future generations and talking to her unborn children about her wishes for them to live in freedom. At the end she feels very clear and centred.

Later I heard from her that her wedding had been a huge success and had been done exactly as she and her new husband wanted it to be without interference from her mother.

This is a good example of being able to honour the ancestors but also turn to a different way of being, more suited to the circumstances we now find ourselves in.

## Conclusion

Even if you believe that it is only possible to bring healing to the client that you are working with directly in the here and now, evidence is building that doctors and therapists need to see their patients in relationship to their family system, not in isolation.

Our social circumstances and conditioning are among the

best predictors of our overall health and well-being and we cannot step into our full potential, with autonomy, until we move out of our personal conscience, beyond the systemic conscience, into the integral or spiritual conscience.

The good news is that shamanic work with family systems and in most cases the modern version of that, constellations, helps us to do just this. These therapies move beyond the belief that you are only working to bring healing to the physically present client to the belief that you are working to bring healing to the whole system. The scope of this work is enormous and when done with sensitivity and care, the acknowledgement and healing of the lineage, their secrets and their entanglements, can pave the way for future generations to be free of intergenerational family conflicts and secrets in addition to autonomously helping the client.

I would like to complete this chapter with a quotation from Osho: *Anything that helps you to attain the fulfilment of your potential is good. It is not only a blessing to you, it is a blessing to the whole existence. No man is an island. We are all a vast infinite continent, joined together in the roots. Maybe our branches are separate, but our roots are one.*

*Realising one's potential is the only morality there is.*

*Losing one's potential and falling into darkness and retardedness is the only sin, the only evil.*[180]

## GLOSSARY FOR CHAPTER 10

**Autonomy**: the right or condition of self-government; freedom from external control or influence.

**Phenomenological**: an approach that concentrates on

180 Osho, 2000. *New Man for the New Millennium* p.183 Osho International Foundation, www.OSHO.com/copyrights

the study of consciousness and the objects of direct experience.

**Symbiotic**: involving interaction between two different organisms living in close physical association.

**Systemic**: something experienced by the whole and not just by the parts.

# CONCLUSION

In this book I have tried to lead you on a journey, starting with what is now well known in science and medicine, even if it has not yet permeated popular culture, and moving gradually to more speculative but crucial territory if humanity is to switch from the paradigm of victimhood of the masses (with an elite of perpetrators and a handful of rescuers) to a new paradigm of widespread autonomy accompanied by the acceptance of self-responsibility.

In this conclusion I am drawing together the various threads I have introduced and making some practical recommendations for spreading and using this knowledge in society.

In my previous book, *Temenos Touch: The Art and Science of Integrated Medicine and Non-local Healing* I relied heavily on the framework of the three Eras of healing[181] developed by Dr Larry Dossey, who served as a battalion surgeon in Vietnam where he was decorated for valour. He then helped to establish the Dallas Diagnostic Association and was appointed Chief of Staff of Medical City Dallas

181 http://www.dosseydossey.com

Hospital in 1982 before releasing his paradigm-altering book, *Recovering the Soul*,[182] in 1989. I briefly recap these Eras below which are discussed in much greater detail in *Reinventing Medicine*.[183]

- Era I believes all forms of therapy are physical and the body is to be regarded as a mechanism that functions according to deterministic principles. Mind or consciousness is equated with the functioning of the brain.
- Era II describes the mind-to-body medical approaches that involve the psychosomatic effects of one's consciousness on one's own body, i.e. what you think affects your health. But mind is still seen as a function of brain chemistry and anatomy. These therapies include psychosomatic medicine, biofeedback, hypnosis, meditation etc. as discussed in Chapter 2.
- Era III sees the mind as unconfined by either space or time: it is boundless. It is recognised that our nonlocal mind may affect healing both within and between people. (Remember from Chapter 5 that nonlocality is the entanglement of particles such that measurement of one impacts another instantaneously, involving information being communicated at least as fast as the speed of light.) Non-contact healing modalities between people in each other's presence, as well as between people distant from each other, become possible with nonlocal mind, as do healings backward and forward in time.

The widely-accepted parts of the new paradigm that I have presented in this book belong to Era II medicine. As I hope I

182 Dossey, Larry, M.D.. 1989. *Recovering the Soul: A Scientific and Spiritual Search* New York, USA: Bantam Doubleday Dell Publishing Group

183 Dossey, Larry, M.D.. 1999. *Reinventing Medicine: Beyond Mind-Body to a New Era of Healing* New York, USA: Harper One

have demonstrated, there is now little scientific and medical doubt of the interconnectedness of the body and the brain, with our physical health being dependent on our emotional and mental health. Alternative therapies which fit into Era II, such as craniosacral treatment, acupuncture, reflexology, meditation, massage, art therapy, theatre therapy, emotional freedom techniques and other hands-on bodywork are attracting billions of pounds from individuals willing to pay for such treatments, but they are also starting to attract health insurance funding and even NHS funding in the UK or the equivalent public sector funding body in other countries. When searching for an insurance policy for my new dog recently I was fascinated to see that most animal insurance now covers complementary therapies in addition to traditional veterinary bills!

The more speculative parts of the new paradigm that I have presented are from Era III medicine. Many traditional shamanic techniques fall into this category, as is healing achieved while in an altered state of consciousness, information downloaded from the inforealm[184] and the energies we can meet with and communicate there, and in some cases connection and communication in the inforealm with past lives or the ancestors.

## Recommendations for action

If society more widely is to move to a new paradigm of self-responsibility, using the full implications of the bodymind and possibly also of the inforealm, then there are a number of

184 to recap, the inforealm is the holographic form of the cosmos where information is stored nonlocally as wave functions in nonlocal space. It is also known as physical space-time, hyperspace, the holofield, the implicate order, the Akashic field, the knowing field or simply the field.

clear, practical steps that should be implemented as rapidly as possible and this is my plea to the decision-makers and those who allocate funding for health and education.

1. Let's teach our children about the impact of stress on the body and also about limbic attractors and the possibilities of neuroplasticity, myelination and epigenetics. They need to know that change in their lives and their ways of thinking and living are possible and that we can use mindfulness and other techniques to control our reactions to events, to build new neural pathways that serve us well and open up opportunities to step into our power and potential, no matter how dire the circumstances in which we find ourselves.

   Such a programme is being introduced by Bessel Van Der Kolk and his colleagues in the United States through the National Child Traumatic Stress Network. His team has developed comprehensive programmes for children and adolescents that they are implementing in schools across the country, providing children, teachers and other care providers with a toolbox of ways to take charge of their emotional reactions. As he reports in *The Body Keeps the Score*: *Our NCTSN programs are working: Kids become less anxious and emotionally reactive and are less aggressive or withdrawn; they get along better and their school performance improves; their attention deficit, hyperactivity, and 'oppositional defiant' problems decrease; and parents report that their children are sleeping better.*[185]

   Numerous publications regarding the importance and benefits of working with children and an array of practical methodologies are available on the NCTSN website.[186]

---

185 Van Der Kolk, Bessel. 2014. *The Body keeps the Score: Mind, Brain and Body in the Transformation of Trauma* p.356 USA: Viking Penguin

186 http://www.nctsn.org/resources/topics/treatments-that-work/promising-practices#q4

2. In a two-part effort to heal causes and not treat symptoms, let's make sure trauma and damage in pregnancy and early childhood are avoided as much as possible. This could be built into sex education in schools, through teaching children about the impact of their actions (toxins/diet/emotions) during pregnancy on the foetus. And scarce resources should be spent on treating problems as early as possible with a much greater emphasis on pregnant women (and their partners) and young children.

   What is becoming increasingly evident is that problems very often start early in life and in the current system, by the time people qualify for help, the traumas they have suffered from (sexual, physical, mental or emotional) may be well engrained in the mind and the body. Early prevention if possible or intervention if necessary would save money in the long run although it would stretch limited resources in the short run. Such action is unfortunately the solution that politicians tend to shy away from, as their attention span tends to be the period of time they are elected to power.
3. Let's teach our medical students about the prevalence and impact of stress and trauma, the mind-body connections and the connections between the brain, mind and consciousness. They need to be aware of the benefits to society of healing the root causes of disease through neuroplasticity and epigenetics, and not focus so heavily on just curing symptoms through physical interventions and pharmacology.

   They should be taught about the benefits of an integrated healthcare approach and of encouraging autonomy rather than dependency through all the factors identified as relevant to our health, such as nutrition, exercise, meditation, avoidance of toxic products in our homes and most importantly of all, belonging to a supportive community, which increasingly often may be outside our family system.

It would be beneficial if all clinicians from any discipline were taught about the placebo/nocebo impact their words can have and the extent to which it is important to work in partnership with their patients, treating them as the human beings that they are and not objectifying them from positions of authority.

There are steps being taken in this direction. In the UK there is the British College of Integrative Medicine[187] and in the USA a well-established Integrative Medicine training programme in available at the University of Arizona.[188] But much more needs to be done. These programmes should be the norm, not the exception.

4. Let's practise as well as teach integrated healthcare. Medical centres offering the full range of integrated health facilities need to be widely available with alternative therapies (which are still too often available only to those able and willing to pay privately), being much more generously funded.

   I repeat here that although this would appear to increase the health budget initially, in the long term it would reduce the budget considerably. The focus would be on prevention followed by real healing of causes, not curing symptoms via constant medication. The NHS in England alone spent £15.5 billion on medicines in 2014/15.[189] And it is in the interests of the pharmaceutical companies to keep people dependent, that is using medications indefinitely to keep symptoms under control.

---

187 http://www.integrativemedicine.uk.com/index.php

188 https://integrativemedicine.arizona.edu/education/imr.html

189 http://www.pharmaceutical-journal.com/news-and-analysis/news/nhs-drug-spending-rises-by-8-to-155bn-in-england/20200096.article

According to the Health and Safety Executive, in 2014/15, 9.9 million working days were lost to work-related stress, anxiety and depression[190] at an estimated cost of £6.5 billion.[191] The OECD estimates that mental health problems cost the UK £70 to £100 billion each year.[192] Treating problems at their source, as early as possible, and giving people the tools they need to be empowered has the potential to cut both these human casualties and financial costs significantly, and widespread integrated healthcare is the way to put people at the centre of their own healthcare.

The Royal London Hospital for Integrated Medicine is one example of the new paradigm in the UK, whose full range of services can be viewed on its website.[193] In the USA there are a number of centres now offering a fully integrated healthcare service, such as Duke Integrative Medicine[194] and the Osher Centre for Integrative Medicine.[195] Kaiser Permanente is one of the USA's largest not-for-profit health insurance plans, serving more than 10.6 million members, and it is embracing complementary health enthusiastically because that is what its members want, it's cheaper and more effective.[196]

5. Let's train our talking psychotherapists working with

---

190 http://www.hse.gov.uk/statistics/causdis/stress/

191 http://recruitmentbuzz.co.uk/work-related-stress-costs-uk-economy-nearly-6-5bn-each-year/

192 http://www.oecd.org/els/emp/MentalHealthWork-UnitedKingdom-AssessmentRecommendations.pdf

193 http://www.uclh.nhs.uk/ourservices/servicea-z/intmed/pages/home.aspx

194 https://www.dukeintegrativemedicine.org/about/

195 http://www.osher.ucsf.edu/

196 https://healthy.kaiserpermanente.org/health/care/!ut/p/a0FchBCsMgEEDRs-QAw0QNknYnbecKre4GO6SCmiCSXr928-EDPjCUPIMG_e0V87jfZTapV05j9bhp0CRd4qpCj4xYDgab4XR1x0ix4_8jVtPMQv61eqFbsYBEc2g1GMGR6SBILncjSVnF41HKevXTdMPr8pP7g!!/

the brain to also understand and use the links between mind and body, left- and right-brain. Instead of being prohibited from physical contact with clients they should be encouraged to respectfully access the cellular memories that are held in the body.

There is more and more evidence that the most long-lasting, successful therapies, which truly engage the client in change, are emotionally and empathically focused, right-brain to right-brain, not verbal, left-brain to left-brain, and the work of McGilchrist, Levine, Van Der Kolk and many others has demonstrated the connection between the right-brain and the physical body. The left-brain can acknowledge the story of our traumas, but our unconscious reactions in new situations are programmed from the body. To become more autonomous we need to reprogramme our reactions, which can only take place through working directly with the body and allowing the memories which are stored there to be accessed, acknowledged and released safely.

6. Let's give proper funding to explore the potential of working with altered states of consciousness, so that people can have the opportunity to experience expanded consciousness and spiritual connection in a safe setting. We already have a growing range of meditation centres, ecstatic dance teachers and holotropic breathwork teachers. These various outlets provide the right environment for many to reach an altered state of consciousness in a safe space, but I also strongly advocate the funding and provision of centres for the monitored use of hallucinogenics in a ceremonial setting, accompanied by appropriate professional follow up if necessary.

The previously mentioned Heffter Institute and Beckley Foundation provide centres for hallucinogenic research in the USA and the UK respectively. The former has published highly encouraging studies regarding the efficacy of psilocybin for helping to treat cancer-related anxiety and depression,[197] addiction,[198] and depression.[199] The latter has published an impressive array of results regarding the efficacy of LSD, psilocybin and MDMA for depression, anxiety, addiction and PTSD, the use of cannabinoids in the treatment of brain cancer and the benefit of LSD for cluster headaches.[200] Much more research needs to be done but the evidence base that is building suggests that it would be beneficial for many patients suffering from what have been seen as intractable illnesses to have such treatments much more widely available.

## Difficulties

If all the above recommendations were to be adopted, then the healthcare industry and the health of society could be revolutionised over a decade. I do recognise however that there are huge obstacles to overcome. Not only are there vested interests held by those in positions of power and control, including the pharmaceutical companies. There are also many people who are currently reluctant to step into autonomy.

Most people are already aware that they would benefit from a regular exercise programme, avoiding excessive amounts of fat and sugar, quitting smoking and drinking, engaging in a meditation practice and all the other things that constitute healthy living. But they don't take these actions for all sorts of conscious and unconscious reasons.

It can be much easier to be a victim than to be autonomous.

197 https://heffter.org/cancer-distress/
198 https://heffter.org/addiction/
199 https://heffter.org/neuroscience-research/
200 http://beckleyfoundation.org/science/clinical-therapeutic-actions/

Our society has encouraged the litigious attitude of 'it's not my fault'. We want quick fixes and instant gratification, like the pill or surgery that will make us lose 20 kilos overnight, that will make us feel happy and fulfilled without any effort of our own.

If it is to succeed, the new paradigm needs to be able to demonstrate to people that autonomy is worth the effort. Some of this evidence is coming from the work being done with the terminally ill such as that reported in *Being Mortal: Illness, Medicine and What Matters in the End*[201] where Atul Gawande raises interesting questions about autonomy. He describes how what is emerging from the hospice movement is that what really matters to people as they approach their death is that they have choice and connection with their loved ones, whereas the existing hospital system is often about control and isolation, quantity rather than quality of life, doctors rather than patients making the decisions.

Do we want to live in a nanny state where we hand over responsibility and allow others to decide what is good for us and our loved ones, or do we want to live in a society where we have self-responsibility and live with the actions of our choices?

The measures I am suggesting would allow people to be seen and heard and offered choice and connection on many levels. The results from hospice programmes, meditation studies, school programmes and scientific journals and organisations investigating integrated medicine all tend to show that participants in the new paradigm live longer, with less pain and fewer hospital visits; they spend less of their own or the taxpayer's money, and they report being happier and more at peace with themselves and the world. These are the stories that need to be spread. These are the benefits of

201 Gawande. Atul, 2015. *Illness: Medicine and What Matters In The End* London, UK: Wellcome Collection and Profile Books Ltd.

autonomy that everyone needs to hear about.

The first step out of victimhood is often the hardest. That is why we need to build a culture where there is early intervention in trauma with universal access to supportive therapists and possibly with the use of mind-expanding psychedelics, which may be the quickest and most effective way of opening some people to the possibility and the benefits of autonomy and of connection to a consciousness outside their own inner egos.

Only through such measures can we hope to bring about a new nonlocal healthcare paradigm and a healthier society based on self-awareness and autonomy within our daily lives, but also based on the recognition that although we are in many ways alone, we also have connection to the whole universe on a much wider level than we may previously have recognised.

**Metaphysical musings**

I know that no matter how much you read, no matter the mountain of evidence I provide you with, if you are sceptical of the inforealm and Era III healings the only thing that will truly change your mind will be a personal experience outside of your current belief system. One cannot have an opinion unless one has done the research and in this matter the research can only be experiential, not theoretical. I hope that this book might encourage you to experiment, to step outside your comfort zone, to admit that we don't know what we don't know.

I have been blessed to be able to travel the world and work with a great variety of teachers, enabling me to experience a vast range of altered states of consciousness. While I am in those altered states, the experiences I have all seem totally real, just as real as sitting here tapping away on my computer.

In my work almost every day I journey into the inforealm for clients and the information I receive appears to be highly relevant to them and give them great insight and healing. I don't really understand how this miracle of nonlocal communication is possible and why I (and indeed all human beings) have been gifted with the ability to connect or resonate with the nonlocal information field. All I know from a really practical point of view is that 'it works'.

Yet when I think about it, and try to come up with a full and convincing explanation of how I do it, the answer reverts back to Socrates, who said: *The only true wisdom is in knowing you know nothing.* At this time in our evolution, probably the most pragmatic approach is to acknowledge that we don't fully understand how it works, but we can accept from the physical, real-time evidence that it does.

My well-educated left-brain however has always wanted the understanding as well as the evidence, and that is why I have written my books: to spread the extensive evidence that is emerging and the limited understanding I am achieving.

The closest to a metaphysical model that I can derive from my knowledge at this moment in time is that all living things throughout the cosmos have an energetic vibration. Within our solar system there is a range of resonance for everything that is based on DNA. In our normal waking consciousness we only experience a limited range of frequencies through our sight, hearing, etc. But when we enter an altered state of consciousness we open up to accessing a wider range outside our normal frequencies of capability. It's like seeing outside the normal visual spectrum of light to the higher and lower spectrums.

As suggested in Chapter 9, the way we do this may be via our RNA and non-coding DNA, which is biochemically active and does serve some useful function; indeed the latest research shows that it appears among other things to act as the regulation mechanism for the action of our genes. I get the sense that we can absorb things possibly through the wrapping or unwrapping of sections of the non-coding DNA and/or through cosmic quantum tunnelling within our DNA, which is a step beyond epigenetics.

With this type of model, access to a life-review after death seems relatively easy. Nonlocally in the holographic universe we are capable of accessing everything and resonance with our own recent transmissions into the field will be fairly strong as we are most coherent with our own energetic vibration. Similarly accessing information from our own past lives seems to be a simple extension of this. If, as seems likely and has been speculated by others, each family system, tribe, religion and race also has its own specific frequency of transmission, then accessing those we are or have been close to should also be relatively easy.

Moving out beyond this coherent range of resonance with our immediate tribes, resonance from the archetypical energies known as angels, spirit guides, earth-keepers or animal guides seem to be potentially explicable as they are energies or entities that are within the resonance of our solar system or at a certain range of vibration within the nonlocal field. Thus when we are in expanded states of consciousness we can experience and contact them.

So my own personal metaphysics at this moment are:

- We are all inter-connected, each being drops in the ocean of the cosmic energy field.
- If we choose to we are capable of engaging and communicating with aspects of the all-knowing and entangled nonlocal consciousness. These energies from other dimensions most likely take forms, or we imagine them with forms that are familiar to us, so they may appear to communicate with us as spirit guides, angels,

animal guides, plant spirits, aliens etc. We see a form that we believe in.

- We can use the knowledge that we obtain from the inforealm to create much healthier and happier lives in these bodies.
- We need to be careful about what we do and say in this lifetime as death is not the end of our individual consciousness and we do reap what we sow.
- We are capable of much, much more than we are often conditioned to believe, and we can expand our beliefs with simple physical, mental and emotional reconditioning.

That leaves open the question that I raised in Chapter 6 regarding whether the cosmic field of consciousness contains moral values? And does it care about us? Furthermore, are we creators of our own individual realities because we are so much more powerful than we believe or because there is no greater Creator in charge and hence as drops of the cosmic consciousness we are truly autonomous beyond our wildest imaginings?

I know I don't know!

But I do know my actions don't depend on knowing. My actions can be based on the experiential evidence of what works to give people healthier, happier lives and I hope that by reading this book you will have been encouraged to explore different modalities of healing and expanded states of consciousness, so that you may draw your own conclusions based on your own direct experiences.

# APPENDIX 1

## Some of the Q'ero shamanic practices that I use with clients and their parallels with modern psychotherapy and trauma therapy

### Cleansing

One of the most common shamanic services is to cleanse heavy energy attached to clients, which may have been sent (more or less intentionally) in the form of bad thoughts or curses, by family members, colleagues, or people that perceive they have been wronged in some way. This heavy energy may also be something that the clients have absorbed from others around them in their lives. Or it may be something they have created by their own actions.

As I have already noted, in shamanic communities there is a clear distinction between the curanderos and the brujos – the healers and the sorcerers, and in many societies today people still unfortunately go to the latter when they wish ill on another. Patients from these cultures totally believe in the power of the witch doctor or shaman to harm them, and as a result of that belief they react accordingly when they know someone in the community or family has been to see the brujo to ask for something bad to happen to them. Sometimes they just have an unexplained bad feeling or sickness so they suspect a 'psychic dagger' is embedded in their energy field, even if they don't necessarily know its source.

The possibility of doing harm through our thoughts or our wishes is less accepted in Western culture, but all the work in previous chapters about our ability to transmit and download to and from the inforealm suggests it is possible. The implication is that we all need to be really careful what we say and think about others and indeed most of us have likely stepped into sorcery at some point, perhaps without real intention, from the unthinking or unconscious mind.

I have been taught that as soon as we talk about someone else behind his or her back, wishing them ill or judging them, we are engaging in a form of sorcery. If you listen to gossip you are just as guilty as the person who is doing the gossiping, for you are fuelling those negative statements and intentions. As soon as you recognise the ripples every thought and every action has in the inforealm, you are capable of interfering with others, hurting them through what are known in shamanism as psychic daggers, poisoned darts or black magic (and often labelled in the Judeo-Christian traditions as curses). We send psychic daggers when we say or even think things like *I hate that stupid bastard. I hope he suffers like he has made me suffer!* Or, *How dare she dump me, she's such an arrogant bitch. I hope her next boyfriend dumps her!* This energy vibrates into the inforealm where it is stored and then can be picked up and taken into the recipient's energy field leading to genuine distress. It is particularly likely to resonate coherently when the two people are still connected by the energy cords that grow within family entanglements or close relationships, romantic or professional.

In a cleansing process or ceremony, the shamanic practitioner checks for where psychic daggers or heavy energy may be embedded in the patient's energy field and then removes them, cleansing the area with smoke, incense, sound or herbal remedies, then sealing the area with white light.

Whether you believe the client's perceived psychic attack is real or not, I have already described the power of our beliefs to impact our health. So as you read this, even if you think it is purely placebo, the impact on the client of the curandero removing daggers from their system and giving them protection tools to use in the future cannot be ignored. If the patient doesn't believe in the possibility of such an attack in the first place, the placebo effect of removing a psychic dagger or curse should of course theoretically be reduced.

At a deeper energetic level it has been widely researched and documented that, when shamanic practitioners do this work, the other person who is sending the negative thoughts and bad wishes also seems to feel the change in how the client is interacting with them, even although they are not consciously aware that the cleansing work is being done.

On a personal level, I do believe in the power of the psychic attack, having also felt as if people were sending me negative thoughts or attempting to drain my energy at different times. Indeed I think most of us have felt at some time in our lives that someone is out to get us or is sending us bad luck. I have felt a difference when that negative energy has been removed by a shaman or that cord to someone else allowing them to take energy from me has been cut. Maybe I was simply reacting positively to a treatment for something that was never there, that wasn't real, but when I felt as if I had been cleansed of a psychic attack I can definitely report that I regained my strength and vitality. That much was real and beneficial.

If you have a difficult time accepting this then consider it from the opposite point of view. Do you believe in the power of prayer, of sending good wishes, good luck or forgiveness? That is effective exactly because of the same sort of energetic transmission which can have a profound and tangible effect, whether the recipient is present and aware of your words and thoughts or not.

**Case Study Client N**

Client N is from South America and feels there have been a lot of poison darts sent to her out of jealousy. She has a regular meditation practice and a strong spiritual belief but she feels anything good she tries to achieve is blocked.

I test for psychic daggers using my pendulum which turns clockwise if the energy is good, anti-clockwise if the energy is negative and hangs completely still if there is a total blockage. It seems as if there are what I can visualise as nails through both her feet, preventing her from moving forward. She instantly recognises that as being from her family. I remove those energetically and visualise sealing her feet with white light to fill the holes where the negative energy was stuck with balanced, positive energy.

She feels very relieved and grateful and ready to move forward. The next time I see her she tells me she had felt much better until she decided to go home to South America to visit relatives. She then suffered from a succession of difficulties which she is convinced once again come from someone in the family wishing her ill.

I do some further cleansing and then we do work with the ancestors. I drum and ask her to call in whatever ancestor was excluded from the system, who needs to be seen and acknowledged. Immediately she thinks of one of her grandmothers who passes on several messages to the client and the grandmother says she is pleased to have been seen and her suffering acknowledged.

We then call in her grandfather who brings lots of anger

with him. She is very surprised that he comes because no-one ever talks about him, she has never thought about him, she would never have considered him! He tells her that there are many secrets in the family and part of the story seems to emerge to her. We acknowledge his place as father to the many children he had and then as grandfather to all their children. She feels that healing in the family may finally start.

This is a perfect example of the kind of work we also do in constellations, when someone who did huge harm within the family is ostracised and forgotten and loses their place in the system. But somehow they continue to have an impact until their story is acknowledged and they are seen and heard and given their place once again.

## Soul retrieval

Another service common to many shamanic traditions is to help the client retrieve a part of their soul or their essence that they have lost. This work seems to fit in very closely with the theory underlying much of modern trauma therapy, which suggests that traumatic dissociation results in a split of the psyche into three parts: the traumatised self, the survival self and the healthy self.[202] The healthy self aspires to integration and wholeness. The survival self does everything it can to keep the traumatised part safe, which may mean refusing to look at or acknowledge the trauma, which is suppressed into the unconscious. This survival self creates a way of living which does help us to get by in the world, but it also keeps us split and stuck in the old belief system.

202 Ruppert, Franz. 2012. *Symbiosis & Autonomy: Symbiotic Trauma and Love Beyond Entanglements*. Steyning, UK: Green Balloon Publishing

In a soul retrieval session the first thing is for the shaman and the client to identify the key phrase that is keeping the client stuck. This is frequently something like 'I'm not good enough', 'no-one loves me', 'I always get abandoned' or 'I am afraid to speak my truth'. Then the shaman and the client together have to decide who is going to journey into the inforealm in the first part of the work. Either the shaman can journey on behalf of the client, or they can lead the client on their own journey. Some clients want to do their own journey, and it may seem more obvious that they should journey for themselves. However, particularly if they are very embroiled in their story or have done a lot of work on themselves already, they may be too stuck in the existing neural pathways to journey effectively. They will see what they expect to see.

In these cases it can be more effective for the shaman to journey cleanly, without preconceptions or expectations and without knowing too much of the story. It is also useful to journey on behalf of clients who are afraid they won't be able to see anything – that may be their truth. They may not at this time be able to access the necessary brainwave state to download the information that is stored and available in the inforealm.

In the way I do this process of soul retrieval, the client then lies on a therapy table and then I hold their head with one hand to connect to them and start to drum with the other hand as the journey begins, into the belly of the earth, to the underworld of the unconscious mind. After meeting the guardian of the underworld, first we visit the cave of the original wound, then the cave of the contract made at the time of this wounding in order to survive, then the cave of the lost soul part (the part that was split off at the time of the wounding in order to be safe) and then the cave holding a gift with qualities that would help in the client's life right now. On the way back from the journey we invite in a creature with qualities that would be of assistance at this time.

This journey is relatively quick. It is simply to receive the archetypal words and images that present themselves, not to get involved in understanding the story. That comes in the second part of the work, after the journey, when the client visits and works with all the elements that have been seen, to gain a greater awareness with the intention of bringing about transformation going forward. And of course even if I have journeyed on behalf of the client, it is entirely up to them in the second part of the process to interpret the information received.

To enter the second part of the process the client places stones on the floor to represent the different elements: the core wound, the contract, the lost part, the gift and the creature. Then the client is invited to stand into each of these places in turn, knowing that they can go back as often as necessary to work with each element. They are standing in 'the field', sending out a request to the inforealm to access and download the story of each part, trusting what comes. Sometimes people ask if it is just their imagination? My response is that we have very fertile imaginations but a particular image or story has presented itself out of the millions we could have conjured up. Trust that there has been a resonance of some kind which has brought that particular wave pattern into our conscious awareness.

What qualities does the gift represent? What are the qualities of the creature? How could these be of assistance at this time? If they like the qualities then they imagine those being available to assist them as we move on to visit the core wound, which can be very emotional and even frightening for the client. When the client is visiting the core wound the shaman needs to be able to continue holding the space, ensuring the client feels safe in doing this difficult work.

They may need to ask very simple questions such as what is happening there? Why is that person there? What have they done? Can you see what happened to them before? Is there anything they want to say? Is there anything you want to say to them? Some clients will get images very quickly and easily and some really start to embody the scene presented to them, crying, shaking, reacting in horror and many other potential emotions.

As we do this it is really important to recognise that the core wound is not necessarily the result of the client suffering as a victim. They may perceive in the cave of the core wound that their trauma and splitting come from a time when they were the perpetrator. This can be extremely difficult for some clients to cope with. It brings up guilt and remorse.

Having seen the core wound, the client visits the contract that they wrote with life at the time of this wounding in order to be safe. The first intention underpinning the soul retrieval work is to re-write the contract from this day forward. Not because the old contract was wrong in any way. The client wrote it at a time in the past when they had been traumatised and it was necessary to protect them. But it almost definitely will no longer serve them well today. By holding onto it, it becomes a limiting belief that continues to manifest in their lives. To change the pattern they need to release the limiting belief. They need to re-write the contract. So the shaman asks, what is the contract that the client would like from this day forward?

The client then goes on to visit the lost soul part as the second intention of the soul retrieval work is to reunite this part, which was split off within our psyche for its protection. Once again what qualities does this image represent to the client? Would they like it back in their life? Is it willing to come back and if so is there any conditionality about it returning?

Usually, having visited with all the other elements, we

then go back to the place of the contract and review the client's initial suggestion for their new contract. In particular, if they are bringing the lost soul part with them, how does it feel about the new contract? Often the lost soul part will want a hand in re-writing the contract in a way that serves it and helps it to feel recognised and accepted.

The third part of the work is client homework! We have received the necessary information from the inforealm, letting us see that which is usually hidden by our survivor personality in order to keep us safe. But we need to work with this information consciously to re-integrate the lost part into our psyches and manifest the new contract in our everyday lives. Different people like to do this work in different ways and as far as I am concerned it is what resonates with the client that matters. For instance, if clients have a meditation practice, the new contract can be used as a mantra each day and then they can meditate for a few minutes on the qualities of the animal, the qualities of the gift and the qualities/voice of the retrieved soul part. Other people like to write or draw so they may choose to use the contract as an affirmation each day, or they may like to draw pictures for their wall of the different elements, use elements as a computer screen saver, or even text themselves the new contract a number of times each day!

What is important is to work with the information with as much attention and intention as possible until the new neural pathways, the new ways of being, are really embedded into the physical brain. To achieve this integration of the lost part, try to include it and embrace it in your life consciously. Dialogue with it. What would it like to do today? If there is a choice to be made, what does it want to do? The gift and the creature give us archetypal representations of qualities that may help us as we move to a new way of being and living. The ritual of picturing them in our lives, working with us, gives us an outside resource as we re-integrate a very wounded and delicate part of ourselves that may have been split off for decades (or even hundreds of years if the core wound is being carried in the energy field from a previous lifetime).

The direct parallels with the modern models of trauma seem obvious. The old contract was written by the survival part of the psyche to keep us safe, but it may no longer serve us. To recognise that however we need to see the core wound and understand why we wrote that contract in the first place, or in other words, its source. Then having acknowledged it, we can recognise that we are autonomous and hence free to write a new contract that serves us better at this current time and place.

The lost soul part is related to the traumatised self, the part that we split off to keep it safe. Its qualities, which are likely to have been absent from our lives as they were perceived to put us in danger, are what we can reclaim and integrate in a soul retrieval, and frequently these are qualities such as innocence, joy, beauty, or a voice.

**Case Study Client O**

Client O is a psychotherapist so has done a lot of talking therapy and personal work, but she still suffers from low self-esteem and a profound social anxiety. She feels a lack of purpose and life seems meaningless. The limiting belief that we decide to journey for is 'I'm scared to be a magnificent woman.'

I journey for her as she knows her own stories only too well. The core wound is a woman being burned at the stake after being judged by other women. The contract she wrote with life as a result at the time of that wounding was 'It's not safe to stand out'. The lost part is a woman researching and studying and writing. The gift is a piece of jewellery with beautiful gems and the power creature is a bear.

She comes up with a new contract: 'I am a peaceful thinker who can protect and look after myself.' The lost part brings a number of qualities including achieving goals, determination and fulfilling her potential. The gift connects her with the ancestors and is beautiful and elegant. The bear is protective but not aggressive, and is reliable and consistent. She feels it will really help her to stand her ground.

The lost part loves the new contract and she feels that the session has really helped to reinforce in a very concrete way things that she knew at some level already but had not put together. She now feels she has a set of tools that she can use going forward to step into her potential.

This demonstrates how working in the energy field can connect parts of the jigsaw in a very quick and direct way, giving clients tools to work with on a daily basis that will help them to manifest change in their lives.

## Releasing limiting beliefs

Another service is to help the client to release limiting beliefs that they have taken in as a result of societal conditioning. This is appropriate if clients have a repeating pattern in their lives or feel that they are blocked or stuck, usually without knowing the source of their self-sabotaging behaviour.

To get to the source of the conditioning, perhaps the core trauma that formed the neural attractor pathways, it seems necessary to get out of the head and the known story (or at least the left-brain) and into the body (more closely associated with the right-brain). In psychotherapy or shamanic healing this is known as shadow work.

To help with this I ask the client to lie on my therapy

table and I go to their head and hold under the occiput, at the limbic brain centre, asking them to breathe in deeply through the nose and out through the mouth. With the in-breath I ask them to acknowledge the times they have suffered from this issue and with the out-breath I ask them to imagine that suffering leaving from the cells and from the energy field along with the breath. They continue to do this, gradually going back in time, allowing feelings and memories of their suffering to arise from the body and the energy field.

The intention is for the client to track back in time to the source of the limiting belief that is keeping them stuck, which may mean facing a trauma that has been deeply buried in the unconscious. As long as they are in their left-brain, the survivor personality may try its best to prevent them from seeing this, and the shamanic practitioner or bodywork therapist needs to be able to hold a safe enough space for the client to enter an altered state of consciousness such that the information that will be of assistance to them can be downloaded from the intuition or the inforealm to the right-brain.

Seeing the core wound, the source of a limiting belief, often allows us to release it. The process may show us that what we were conditioned to believe is not the truth and that the person who told us that we were not good enough, were ugly, worthless or stupid, was not acting from love or honesty, but from their own fear, neediness, damage or desire to have power and control. Just this observation often opens the door for us to behave in a different way from this moment forward. The limbic attractors can be reset.

Other times we see that we adopted the belief of someone else to try to please them or make them feel better, but it is not our own truth. It belongs to them, not to us. This acknowledgement allows us to let this belief go and instead honour our own truth and path in life.

When the process of releasing the blockage or limiting belief appears to be complete, I ask for light energy to come in from the inforealm to replenish and re-balance the client and their system. Then I hold the client under the lumbar spine and the heart centre, allowing them to absorb the information and reprogramming that has taken place as a result of our interaction with the external consciousness into the left-brain and the physical body.

**Case Study Client P**

Client P wants to resolve a current relationship situation and heal wounds from the past that she feels are preventing her from progressing in her life. Non-communication is a repeating pattern that she is aware of and we work with the limiting belief 'I don't deserve very much.'

She feels that belief in her heart which is tight and dark and heavy. As I hold her head and she breathes back and back to the source of her limiting belief, she remembers a time when she didn't get good grades at school and her father told her it was because she didn't deserve them. As an adult now I ask what she would like to say to her father. 'I do deserve them, and I deserve love and appreciation and good things.' Her father is dead now and she feels that from where he is now he is sorry for the way he treated her.

From her heart she feels she is warm, loving, open and deserves goodness and kindness and love. It is great for her head to hear that and for her voice to say that. She knows it is true.

We do some further bodywork and her throat and heart say she has not had any boundaries and has been prepared to settle for crumbs. It's not good enough! She realises she needs to communicate what she needs and deserves.

At the end of the session she is resolved to go home and talk to her partner as it is time for their path to be decided.

This shows how these techniques can quickly unlock memories that have been repressed for many years, and also lead to a deep acknowledgement that change is possible.

## Conscious dying or death and rebirth within life

One more long established shamanic practice which is being increasingly recognised and adopted throughout the medical profession is work with the dying, to help people to die more consciously and in a more healed (although not cured) state. Elizabeth Kubler-Ross is one of the most famous of the doctors who paved the way to the modern work with the dying in many hospices and two of her fantastic books are *On Death and Dying*[203] and *On Life After Death.*[204]

In the foreword to the latter, Caroline Myss writes: *Not speaking about death does not, in fact, calm the patient. The truth is the patient knows he or she is dying through the natural knowledge of the soul. To not speak about this process is to deny the human being the essential need to complete unfinished business by collecting the fragments of the soul that long to come together before the soul is called home. It is that completion that ultimately brings the soul peace and calm, making it ready to release itself from this earthly life. And completion requires open dialogue with friends, family members, business associates, and even adversaries.*[205]

Alberto Villoldo's Four Winds School of Healing the

---

203 Kubler-Ross, Elizabeth, Dr. 1969. *On Death & Dying*. New York, NY, USA: Scribner, Simon & Schuster

204 Kubler-Ross, Elizabeth, Dr. 2 Rev Ed. 2008. *On Life After Death* Berkeley, CA, USA: Celestial Arts

205 Myss, Caroline. Forward pp viii–ix in Kubler-Ross, Elizabeth, Dr. 2 Rev Ed. 2008. *On Life After Death* Berkeley, CA, USA: Celestial Arts

Light Body helps to run a website of practitioners available to assist those nearing the end of their lives in the current physical body to die more consciously.[206] There is also a way of using this process within life when someone wants to have a metaphorical death and rebirth, when they want to completely let go of the past and bring in a new beginning.

In this process the death rites are for those people who want to work in 'ayni' or right relationship. Within their own personal growth and development they are at a place of recognising that they start each day anew and want to leave nothing unfinished at the end of each day. For who knows, that night they may die.

When it is a death and rebirth process within the current physical body, the intention is to go through the death experience, saying goodbye to everything we have as if we are going on the journey beyond death today. We want to ensure there is nothing left undone, that could have been said, could have been acknowledged, could have been healed.

In this process the client lies on the bed and the shaman calls in the energies of anyone that the client would like to speak to before passing on. These may be from among the living or the dead. When I conduct this process the client says to each of those called in whatever needs to be said to heal any hurt or wounds before they die, to voice anything they have never been able to voice in life, to tell them anything they have never dared to say or tell.

As shaman within this process I sit in the knowing field, in the place of the person being spoken to and I may get very strong emotions and responses coming from the inforealm. If that happens then I tell the client, 'as I am representing this person, I am feeling…', or 'representing this person, I want to say to you…'. I allow the dialogue to continue as long as

206 http://www.dyingconsciously.org

necessary with each person, then I come back to myself and ask the client who they want to call in next, so that I can step into that next role.

After everyone that the client wants to talk to has been addressed, I count down the client's breath to their death from this current body, then invite the client's energetic aura to detach from the physical body to receive cleansing in the inforealm from those whose wisdom, knowledge and experience is greater than my own. After a couple of minutes, because it is an exercise during life rather than real physical death, I call the cleansed energy body back and ensure that it is reconnected to the physical body.

The intention is that, were the client to die immediately after doing this work, this life would be at peace. I truly believe this work is not just for the client undergoing the session, but for the people they call into the room to connect with and set things right with and for the lineage, both backwards and forwards. This is true healing in the inforealm, outside conventional space and time.

Having gone through death, the next part of the exercise is rebirth where the client considers what they want to manifest in the future, from this moment onwards. To assist with this I hold each of the lower four chakras in turn, the root, sacral chakra, solar plexus and heart. I encourage the client to feel what they want to bring into their lives from each of these perspectives, each associated with a power animal and connected with the earth, their emotions, their life's purpose and their soul's purpose. After the feeling and the images and the intentions have bubbled up at each chakra we start at the root again and I repeat what the client wished for, as they themselves hold each chakra in turn, allowing that new way of being, the information they have received from the inforealm, to sink into the physical body from the energetic field.

This proves to be a profound and life-changing exercise for

most of the people I have been honoured to have shared this work with and ideally it is followed up by people making sure there is nothing left undone each day of their lives henceforth.

For those who are actually dying, this process allows completion, closure and potentially very deep healing of long-standing rifts within the family prior to the person's death, but without the judgmental aspects of The Last Confession carried out within the Catholic Church which assumes that all that needs to be heard is our list of sins.

**Case Study Client Q**

Client Q is a complementary therapist who has done a lot of personal work. She was abused as a child and now has addiction and self-sabotaging issues. After several other sessions we do a death and rebirth within life to try to clear out the old patterning and bring in a new way of being. During the death process she calls in a number of people, including her parents, her brother, several ex-partners, her abuser, her grandmother. After that I do the death spiral, unwinding the energy body and releasing it for cleansing before bringing it back and re-attaching it.

Looking forward from this day, from the root she would like to bring in love, feeling safe in her own house, having stability and feeling financially secure. From the second chakra she would like to step into her creativity and attract a partner. From the third chakra she would like to say yes to joy, happiness, self-confidence and a sense of self-worth. From the fourth chakra she would like to open her heart, travel more and connect with eagle.

This is a good example of complete closure to an old way of being, with an array of positive affirmations for the future.

## Impact

In shamanic healing sessions the therapist often knows very little about the client's background. The key is to focus on the core wounds that are keeping the client stuck, or energetic interference that is harming the client.

By moving the session quickly into the physical and energetic bodies as the client lies on a therapy table, the left-brain does not get a chance to repeat and get stuck in its story. Shamans don't collude with stories and limiting beliefs, they work instead to change perceptual states and beliefs. Rattling and drumming can be used to assist in journeying to the inforealm by disrupting the left-brain and helping to engage the right-brain. Breathwork can be used to assist the client to get deeply in touch with the body and not just the brain. Rocks can be used as physical representations of energy blockages and burdens, along with other props such as rolled up blankets to represent dead bodies, small cushions to represent the inner child and so on.

Having done thousands of shamanic healing sessions with hundreds of clients over a decade, what really comes through is:

- how almost everyone is capable of journeying,
- how deep people can go in a very short time, and
- how quickly change can be instilled when we work through the energy field and the body rather than through language and the left-brain.

The people who do not seem to benefit so much are those who are not really ready to do their shadow work and those who unconsciously benefit from holding on to a victim mentality. They may say they want things to be different, but as an extension of our quick-fix society, actually they often just want someone to fix them and their lives without making any effort themselves. That is why I categorically will not take appointments for one person made by another friend or relative, no matter how well intentioned. There is no point in someone coming to see me if they don't want to do their own work.

It is also the case that many of my clients are therapists themselves, or have been in psychotherapy (possibly for many years), or have been on antidepressants. They come for a different approach because these other options have not worked for them. What I hear over and over again is that they feel they have achieved more in one shamanic session than in multiple sessions of other therapies. I believe this is because with shamanic healing we take a much more systemic view of the client and their issues, and allow information to arrive from a huge field, whether you wish to label that the deep internal unconscious mind or the omniscient external cosmic consciousness.

# APPENDIX 2

## Working with the master trees of the Amazonian rainforest and the plant medicines ayahuasca and wachuma

I have described how it is possible to access the inforealm, or the cosmic consciousness, through a variety of practices. In this appendix I want to describe just a couple of my own experiences, journeys and conclusions resulting from drinking plant medicine and working with the master trees of the Amazonian rain forest. I repeat the warnings I gave earlier – these are hallucinogens with a powerful impact and the impact they will have on you personally if you decide to engage with them depends heavily on the set, setting and intention.

I described my first experiences with ayahuasca (DMT) in *Corporate Bitch to Shaman*. Looking back, when I first went to the Ashi Meraya[207] centre in 2010, deep in the Amazonian jungle outside Iquitos, Peru, to work with the Shipibo shamans and their medicine, I had no idea of what I was about to engage

207 Ashi means spiritual and the Merayas were the top level of shamans, the shape-shifters, although according to Maestro Heberto who owns the centre, there are no Merayas anymore. He learned his skill initially from his grandfather, who was possibly the last Meraya.

with and what to expect. Perhaps that was a good thing. Had I realised the power and the possibilities, I might have been afraid to drink Mother Ayahuasca as the brew is known in the jungle.

My second visit was in 2013. On this occasion when I arrived once more at the airport in Iquitos, on my flight from Lima, I was greeted by a huge, complete rainbow right outside the airplane window as we taxied from the runway to the terminal. In the Q'ero shamanic tradition that I primarily work with, the rainbow represents the bridge between the worlds, the four-dimensional world of everyday space-time and the nonlocal world outside conventional space-time, so in my journal I noted, *Thank you, thank you, thank you for the auspicious sign that this is where I am supposed to be for my journeying to continue.*

Ashi Meraya is at least 90 minutes outside Iquitos by moto-rickshaw, the ubiquitous motorcycles with open-air passenger cabins hooked on the back. That is when it is dry and you are able to drive all the way, rather than walking through knee-deep mud for at least part of the journey to reach the destination. On arrival I was delighted to find that they had installed indoor, private bathrooms in each of the jungle cabins, compared with the shared external facilities that I had had to use on my first visit – a huge benefit when one is dealing with the after effects of the plant medicine!

Going to sleep that first night I was reminded of the intensity of the noise of the forest, with a cacophony of sound from the many mammals, birds, insects and amphibians that surround the jungle cabins. And then as it started to rain (as it frequently does, even in 'dry' season) the pounding sound of the raindrops on the corrugated roofs of the cabin added to the realisation that I was truly in the midst of nature, with her huge power well beyond that of us mortals.

It is very important to prepare and purify your body to

allow the plant medicine to work most effectively with you, so as on all occasions when working with ayahuasca, I had already been dieting in preparation for the retreat, which means no salt, sugar, pork or spices and as little fat, dairy or meat as possible – certainly no alcohol or recreational drugs or other pharmaceutical products that might interact with the DMT.[208] At the centre the diet continues to be limited to potatoes, rice, pasta, lots of vegetables, legumes, a little fruit and herbal teas.

In addition, the next day, in preparation for working with the plant medicine I started dieting with the juice from the bark of three of the master trees for three days, accompanied by sweat lodges, leaf and flower baths and smoking the pure tobacco that is known as mapacho, to release toxins from my body and introduce me to the spirits of the various plants and trees that I was going to be working with in ceremony.

I was also re-introduced to the master trees of the jungle that they are fortunate enough to have at Ashi Meraya, including:

**Chullachaqui caspi** (*tovomita*), known as the guardian of the jungle. It helps us to access all the spirits of the forest – the plants and trees but also the little people including elves, sprites and fairies. The local people pray to chullachaqui before undertaking any major venture, such as hunting, building a new house or starting a new project and before working with any other plant medicine you drink a potion made from the

208 Any teacher or centre offering an ayahuasca ceremony without asking if you have been dieting correctly and without asking if you are on any medication should be avoided at all costs. Anti-depressants are one of the main contraindicated medications, as they are frequently based on MAOIs. As the ayahuasca vine itself contains the MAOIs necessary to prevent the breakdown of the DMT from the chacruna leaves in the gut before it reaches the brain, a double dose of MAOIs could allow too much DMT through to the brain.

bark of chullachaqui, to prepare and protect yourself and give you access to the rest of the forest spirits.

**Remo caspi** (*pithecellobium laetum*), known as the tree which allows you to find the rest of the medicinal plants. Shamans diet with remo caspi for at least 6 months, so they can learn to diagnose illness and know what plants to use to heal others.

**Tamamuri** (*Brosimum acutifolium*), known as a feminine tree spirit which will help you to be receptive to spiritual energies. It is a tree of love and connection and grounding.

**Renaco** (*ficus*), known as a feminine tree spirit and a master tree of love. Renaco wants us to be joyful.

**Wimba** (*Ceiba samauma*), known as the father of all trees. It is associated with thunder and lightning. Also the shamans teach that you can learn well or learn badly. The curanderos (healers) and the brujos (sorcerers) both learn from wimba as it is recognised as the most powerful of all the trees but it has twin energies and you can work with either side. It is a very difficult tree to diet with and it requires a lot of discipline as you need to drink or smoke the powdered bark for three months.

What really strikes me every time I go to the jungle is that all the master trees are home to so many other plants and animals, birds and insects. They are a perfect demonstration of symbiosis and the inter-dependence of all living things.

I see how important it is for all of us that the shamans and their knowledge should be kept alive and preserved. These men and women are the wisdom keepers of the forest. They have such connection with the plants and such vast knowledge. They spend their lives in the forest, working with the plants, dieting on the plants, learning all their properties and how to prepare them, alone or in combination, to physiologically heal all sorts of illnesses and disease as well as allowing access at the mental and emotional levels to altered states of consciousness.

All this knowledge would be lost if it were not for these people keeping alive the ancient wisdoms and traditions. The world owes them a lot and it is essential that they and the forests they tend are not swamped and eliminated by modern society.

### Ayahuasca ceremonies

Ahead of any plant medicine ceremony, it is very important to set an intention. The brief descriptions below are snapshots of what has happened to me in a couple of the ceremonies that I have participated in, spanning six years. I have not included all the ceremonies or all the details, just enough I hope to give a flavour of what can emerge.

**Ceremony 1**: My intentions were to surrender to the wisdom, knowledge and experience of the plants, which is greater than my own. To see where and how I should be working to be of best service. To ask for cleansing of anything that is not mine and that does not serve me.

As I sat waiting for the medicine to have its effect, I was focusing on my intentions. After a little while I began to get some pretty, spiralling rainbow lights and flashing images of people's faces. Then I lay down and the nervous spasms started, jarring my body. Two of the shamans were with me, singing and cleansing for what seemed like a long time, and one told me that he thought I was under poisonous psychic attack.

It started to rain, torrential, pounding rain on the tin roof and I started to vomit and vomit. I knew I had to release the heavy energy inside me but it was fighting with the ayahuasca which was trying to get it out of me. A shaman was in front of me, circling and circling a lighted cigarette in spirals in front of my third eye, opening my vision to see and release whatever was attacking me.

Another shaman then took me outside and asked me to kneel on my hands and knees on the earth. I became like a jaguar and I was growling and screaming to try to let go of what felt like an alien being inside my intestines. I kept thinking 'I can't do this alone, I need help', and of course help was there in the form of the medicine and the shaman and the spirit of jaguar, but it was also shown to me very clearly that I have to do my own work and that no-one else can do it for me. At one level we all are totally alone, and I had to find my own strength and use my own voice to talk to the entity and release it to the light. It's the constant pull between knowing that we are all interconnected and one, yet we can only do our own work within that interconnected inforealm.

**Ceremony 2**: In the next ceremony the shaman asked me to take a larger quantity of a more gentle plant medicine plus a lot of water a little while after drinking the ayahuasca, to help me to vomit as much as possible to clear any remaining heavy energy in my system. He had me lie down as he worked to clear my second chakra. Even before he started I could feel whatever entity was still inside pulsating and I felt like screaming. It was as if something inside me wanted to fight and not let go, not leave. Anyway, the shaman did manage to extract it and after that I felt a little better. Then he sang the icaros and asked me to focus on the eagle archetype. I was kneeling, trying to fly like eagle and it was beautiful except that I felt as if my left wing was weak or broken. It made me realise that since arriving I had had no pain at all in my shoulders and arms, which had been suffering a lot of pain and stiffness before leaving London, despite physiotherapy, massage and acupuncture. Not long after that I had gut-wrenching vomiting, after which I felt much better and decided I could now enjoy the rest of the evening!

I saw wonderful rainbow spirals dancing and intertwining and weaving, then a long tunnel that I was travelling through, spiralling and spiralling as I went towards the light. It was a very beautiful ceremony and at the end of it I had a sense that the real work can start now – I am clean, the poisoned darts that malicious people have sent to me have gone, and the immersion is now able to take place.

**Ceremony 3**: As the medicine took effect, there seemed to be a lot of different animals in the ceremony room, but the overwhelming sense was of a huge serpent above me. Then the shaman came to sing the icaros in front of me and, as he put his hands on my head to transmit the power of one of the master trees, it felt as if he was enveloping me with the wings of a giant insect.

One of the very clear and beautiful visions from that night was of a tunnel, then a figure at the top of the tunnel standing with an outstretched arm. It was releasing a fountain of sparks down from its hand and it seemed like I was being bathed in a shower of white light. Another time I went up the tunnel again and this time there was a wolf at the top, looking all around. It wouldn't talk to me or show me anything, although I asked it to. A third time I went up and there was a man who turned into a woman and then the being told me it could take whatever shape I believed in.

I got the sense once again that we always have to do our own work, and also a sense of achievement, accomplishment and strength. I started to understand that the spirits or energies of the other dimensions appear to us in whatever way they think we can understand. They are not form-bound, but our limited brains need a form that we can label. We cannot perceive anything we don't have a label for.

**Ceremony 4**: White lights against black (like stars in the night sky) and a beautiful Asian-Indian girl came first, and very quickly some big orange/brown/black insects appeared and my hands felt immobilised and very heavy as the insects did some sort of operation on them. Then they moved onto my head and did work there. It felt as if they were implanting something. They moved on again and I lay down for a bit and I experienced lots of spiralling tunnels, sometimes going down into the earth and sometimes up and up and up into the stars. Sometimes weird scary faces or objects would appear in the tunnels but it seemed that if I laughed at them they would just melt away and I was able several times to emerge out into the stars.

Then there was a succession of worlds that I was passing through very quickly and in total I met – or viewed would be more accurate – hundreds of people in rapid succession. These scenes were totally real and I felt completely immersed in them. I was not in the ceremonial room or even aware of the ceremonial room. I was on different surfaces with the open sky above me, or sometimes a different room or under the earth. Sometimes during ceremonies I feel as if I am observing scenes in a different dimension from the outside, but on this occasion I was totally immersed there. These alternative dimensions were my reality.

There was one point when I don't remember exactly what had been happening but I seemed to get dropped back into the temple from quite high up and I landed back into my body with a real jolt which made me jump.

Then there was an occasion when I was trying to pull something out of my mouth like a hair or a piece of fine wire. A spirit appeared in front of me and told me to stop! They were trying to operate on my painful back but had to anaesthetise me first, so if I had to see what they were doing they would show me, but stop interfering in their work! They opened another window in my vision and it seemed as if I was inside a blue alien spaceship capsule and they had a range of really sophisticated instruments laid out on an operating table. The vision closed and I let them get on with it.

Finally as the shamans were singing, another beautiful

spirit appeared, very feminine and gentle and she asked me if she could do one more thing. I thanked her for being there still, having stayed so long. She was made of orange and white spinning light but I also got a sense of very fast fluttering like dragonfly wings. She got some sort of probe out, very fast spinning orange and white light, and seemed to implant something in my brain.

**Ceremony 5**: I asked to download anything that would be of benefit to me or my clients or my teaching or writing, particularly regarding how the wisdom and consciousness communicates with us. Tunnels and lights gradually started appearing and I got visions of banks of screens and flashing lights and computers in a hemi-spherical space ship. It was huge and looked like the set of a science fiction movie, definitely like a space ship.

Then they seemed to show me cords with little hooked devices coming down and it was as if they are implanting these devices, which seem to come from the space ship control room, into people's heads through their ears. I got the sense they were trying to show me but I couldn't understand so I felt a bit stupid! There were lots and lots of black lines with red dots at the end, all interconnecting and exploding like molecular diagrams, and then there was another demonstration with energy downloading but again I didn't fully understand it.

Then I went to a scene where I was lying in an open-air shed, on a bed, by an open-to-the-air window, and a string of people were filing past me. It seemed as if they were leaving, evacuating wherever we were. I felt really weak and tired and didn't have the energy to get up and go with them, but then George was one of the people in the line and he reached out his hand and told me I had to come. If I didn't I would be left behind. I said I didn't have the energy and I would have to be left behind to die, but he encouraged me to come and the spirits were telling me I had to make the effort, so I physically got up and crawled over to lie beside him in the ceremony room.

Finally when I lay down there was a woman working on my head and she told me to turn my head so that she could work on the back of my head which I felt was to bring some healing into my back which had been very painful. Towards the end I got some visions of going out into the stars – just space and stars and some other beautiful colours and lights.

### Wachuma (San Pedro cactus) ceremonies

Ayahuasca is the hallucinogenic plant medicine of the jungle. The hallucinogenic plant medicine of the mountains is known locally as wachuma and it is made from the San Pedro cactus. It has a very different energy and leads to a very different kind of experience. The ayahuasca is usually drunk at night, in total darkness inside a temple, whereas wachuma is taken in nature, during the day. The main active ingredient is mescaline, with the chemical composition 3,4,5 trimethoxyphenethylamine.

**Ceremony 1**: Once again I am back in a forest, but this time of sweet smelling eucalyptus. My intention is to get in touch with the divine mother having a human experience, and allow the support, love, nurturing and the compassion of mother earth to allow me to open my heart.

For a long time it seems as if I can see the photonic emissions of the trees and hear them talking to me. Mother earth will nurture me, but I also need to protect her and protect the earth-keepers, the holders of the plant medicine. What I receive as another really strong quality during the ceremony is forgiveness. Mother earth forgives us despite all the pain and suffering we cause her.

Later, when I go above the path to sit in the sun because I

am getting really cold down by the river, I can see green energy coming out of the earth, right down the mountainside, like a green aura. It's always there, and I ask that I may always be allowed to see it. They tell me they are always there, trying to speak to us.

The overwhelming sense I get is that my purpose is to protect and promote the plant medicine and also the wisdom keepers of the plant medicine, those who have dieted the plants and lived with them such that they can always hear and feel and see what the plants are trying to communicate.

**Ceremony 2**: Initially I went and lay down on the grass with a rock. It felt as if I had to hold on quite tight to the rock as the earth is spinning so fast that I could easily fly off. Then I got a vision that the gravitational pull might change slightly so that anything without deep roots flies off into space. Humans that want to stay here will need a cave, underground, and a deep connection with the earth, else they will be thrown off into space.

After that I spent a long time going around the garden talking to the different trees and trying to learn their dance. I realised I must always ask permission from the tree spirits before touching a tree. I kept getting flashing red lights in huge strings, which seemed like a sort of morse code of energy that allows the trees to communicate. Also rainbows of light energy flowed through everything. Connectedness, we are all one.

Then I sat for a while on a tree stump that looked like a frog with my back against the beautiful silver bark of a tree and I went right 'out there'. I had times of really seeming to be able to fly like eagle.

Then George came over to join me and we went around the garden again talking to several trees together. We could just feel the oneness of the energy flowing through us and the trees and every living thing in a very beautiful connection.

One practice resulting from the experience is that I must always remember the spirits of the plants that I am eating and thank them. Anything I eat, anything I drink. Remember the spirits of all the plants and animals involved in all my food and know that I am ingesting their light, their information and energy as I eat them.

**Ceremony 3**: After drinking I lay down for a bit and then I went to stand on one of the eucalyptus trees above the river thinking it has the best view because it can see down the valley as well as across the river to its friends on the other side as well as being connected to the water in the river and the rocks and the mountain above. I was holding some thin new growth and the wind started to blow and the tree was moving and bending and playing in the wind. It was very beautiful and I felt very relaxed and flexible. At another point with a different tree I leaned against it and the sun was shining on me from the front with the tree supporting me from behind and I got a beautiful line of white light which expanded and expanded and I experienced a real sense of Oneness. We need the sun and the energy of the sun on this planet, it feeds everything else and we, the rocks, the plants, everything is that energy.

Later I went down to sit in the river, on a rock, and started seeing all the animal spirits inside the rocks. Sitting on a rock it seemed as if the rocks are a bit jealous of the trees because the trees can move and sway in the breeze but the rocks are fixed. On the other hand they are there for much longer than the trees which come and go. Then I climbed up and sat against another big tree in the sun. There I got a complete sense of merging into mother earth, really becoming one with the tree and the earth. I started getting lots of red/orange/yellow and I seemed to be able to transform into eagle and fly. As I flew down the valley and then over to the Amazon I got a sense of the earth heating up – starting to burn up, and the message seemed to be that it can't survive like this for much longer. There was so much colour but all fire colours, whereas when I was just holding the trees there was a lot of green and blue, much cooler colours.

## Impact

I have spent many hours trying to figure things out with the rational part of my brain. Is what I experience in altered states of consciousness real? Indeed what is reality? Are we all constantly surrounded in our everyday lives by a host of spirits or energies that we are just too limited to see but which we can communicate with when we open our minds?

The truth is I don't know and sometimes I just need to accept that things can happen even though I don't understand them. Sometimes I need to accept that practices are useful to me even though I can't explain how they actually work. This applies so often in my everyday life, for instance when I use a mobile phone or fly in a plane, even though I could not attempt to design or build either.

My beliefs may change over time as my range of experience expands, and my technical understanding may change over time as science advances. So I make no pretence that what I believe right now is 'the truth'.

The closest I can get at this time to a communicable understanding of the reality of what people experience in altered states of consciousness is that when we take DMT from exogenous sources, or produce DMT endogenously, it helps our human brain receptors and our DNA to resonate at different frequencies from normal and therefore we become capable of transmitting and receiving information that is not usually accessible to us. This could be likened to wearing a hearing aid that expands the range of sound we can hear, or wearing glasses that allow us to perceive infrared or ultraviolet wavelengths.

Since plants and trees and all living things are made from DNA they all have their own vibrational frequency and it seems as if the master trees in particular may have a wider range of resonance than we do. So they can resonate with the inforealm and the holographic universe to access information from it. When we are also dieting with different plants and inviting in the spirits of the trees we can start to resonate with them, thus gaining access to some of their wisdom. So my conclusion is that yes, we are surrounded by a host of spirits or energies that we are just too limited to see in our normal states of consciousness.

Beyond that, is there an array of guides, earth-keepers and entities that have greater wisdom, knowledge and experience than us and which we can communicate with when we open our minds? My personal experience inclines me to say yes. But because we human beings tend to see what we believe rather than believing what we see, I think the forms these energies take or the way they appear to us changes, depending on our own belief systems.

So in the past the Irish may have perceived these energies as leprechauns, the Scottish may have perceived them as fairies, the Italians and Spanish may have perceived them as winged angels, the Native Americans may have perceived them as wolves or eagles, whereas modern atheists perceive them as 'greys' or other alien representations from populist movies.

It would appear to be supreme arrogance however to assume we are alone in the universe, never mind being at the pinnacle of intelligence. Other energies are capable of so much more and are willing to help us if we will just ask and open ourselves to our true potential, acknowledging our tiny place within a spectacular and magnificent entangled universe. We are drops in the ocean.

# BIBLIOGRAPHY


Al-Khalili, Jim and McFadden, Johnjoe. 2014. *Life on the Edge: The Coming of Age of Quantum Biology* London, UK: Bantam Press.

Aurobindo, Sri. 2001. *A Greater Psychology* Pondicherry, India: Sri Aurobindo Ashram Publications Department

Bischof, M. March 2005. Biophotons – the Light in Our Cells in *Journal of Optometric Phototherapy*

Bohm, David. 1980. *Wholeness and the Implicate Order* UK: Routledge & Kegan Paul

Botkin, Allan L. PsyD and Hogan, R. Craig, PhD. 2005, 2014. *Induced After-Death Communication: A New Therapy for Healing Grief and Trauma* Charlottesville, VA, USA: Hampton Roads Publishing, c/o Red Wheel/Weiser, LLC Newburyport, MA, www.redwheelweiser.com

Brodie, Evelyn M. 2013. *Corporate Bitch to Shaman: A journey uncovering the links between 21st century science, consciousness and the ancient healing practices* Beauchamp, Leicestershire: Matador

Brodie, Evelyn M. 2015. *Temenos Touch: The Art and Science of Integrated Medicine and Non-local Healing* California, USA: Waterside Press

Brown, David Jay. 2013. *The New Science of Psychedelics: At the Nexus of Culture, Consciousness and Spirituality* Rochester,

Vermont, USA: Inner Traditions International and Bear & Company, http://www.Innertraditions.com

Buchanan, Lyn. 2003. *The Seventh Sense, The Secrets of Remote Viewing as Told by a 'Psychic Spy' for the U.S. Military* New York, NY, USA: Paraview Pocket Books

Chia, Mantak and North, Kris Deva. 2009. *Taoist Shaman: Practices from the Wheel of Life* Rochester, Vermont, USA: Destiny Books

Cresswell, J.D., Way, B.M., Eisenberger, N.I., and Lieberman, M.D. 2007. Neural correlates of dispositional mindfulness during affect labeling. *Psychosomatic Medicine, 69*

Dossey, Larry, M.D. 1989. *Recovering the Soul: A Scientific and Spiritual Search* New York, USA: Bantam Doubleday Dell Publishing Group

Franke, Ursula. 2003. *The River Never Looks Back. Historical and Practical Foundations of Bert Hellinger's Family Constellations* Heidelberg, Germany: Carl-Auer-Systeme Verlag

Gawande, Atul. 2015. *Being Mortal: Illness, Medicine and What Matters in the End* London, UK: Wellcome Collection and Profile Books Ltd

Gladwell, Malcolm. 2008. *Outliers: The Story of Success* London, England: Allen Lane

Glass, R.M. 2008. Psychodynamic psychotherapy and research evidence. Bambi survives Godzilla? *The Journal of the American Medical Association*, 300.

Halifax, Joan, PhD. 1991. *Shamanic Voices: A survey of visionary narratives* New York, NY, USA: Viking Penguin. Reproduced by permission of Brockman, Inc.

Hancock, Graham. 2005. *Supernatural: Meetings with the Ancient Teachers of Mankind* London, UK: Century, Reproduced by permission of The Random House Group Ltd.

Hancock, Graham. 2015. *The Divine Spark: Psychedelics, Consciousness and the Birth of Civilization* London, UK: Hay House, Inc.

Hoffer, Abram and Osmond, Humphrey. 1967. *The Hallucinogens* New York: Academic Press

Huxley, Aldous. 1945. *The Perennial Philosophy* USA: Harper and Row

Kalsched, D. 2005. Hope vs. Hopelessness in the Psychoanalytic Situation and in Dante's Divine Comedy in Lynn Cowan (Ed) 2005 *Barcelona, 2004, Proceedings of the Sixteenth International Congress for Analytical Psychology* Einsiedeln, Switzerland: Daimon

Kirsch, Irving, PhD. 2009. *The Emperor's New Drugs: Exploding the Antidepressant Myth* UK: Random House

Kubler-Ross, Elizabeth, Dr. 1969. *On Death & Dying*. New York, NY, USA: Scribner, Simon & Schuster

Kubler-Ross, Elizabeth, Dr. Rev Ed. 2008. *On Life After Death* Berkeley, CA, USA: Celestial Arts

Laszlo, Ervin. 2007. *Science and the Akashic Field: An Integral Theory of Everything (Second Edition)* Rochester, Vermont, USA: Inner Traditions International and Bear & Company, http://Innertraditions.com

Laszlo, Ervin. 2009. *The Akashic Experience: Science and the Cosmic Memory Field* Rochester, Vermont, USA: Inner Traditions International and Bear & Company, http://Innertraditions.com

Levine, Peter A. PhD. 2010. *In An Unspoken Voice: How the Body Releases Trauma and Restores Goodness* Berkeley, California, USA: North Atlantic Books

Lewis, Thomas, M.D., Amini, Fari, M.D., Lannon, Richard, M.D.. 2000. *A General Theory of Love* New York, USA: Vintage Books, Random House

Lipton, Bruce H. PhD. 2005. *The Biology of Belief* Carlsbad, CA, USA: Hay House Inc.

Mason Boring, Francesca. 2012. *Connecting to Our Ancestral Past: Healing through Family Constellations, Ceremony, and Ritual*, Berkeley, California, USA: North Atlantic Books

McGilchrist, Iain. 2009. *The Master and his Emissary: The Divided Brain and the Making of the Western World* New Haven and London: Yale University Press

McMoneagle, Joseph. 1993. *Mind Trek, Exploring Consciousness, Time and Space Through Remote Viewing*. Charlottesville, VA, USA: Hampton Roads

Morehouse, David. 2000. *Psychic Warrior, the true story of the CIA's paranormal espionage programme.* UK: Clairview

Myss, Caroline. 1997. *Anatomy of the Spirit* London, UK: Bantam, Reproduced by Permission of The Random House Group Ltd.

Narby, Jeremy. 1999. *The Cosmic Serpent, DNA and the Origins of Knowledge* New York, NY, USA: Jeremy P. Tarcher/ Putnam

Nisbett, Richard E. and Cohen, Dov. 1996. *Culture of Honor: The Psychology of Violence in the South* Boulder, Colorado: Westview Press, Inc.

Osho, 2000. *New Man for the New Millennium* Osho International Foundation, www.OSHO.com/copyrights

Pahnke, Walter N., Kurland, Albert A., Unger, Sanford, Savage, Charles and Grof, Stanislav. 1970. The Experimental Use of Psychedelic (LSD) Psychotherapy in *Journal of the American Medical Association* 212

Pribram, Karl H. M.D. 2013. *The Form Within: My Point of View* Westport, CT, USA: Prospecta Press

Rankin, Lissa, Dr. 2013. *Mind over medicine: Scientific Proof That You Can Heal Yourself* Carlsbad, CA, USA: Hay House Inc.

Romijn, Herms. 2002. *Journal of Consciousness Studies, Volume 9, Number 1, 1 January 2002,* Imprint Academic

Ruppert, Franz. 2012. *Symbiosis and Autonomy, Symbiotic Trauma and Love Beyond Entanglements* Steyning, UK: Green Balloon Publishing

Schneider, Jakob Robert. 2007. *Family Constellations: Basic*

*Principles and Procedures* Heidelberg, Germany: Carl-Auer-Systeme

Schore, Allan N. 2012. *The Science of the Art of Psychotherapy* New York, USA: W.W. Norton & Company

Sheldrake, Rupert. 2013. *The Science Delusion* London, UK: Coronet, Hodder & Stoughton Ltd.

Siegel, Daniel J. M.D. 2010. *The Mindful Therapist* New York, NY, USA: W.W. Norton & Company, Inc.

Singh Khalsa, Dharma, M.D., and Stauth, Cameron. 2001. *Meditation as Medicine* New York, NY, USA: Fireside

Strassman, Rick, M.D. 2000. *DMT: The Spirit Molecule* Rochester, Vermont, USA: Inner Traditions International and Bear & Company, http://www.Innertraditions.com

Strassman, Rick, M.D., Wojtowicz, Slawek, M.D., Luna, Luis Eduardo, PhD, and Frecska, Ede, M.D. 2007. *Inner Paths to Outer Space* Rochester, Vermont, USA: Inner Traditions International and Bear & Company, http://www.Innertraditions.com

Targ, Russell. 2004. *Limitless Mind, a guide to remote viewing and transformation of consciousness* Novato, CA, USA: New World Library

Tegmark, Max. 2000. Importance of Quantum Decoherence in Brain Processes in *Physical Review E: Statistical Physics, Plasmas, Fluids, and Related Interdisciplinary Topics* 61

Van Der Kolk, Bessel. 2014. *The Body Keeps the Score: Mind, Brain and Body in the Transformation of Trauma* USA: Viking Penguin

Van Lommel, Pim, M.D. 2010. *Consciousness Beyond Life: The Science of the Near-Death Experience* New York, NY, USA: Harper Collins Publishers

Van Wijk, R. 2001. Bio-photons and Bio-communication in *Journal of Scientific Exploration* 15, no 2

Villoldo, Alberto, PhD. 2009. *Courageous Dreaming: How the Shamans Dream the World into Being* London, UK: Hay House, Inc.

Watt, D.F. 2003. Psychotherapy in an age of neuroscience: Bridges to affective neuroscience. in J. Corrigall & H. Wilkinson (Eds), 2003. *Revolutionary connections. Psychotherapy and neuroscience.* London, UK: Karnac Books

Weiss, Brian, Dr. 1988. *Many Lives, Many Masters: The true story of a prominent psychiatrist, his young patient and the past-life therapy that changed both their lives* USA: Simon and Schuster Inc.

Woolger, Roger J. 1987. *Other Lives, Other Selves: A Jungian psychotherapist discovers past lives* New York, USA: Dolphin/ Doubleday, Inc.

# INDEX